Politics and Society in Twentieth-Century
SPAIN

Modern Scholarship on European History
Henry A. Turner, Jr.
General Editor

Politics and Society in Twentieth-Century

**Edited with an Introduction by
STANLEY G. PAYNE**

Modern Scholarship on European History

NEW VIEWPOINTS

A Division of Franklin Watts
New York London 1976

Acknowledgments

The editor wishes to express his appreciation to the following for permission to translate and/or to publish selections included in this volume: the editors of the *American Historical Review* and Gabriel Jackson for "The Azaña Regime in Perspective (Spain, 1931–33)"; the University of Kentucky Press and Edward Malefakis for "Internal Political Problems and Loyalties: The Republican Side in the Spanish Civil War"; The Westermarck Society and Juan J. Linz for "An Authoritarian Regime: Spain"; and the Fundación FOESSA and Amando de Miguel for "Spanish Political Attitudes, 1970."

Library of Congress Cataloging in Publication Data

Main entry under title:
Politics and society in twentieth-century Spain.

(Modern scholarship on European history)
Includes bibliographical references and index.

CONTENTS: Gómez, X. T. The functioning of the cacique system in Andalusia, 1890 – 1931.—Meaker, G. Anarchists versus syndicalists: conflicts within the Confederación Nacional del Trabajo, 1917 – 1923.—Jackson, G. The Azaña regime in perspective (Spain, 1931 – 1933). [etc.]

1. Spain—Politics and government—20th century—Addresses, essays, lectures.
I. Payne, Stanley G.
DP233.P58   320.9'46'08   75-38923
ISBN 0-531-05382-2
ISBN 0-531-05588-4 pbk.

Copyright © 1976 by Stanley G. Payne

Printed in the United States of America

CONTENTS

Introduction

Political commentators in the North Atlantic countries have found the civic affairs of twentieth-century Spain to be puzzling, tumultuous, and atypical for a West European country. The situation is less perplexing when it is understood that the social and economic structures of Spain have been those of a South European or Mediterranean country rather than of a developed Northwest European state. During the late nineteenth and early twentieth century Spain was governed by a liberal constitutional monarchy, which was fairly typical of most of Southern and Western Europe. It broke down under the manifold pressures of incipient democratization, social and economic change, radical dissent, and the frustrations of colonial war in Morocco. This breakdown paralleled the common collapse of liberal government throughout Southern Europe in the 1920's and 1930's.

The most unique feature of twentieth-century Spanish politics was the introduction of a liberal democratic Republic in 1931, near the trough of the great depression. This momentarily ran counter to the anti-democratic and authoritarian trend common to all Southern and Central Europe at that time. The anomaly of the Spanish Republic can be explained by several factors: (a) the failure of the Primo de Rivera dictatorship of 1923 – 1930 to offer any authoritarian alternative to liberalism on either a philosophical or systematic basis, leaving the principles of liberalism and the left almost unchallenged; (b) the unique geographic position of the Hispanic peninsula, enabling Spain to avoid involvement in European wars since 1815, and hence escape the pressures of militarism and national rivalry; (c) the remarkable weakness of nationalism in twentieth-century Spain, depriving potential rightist elements of their strongest source of support; and (d) the fact that Spain, like France, did not at first feel the same proportionate effects of the depression experienced by industrialized countries.

The Spanish Republic began with general goodwill and relative moderation in 1931 and ended in sharp polarization, violence, and protorevolution in 1936. It constituted a remarkable political experience, indeed the only example in recent times in which an advanced democratic polity has completely disintegrated without major foreign interference or war. Much of it had to do with the climate of the times, for if uniquely Spanish conditions permitted the inception of the Republic in 1931, the country could not subsequently escape the influence of extreme reactions of right and left emanating from abroad. Nearly all other countries facing Spain's political and structural problems had succumbed to authoritarian rule by 1933. In Spain, however, the peninsular climate of continued democratic liberalism and growing intemperance permitted the mobilization of increasingly sharp and polarized antagonisms that eventually broke out in the Civil War of 1936. The 1930's offered an exceedingly adverse climate for democratic experiments. Perhaps the most atypical factor in Spain was that, whereas elsewhere in Southern Europe the initiative was taken by the authoritarian right, here it was taken by the revolutionary left. Since, however, the Spanish left was not a bloc but a heterogeneous constellation of mutually competitive and normally mutually antagonistic groups, it was ultimately not in a position to win the power struggle of 1936 – 1939.

The Franco regime that won the Civil War was not primarily a fascist movement of national revolution but a syncratic combination of rightist and middleclass elements joined together as a counterrevolutionary movement under General Franco. Once more Spain's geographical position, combined with Franco's astute diplomacy, enabled the country to escape involvement in World War II, and also enabled the new Franco regime to avoid the fate of all other fascist and right-wing dictatorships in Southern Europe between 1941 and 1945.

The Franco regime governed Spain throughout the entire postwar era of resurgent liberal and social democracy in Western and Southern Europe. During that period it became increasingly moderate and tolerant, permitting greater expression of partial pluralism, yet the basic principle of authoritarian rule remained unaltered. During the nineteenth and early twentieth century Spain was somewhat unique in trying to adopt advanced liberal and democratic forms of government for which a poor and illiterate society was fundamentally unprepared. Since 1950 it has undergone a great process of industrialization, accompanied by social mobility and expanding education that has made of Spain a developed or at least semi-developed country. The result has been a growing contradiction between the increasingly advanced structure of Spanish society and the authoritarian structure of government that permits only minimal and indirect participation and representation. This constitutes the basic civic dilemma of Spain's recent past and near future.

1

The Functioning of the Cacique System in Andalusia, 1890 – 1931

Xavier Tusell Gómez

(Translated by Ann Kaenig Fleming and Shannon E. Fleming)

Spain was the first of the larger South European countries to introduce the modern Northwest European system of parliamentary government and nominally democratic elections. The restored constitutional monarchy of 1875 – 1931 managed to achieve political stability on the basis of reformist oligarchic rule by two alternating parties—one Liberal and one Conservative—that slowly evolved in a more openly democratic direction. The introduction of universal male suffrage for Spanish elections in 1890 did not, however, achieve a functional system of liberal democracy. More than half the population remained illiterate and the formal system of democratic elections was in fact operated in most parts of the country by means of boss rule (caciquismo), government manipulation, indirect clientage relationships, and in some cases outright coercion. During the first decades of the twentieth century this system began to evolve into one of more genuine and direct electoral democracy in the larger cities and in a few of the more advanced provinces, but in much of the country electoral manipulation and control persisted to some de-

*gree right down to the overthrow of the parliamentary sys-
tem by the* Primo de Rivera *pronunciamiento in 1923.*

*Xavier Tusell Gómez, the author of the following article,
is professor of history at the University of Madrid. Born in
1942, he is the most active younger scholar in the field of
recent Spanish history. In addition to a* Historia de la
democracia cristiana en España *(Madrid, 1974), he is the
author of several volumes of regional electoral analysis
and electoral sociology, including* Las elecciones del
Frente Popular en España, 2 vols. *(Madrid, 1971). This article[1] analyzes the obstacles to representative elections
and political democracy in one of the more backward
though heavily populated regions of Spain.*

In recent years the field of contemporary Spanish history, which had previously been studied in a traditional manner (biographies, for example), has
been opened to procedures used in other social sciences such as political sociology. It is clear that these new methods may be very productive, but the
danger exists that such procedures may follow excessively mimetic patterns.
This has occurred with the application of electoral sociology (such as was
elaborated by French and British specialists) to Spain before 1931. From 1931
to 1936, when Spain had a political system based on general mobilization,
mass political parties, and mostly honest elections, elections can be studied
following the same criteria as in other countries. On the other hand, before
1931 the utilization of these procedures not only is not productive but can even
be seriously erroneous, for the simple reason that if we judge the period
1890 – 1931 from the point of view of functioning democracy, it was not that
the political system suffered more or less from corruption, but that corruption
was the system. No doubt such an interpretation has an axiomatic content
which one should avoid. Perhaps it would be much more just (or more correct)
to say that the system of political life which existed in Spain in previous periods
was simply different from the democratic. Defined by Joaquín Costa as "oligarchy and bossism," its main bases as well as its praxis were far from being
democratic: Rather it was a political system characterized more as a corruption of democracy, because it constituted a state prior to it.

In good measure the error of utilizing in an excessively mimetic manner the
procedures of electoral sociology arises from the national dimension with
which the study of the political system or electoral results has been approached. Greater accuracy may be achieved by limiting the frame of refer-

ence to the region. The present article will study the functioning of the *cacique* system in Andalusia, but many of the conclusions that may be drawn from it are valid for the rest of Spain.

1. The *encasillado* (formation of a list of electoral candidates approved by the government).

A fundamental mechanism for understanding the political system of the Spanish Restoration with regard to making elections, but not only in this aspect, is what, in the language of the period, we could term "encasillado."[2] This is usually defined as government intervention in elections, but it is necessary to state precisely what this means, because otherwise one may get the erroneous impression that the government arranged to have elected to the Congress of Deputies or the Senate those whom it wanted or intervened in the electoral contest in a anecdotal or superficial manner. The true etymology of the word "encasillado" permits us a more correct view: *"Encasillar"* means the same as to put in a pigeonhole each deputy or senator. Other terms commonly used by politicians of the period to refer to elections are "to fix," "to prepare," "to organize" the elections. All of them indicate governmental intervention which, nevertheless, does not have, as the terms themselves indicate, completely free hands in the electoral process.

The encasillado was essentially a pact. Not a pact among equals, of course, but a pact in which the government, by virtue of being the government, had a certain preeminence. If the government did not intervene in elections, the local and provincial factions, when they were not violent, would probably have led the country into chaos at the moment of each election. Therefore, the government intervened in elections but at the same time came to terms with the existing power groups of the country. That the encasillado was a pact indicates that in many instances it was not easy to elaborate: Therefore, it gave rise to complicated discussions months in length and requiring the full attention of the government (the Liberal leader Moret, for example, had a notebook in which he wrote very exactly the alternatives to which the negotiation was subject).

Who intervened in such a delicate process? On one occasion Costa wrote that the oligarchic and cacique system was based on three steps: the local caciques, the "oligarchs" at the national level, and, as a link between them, the civil governors. This affirmation seems certain. On the national level, of course, the most important role is in the hands of the prime minister and his minister of the interior. The President held final authority, but his role was customarily indirect: In the elections of 1907, for example, the Conservative prime minister Maura limited himself to giving some general indications and occasional advice to the minister of the interior. This had as its purpose to pair the list of candidates in a concrete manner, stating precisely for each district the candidate who might count on the support of the government or, at least, on its approval (in short, the encasillado candidate).

On the national level, the head of the party out of power also intervened as an interlocutor since it was necessary to satisfy him, at least partially, so that he would not offer secret opposition should he feel himself without the cooperation of the government. A more severe problem arose when, as the number of political groups increased, it became difficult to know precisely who was the valid interlocutor for the interior minister. Other figures also intervened in the elaboration of the encasillado at this level. Candidates who were strong in their local districts (whether or not they belonged to the party in power) asked the government for confirmation of their inclusion in the encasillado (which was usually granted to them). There were also the candidates called *cuneros* (candidates elected by the influence of the government), who had no influence in the district, but whose election was important to the government. Among these, there were two kinds (or at least this distinction was made by the Liberal leader Conde de Romanones, as may be found in his archive). Candidates who lacked any personal support were usually journalists or professional politicians for whom each party leader had "disposable districts" or "districts to offer," because there was no existing political force in these districts and, consequently, they accepted whatever was decided in Madrid. On the other hand, those which Romanones called "money candidates" had in their favor the possibility of buying votes, so that it was possible to send them to more difficult districts. In any case, as time passed the "disposable" districts decreased and the party leaders in power were obliged to postpone indefinitely numerous candidates who sought a seat in the Cortes.

At the provincial level principally the civil governor and the provincial head of the party in power intervened in the elaboration of the encasillado. Of course, the civil governor was not merely an administrative functionary but also represented the government politically (and did so, of course, with much greater loyalty than the provincial head of the party), yet it would be too simple to condemn him for his intervention in partisan politics. In many instances the civil governor was the representative of more modern politics than the provincial party head: Toward the end of the nineteenth century one of the governors of Jaén complained that a policy of patronage violence dominated his province ("everyone has a Moor inside," he said) and he asked for a civil government "with a view toward Europe" from his superior. In any case the good civil governor was not the one who imposed the government's candidate by brute force, but rather the man who enabled that candidate to triumph by means of friendly negotiation. On the other hand, the provincial party chiefs manifested greater bellicosity against opponents when their patronage organization was solid.

At a local level it was necessary for each candidate who wanted to win "to have the mayors," that is to say, to control the municipal authorities (not the voters, since these were fictitious). For this it was not even necessary to belong to the same party: The Conservative candidate for Cazorla (Jaén) in 1907 complained to the minister of the interior that the Liberal mayors of the district were being replaced (they supported him even though they were Liberals and he was a Conservative, for the simple reason that they had earlier been supporters of a relative). It was common for the municipal authorities to resign in favor of those who were in power at election time or to support the official candidates: In general the minister of the interior also preferred in this respect agreement rather than violence. Nevertheless, in case of resistance the government had abundant means of persuasion: Local administration was so deficient that a severe application of the law permitted the dismissal of all necessary municipal officials and this on occasion was done.

All these elements were a part of the encasillado and thus we see why it is so difficult to elaborate. In spite of this the cases in which the encasillado did not exist are very rare. So it happened, for example, that in some districts two candidates from the same party in power faced each other (and the government was indifferent to the result), but at the provincial level an at least partial encasillado was always found. Having concluded the negotiations, the minister of the interior sent a telegram to each civil governor designating the official candidates and stating that "the government will view with pleasure their triumph" (which, of course, except for very exceptional cases, normally occurred). Concerning the specific composition of each encasillado, a general rule cannot be established, but in Andalusia the usual result was that all the rural districts before 1900 and a majority of them until 1920 were won by the party in power. The provincial capitals elected (with the exception of Sevilla) three deputies, two from the majority and one from the minority, who were covered respectively by members of the party in power and the opposition. This list of candidates was, in reality, a united candidacy against eventual candidates from those opposed to the system.[3]

2. Urban environment and rural environment with regard to the encasillado.
What has been said is valid for all Andalusian elections whatever the environment in which they were held, but in reality provincial capitals and the rural en-

vironment behaved differently with regard to the encasillado. In general this behavioral difference (fundamental for understanding Spanish contemporary history) was due to the former's superior modernity.

In the urban environment official candidates were usually the provincial leaders of the two dominant parties, professional politicians who could at least count on something similar to popular support. But perhaps more characteristic was the fact that since public opinion existed to some degree, those not included in the encasillado could turn to the electorate. Since economic interest groups might occasionally mobilize voters, they might not accept outside candidates imposed from Madrid (in reality this was usually infrequent, except in Almería). Moreover, there were occasions in which strong protest arose against administrative corruption (for example, in Granada beginning in 1918 against the Liberal cacique La Chica) and, finally and most importantly, the forces at the margin of the system were considerably stronger in the cities than in the rural environment. Of the 122 elections in Andalusian provincial capitals that have been studied, in 83 there was a true contest, in 78 there were candidates opposed to the system, and in 56 there was a contest between the two official parties. The competition had as a logical consequence the existence in the elections, at least in some instances, of an electoral campaign.

In spite of this the government had, independently of the encasillado, another series of procedures to put pressure on the voter, which received the generic term of *pucherazo* (falsifying of an election). In each urban center of the provincial capitals one common form of fraud derived from the composition of the electoral lists and of the action of the inspectors (in 1918 in Almería there was a precinct of 124 voters which returned 9,015 votes for the official candidate). The existence of *embolados* or *micos* (individuals who substitute for the voters) was also frequent, especially in Almería and Cádiz. Buying votes was a relatively late phenomenon, practiced in many instances by candidates who were not encasillados (although not those with an ideological motivation). By the twentieth century the buying of votes was quite common in Almería, Cádiz, and Granada, being also combined at times with distribution of wine and brandy. By 1920 it was calculated that an urban election could cost at least 50,000 or 60,000 pesetas.[4]

Of all these methods, the most efficient means that the government had of obtaining their desired majority was a form of gerrymandering. In spite of having made the above distinction between the urban vote and the rural vote it is important to point out that the distinction was not as clear as might appear at first glance. In reality all the urban circumscriptions included a large number

TABLE 1−1.

Results from the villages of the circumscription of Málaga in the 1905 election

Villages	Percentage of voters	Votes for the official candidate	Republican votes
Alhaurin Grande	90.7	750	
Alhaurin Torre	94.9	575	
Benalgabón	94.6	439	
Casabermeja	91.5	545	61
Churriana	87.0	251	
Moclinejo	79.4	157	
Olías	78.5	190	
Torremolinos	87.0	295	
Totalan	16.3		63
Totals	86.7	3,202	124

Source: Archivo Municipal de Málaga, Legajo #563.

TABLE 1−2.

Percentage of votes obtained in the urban center by each candidate in several multiseat elections from the circumscription of Sevilla

Year	Conservative	Liberal	Republican	Catholic
1903	27.2	33.3	58.4	28.2
1907	19.3	20.6	41.7	50.6
1910	23.2	33.1	44.9	----
1916	50.9	52.3	55.8	53.7
1919	49.8	42.4	61.9	----
1920	37.8	35.7	52.3	63.2
1923	35.4	39.0	63.5	45.3

Source: Boletín oficial de la Provincia de Sevilla.

of villages in which governmental pressure could be exercised more easily than in the urban center itself and which, consequently, always returned a notable majority for the official candidates. Since in all the provincial Andalusian capitals, except Sevilla, the number of voters in the villages was superior to the number who resided in the urban center, it was very simple to compensate for an urban defeat with these rural votes. Two good examples of what has just been said are found in Tables 1-1 and 1-2. In the first are the results of the

1905 election from the towns of the circumscription of Málaga; they should not be considered exceptional, but rather representative of a form of habitual behavior. As may be seen, the percentages of voting are theoretically extremely high (in reality, what is certain is that they did not vote) and the results favor the official candidate. In Table 1-2 one can see how, in another provincial capital (Sevilla), the percentage of votes obtained by the candidates of the two parties of the *turno* (Conservatives and Liberals) in the urban center is commonly found to be much below the percentage obtained by those political groups whose votes are secured due to an ideological motivation (Republicans and Catholics): In this manner it is again proven that only in the urban environment did there exist a certain ideological motivation at the time of voting. As one may imagine, in the villages belonging to an urban circumscription governmental pressure was more frequent and heavy. While in general the cacique system was based on other methods distinct from violent imposition, it was not strange that violence should occur in the urban environment (although it would be exaggerating to say that it was common). From the more modern character of electoral behavior in this environment and from the fact that the government, nonetheless, did not lack means of pressure is derived the importance which was conceded to the results in the cities, which could even totter ministers of the interior in case of not being favorable (as occurred, for example, in the case of Maura in 1903).

In spite of the government's pressure, the urban environment showed a certain independence: Of 122 elections, in 100 the encasillado was victorious and in 22 the deputy elected was a candidate from parties at least opposed to the prevailing political system. If the number of victories of the latter was not higher, it cannot be attributed solely to governmental pressure but also (and even especially) to the lack of a constant and durable political mobilization in the urban environment (the only one in which there was at least some prospects for it). According to official data, the percentages of votes in the urban center would have been generally less than 50 percent, but since this percentage also includes the falsified votes, one must conclude that it is very probable that in normal conditions less than 25 percent of the population actually voted. As for the results, one may say that the provincial capitals behaved in a manner similar to large cities such as Madrid and Barcelona. In wards of modest social origin, mobilization was commonly much less and much more occasional than in other wards. For example, in the plebian Granadine ward of Sacromonte in 1901 there were 159 voters, of whom 112 were illiterate and only 2 voted; in the sixth precinct of district VIII of the city of Córdoba in 1920 there were 419 voters, of whom 237 were illiterate and only

57 voted. As is natural, it was in these districts that the Republicans obtained a high number of votes.

Although the electoral behavior of the urban circumscriptions was far from model, one may term it exemplary in comparison with that of the rural districts. There not even the fundamental requisite for a true election existed: that is to say, competition. The most frequent occurrence was that in rural districts not even half of the total number of elections was truly contested. Sometimes the situation was even worse: In two districts (Aracena in Huelva and Albuñol in Granada) during thirteen of sixteen elections for the period 1891 – 1923, there was no contest, either because there was only one candidate (from 1907 on, according to Article 29 of the electoral law, if there was only one candidate that candidate was elected automatically) or because when there were several candidates, it was a matter of fictitious candidates who obtained only a dozen votes. Since there was no competition, there was no true electoral campaign. At most, the official candidate toured the district in a true "excursion" (at least it was called thus by the press) in which there were no speeches of an ideological content but rather banquets during the course of which the candidate would allude to the beauty of the women of the region or to the patron saint of the area.

Under these conditions and given the disposability of rural districts according to the decisions of the minister of the interior, direct violence or corruption were normally unnecessary. When they occurred, the procedures were naturally more primitive than in the urban environment. The buying of the rural vote is, for example, a quite late and exceptional phenomenon, even in spite of the fact that already in 1907 the Liberal Conde de Romanones spent 35,000 pesetas to buy a district when he was pursued from the interior ministry by the Conservative La Cierva. On the other hand, the collaboration of those who, because of their economic status, had as dependents a large number of voters was much more frequent. In Córdoba, for example, the laborers from the noble houses were regularly induced to vote for the government's candidate and the same was true of the miners in Ríotinto. Governmental intervention in the electoral process was not limited to the formation of electoral lists but also took the form on occasion of sending governmental delegates (in 1907 Cierva named 250 for all of Spain), who favored with their actions the official candidate, or in the posting of the Civil Guard, who, in theory, were present to maintain order but in actuality were to prevent protest in case of fraud. This also included violence, above all in the provinces of Almería and Granada where caciquismo appears to have had a "South American" aspect. It is very probable that all elections prior to 1916 in both provinces involved at least one death and the presence of what the press described as "shotgun squads."

The most serious part of this generalized corruption is that it was difficult to prove. When at the beginning of 1907 it was decided that the Supreme Court and not a commission of deputies should decide on the validity of election certificates, one thought that the partisanship shown in judging them would finally disappear, but it wasn't that way: In Andalusia for the period 1890-1923 less than 5 percent of the election certificates were considered as suspected of fraud (in Almería it was somewhat more than 12 percent), when the truth is that, if we apply strict criteria, practically all elections in rural districts should have been annulled. In a certain sense the intervention of the Supreme Court was counterproductive since it required that the defeated candidates prove corruption by means of absolutely authentic testimony (as, for example, the presence of notaries who could verify it). As is natural by this method, and starting with the presumption that all elections were valid, it was very difficult to prove the contrary, apart from the fact that there are numerous testimonies according to which the notaries were arrested, their cars damaged, shot at, and so on (the instances of the least violence occurred when the notaries assigned to opposition candidates were sexagenarians).

The official results of elections in rural districts simply cannot be taken seriously. When the most common occurrence was no competition at all, the voting percentages were usually placed between 60 percent and 70 percent of the electorate. Submission to the encasillado was practically absolute: In the period 1890 − 1931 candidates opposed to the system were elected only on thirteen occasions out of almost one thousand contested seats. This meekness to the encasillado is, of course, the most characteristic feature of rural behavior, but, nevertheless, it is possible to establish a difference between at least two types of districts, a difference which was already noted by Ortega y Gasset in his article *The Redemption of the Provinces.* There were districts which may be defined as "meek" because in them the normal course was to follow faithfully the evolution of national politics: They always elected a deputy from the same party as the president of the Council of Ministers. A typical case is that of the Utrera district (Table 1-3) which in the sixteen elections during this period always followed this practice. As may be seen, it was also normal in Utrera to have no competition (there are two cases of opposition between members of the same party, which shows the lack of ideological motivation in rural political contests). On the other hand, there were districts "with stable cacique systems" which, since they were dominated by one individual or one family, did not change political persuasion from one election to another (originally these were rare but, as we shall see, they gradually increased in number). A good example is found in Carmona, monopolized by the Conservative Domínguez Pascual family from the end of the nineteenth century until 1923, habitually without opposition, especially from the Liberals (Table 1-4). With regard to a possible relationship between the degree of economic evolution and political behavior, it may scarcely be said to exist. There are, of course, no differences of behavior between Conservative and Liberal districts, because these distinctions do not mean anything at the local level. At most it is possible to establish a certain link between districts with a greater inclination to electoral violence on the one hand and poverty on the other (which occurs in Almería) or between the high level of illiteracy (greater than 80 percent) and the complete absence of competition (which occurs in the interior of the province of Málaga). In reality there are only two districts in Andalusia (out of some fifty) which exhibited (and not always) electoral behavior that may be compared to the normal model in countries with liberal institutions: Montilla and Valverde del Camino.

TABLE 1−3.
Electoral behavior in a "meek" district: Utrera

Election	Percentage of votes among all voters		
	Liberal	Conservative	Republican
1891		46.7	14.2
1893	74.4		
1896		59.8	
1898	75.1		
1899		89.2 (two Conservative candidates)	
1901	71.9		
1903	31.7	36.5	
1905	70.3		
1907	29.7	38.1	
1910	Article 29		
1914		73.7	
1916	Article 29		
1918	38.7	35.2	
1919		Article 29	
1920		59.3	
1923	50.1 (two Liberal candidates)		

In Montilla a Republican tradition existed which, linked with the later appearance of socialist trade unionism and Catholic trade unionism, resulted in a

TABLE 1—4.

Electoral behavior in a district with a stable cacique system: Carmona

| Election | Percentage of votes among all voters | | | |
	Domínguez Pascual	Liberal	Republican	Others
1891	31.6		26.2	
1893	34.8	16.8	5.5	
1896	52.5			
1898	52.8			
1899	43.9			
1901	40.4			15.4
1903	30.1		13.6	
1905	56.6			
1907	24.7			
1910	45.7			20.6
1914	Article 29			
1916	Article 29			
1918	43.1			
1919	Article 29			
1920	41.9			
1923	41.1		10.6	

contest in fifteen of the sixteen elections. In Valverde del Camino, the district which includes the Ríotinto mines, it was also socialism which enlivened the contest, but only in the final phase.

3. Oligarchs and caciques.

The ruling class, judged as inept, forms one of the most frequent sources of protest against Restoration politics on the part of intellectuals. Does this vision correspond to reality?

A principal feature, which is surprising (in spite of having been pointed out by Linz), is the small role of the nobility. In spite of latifundism, only 13 percent of the deputies and 25 percent of the senators elected in Andalusia from 1890 to 1923 were nobles. This proportion also tends clearly to diminish: While at the end of the nineteenth century the proportion is 20 percent among deputies and 40 percent among senators, in the final phase both proportions are reduced by half. It is also necessary to bear in mind that this nobility is not of old lineage (from the eighteenth century or before) but a relatively recent nobility:

As an example it is sufficient to indicate that in 1923 of the eight nobles who were elected deputies from Andalusia, five had obtained their noble title during the reign of Alfonso XIII. As the only exception to this general rule, one may cite the case of specific districts, as, for example, Utrera and Jerez de la Frontera (both regions of large latifundios) in which the nobility does play an important role. The province of Cádiz elected an exceptional 24 percent of noble deputies.

The limited importance of the nobility among the parliamentary elite does not exactly mean that the nobility had lost its social prestige (it exercised it by other means; for example, through the king) nor that the link between political power and economic preponderance did not exist. With respect to the latter, quite the opposite occurs: The most frequent occurrence is that political representatives figure in the lists of the largest taxpayers. For example, of the ten largest taxpayers in Jerez, six had had parliamentary representation through one party or the other; in Málaga the three largest taxpayers from the same period had also been deputies or senators or both. At any rate this situation which is found in urban districts occurs even more clearly in rural areas. In provincial capitals it was common for the leaders of the Conservative party to belong to the families of greatest economic importance (the Rodríguez Acosta in Granada, the Larios in Málaga, the Ibarra in Sevilla, and so on), but it was not always the same among the Liberals. On the other hand, in the rural districts, when they did not receive cunero candidates from Madrid, the normal practice was a contest among the families who were the most influential from the economic point of view: Thus it was in the Posadas district between the Gamero Cívico and the Calvo de León, the largest taxpayers and the respective representatives of the Conservative and Liberal parties, until the latter ended by monopolizing politics in the district with two brothers dividing the representation of the respective parties. It is also curious that when an electoral contest was waged between two economic sectors of a district, it was the most dynamic sector which triumphed: So it was in the Cádiz district of Medina Sidonia where the tunny fisheries of the Liberal candidate Romeu drove out the agricultural wealth of the Conservative candidate the Marqués de Negrón.

In short, one may say that the three characteristic types of politician in Andalusia during the period were the cunero, the notable, and the cacique. The first came from an urban environment, was usually a person of political importance (a young relative of some politician at the national level, for example, which explains why the directing elite had numerous young members) or an intellectual (a journalist or a writer) who was elected by a "disposable" district normally in an underdeveloped region (in Almería 80 percent of the representatives were not born in the province). It thus happened very frequently that illiterate districts were represented by great figures of the intellectual world who had obtained their posts through governmental aid, in such a manner that there existed a considerable difference between the representatives and their constituents, with the former being greatly superior to the latter. Two districts with a percentage of illiteracy around 80 percent, Sorbas (Almería) and Huescar (Granada), were represented by men of stature in the intellectual world: the writer Azorín and the "Regenerationist" journalist Morote. The "notable" was that person who was firmly linked to the district in which he had vested interests and from which he derived his political influence. The term "cacique" should be reserved for those professional politicians whose form of action did not differ too much from that of the "boss" in United States politics; congenial (they are usually called by affectionate names: the cacique from Sevilla was "Perico" Rodríguez de la Borbolla, an old Republican), their power derived from the patronage that they practiced with regard to the electorate and from their role of promoter for concrete material advantages from the central government for their constituents.

Concerning the typology of the politician of the period, however, it is necessary to make two remarks: In the first place, they occurred in the Conservative as well as the Liberal party (although logically the "notables" were more frequent in the Conservative party, at least at an urban level) and, in the second place, the most normal occurrence was that every politician was a composite of the three types. What is clear is that this triple typology shows us the fundamental characteristic of Spanish politics of the period: the absence of ideological motivation. In the case of the notable or the cacique this is clear, but it is also true in the case of the cunero, who habitually is motivated by having a place in the Cortes and not by convincing his constitutents (the anti-clerical Morote, for example, avoided espousing his ideas in his district).

Politics was essentially the kingdom of the favor and, therefore, we should accept the definitions of Unamuno, according to which in Spain the politician was "a gentleman who distributed destinies" and the citizen "a gentleman who is looking for a destiny." The best proof may be obtained by simply glancing at the archive of any political personage of the period: The researcher feels overwhelmed by files and files in which are found all kinds of recommendations for positions or favors from that of the canon to that of the mailman, including those from the bullfighter and the wet nurse. It was so extreme that one of the politicians of the period established an ordered system of the letters of this type that he received. Cierva, for example, had an alphabetical file in which he kept each person helped by him, with a description of the favor, and Romanones, when he appointed civil governors, used sheets of paper with columns for "the recommended" and "the recommender." The favor was, in short, the great political mechanism of the period. A deputy owed everything to his constituents: Azorín, for example, was obliged, for one of the caciques from Sorbas who had supported him, to request the lease of some mines in the area. A good deputy was, above all, one who obtained from the state advantages for the district which he represented: Natalio Rivas, cacique from the Alpujarras in Granada, stated on one occasion that when he was a minister he had managed to use 2.5 percent of his ministerial budget in his district; if all the other deputies had done the same thing the state budget "would have been decimated." If a national party leader should refuse to accept the budget for public works in a province from the leader of his party in that province, it was, of course, a sufficient motive for the latter to change to another political group.

Related to the fact that the favor was the fundamental political mechanism was the supposed administrative corruption. In reality this corruption has been considerably exaggerated. Pérez de Ayala who, as an intellectual, tended to multiply the objections to the political system, stated on one occasion that the greatest evil of professional politicians was not their corruption but their stupidity (with this word he alluded to their lack of broad vision and to their lack of ideological orientation). It is true that there were caciques who acted only to their own advantage, as the above mentioned La Chica, but the prototype of the good cacique did not benefit personally from his political activity and he died poor (as in the case of Rodríguez de la Borbolla) even if he had been wealthy previously (this occurred with the Conservative cacique from Huelva, Burgos y Mazo). However, the moral rules of behavior were clearly radically different in a political system such as is described here and in a democracy: If the politicians themselves did not benefit from their positions, their subordinates surely did in such a manner that one could apply to them the phrase coined for the Mexican regime of Porfirio Díaz (they didn't rob but they permitted robbing). In any case the political career was conceived of as an administrative career in which the favor, even among family, also predominated. In 1923 some 120 deputies and senators were members of an ex-minister's family. So it was, for example, that Romanones had in the Cortes his three sons, one son-in-law, and three nephews, and Maura had one son, a son-in-law, and two nephews. Politics had a rigorous *cursus honorum,* which explains why one habitually obtained the position of minister only at an advanced age.

Under these conditions as one can easily imagine, there does not exist what is commonly understood as a politician party, not even "of notables,' or of cadres. At a national level, for example, the Liberal Circle in Madrid in 1920 counted on only 96 members and expenses of 15,000 pesetas annually. At the Andalusian provincial level the situation was even more significant: There scarcely existed a handful of societies which did not have a purely political purpose (for that reason they received the names of *"casinos,"* *"tertulias,"* *"circulos"*) and only a minimum membership. The most normal thing was for political meetings to take place in the local leader's own home. Practically speaking, the parties were no more than groupings of personal supporters to whom ideology mattered little. For example, at the end of the nineteenth century the provincial deputation of Huelva was divided between Conservatives and Liberals, but in reality there really existed five groupings, three of which stood for the Conservatives and two for the Liberals. It is logical that changes of political affiliation were very frequent: Sánchez Guerra was the Liberal represenative from Cabra (Córdoba) at the end of the nineteenth century opposed by the Conservative Marqués de Cabra. When the former, like all the followers of Gamazo including Maura, changed to the Conservative party, his competitor in Cabra also changed party in order to continue opposing him. At any rate, the fact that the parties were based on patronage does not mean that they were followings who did not get along well. As we already know, they commonly made agreements. There were even family reasons for their doing so: In Cádiz the provincial leaders of the two parties were the Gómez Aramburu brothers.

4. The evolution of the cacique system and the impotence of its opposition.

The preceding summary permits us to conclude that the prevailing political and social system in Spain during the period was clearly not that of a traditional society nor that of a liberal one. If the first case were true, those who governed would not have governed. To achieve the second, it would have been necessary for an ideological mobilization and honest elections to have existed. Without doubt the Spanish situation was transitional between one state and another, but the final phase of its evolution was patently clear: a democracy with a general political mobilization. Departing from these premises, it is fitting to ask to what point an evolution occurred in the period from 1890 to 1923, at least from the Andalusian view.

Among the promoters of change one could cite, in the first place, the forces situated on the margin of the political system who could effectively attain a mobilization of the masses (as was attained in fact in other Mediterranean countries, such as Italy). However, the truth is that these forces, situated to the left and to the right of the system, were totally incapable of effecting a fundamental change in political life.

The Andalusian Republicans had considerable strength in the provincial capitals and in some rural districts (Montilla, Jerez), but their strength decreased throughout the period and their methods differed little from those of the politicians within the system. A first proof of the weakness of Republicanism in Andalusia (and throughout Spain) is that, although they were the fundamental alternative to the Restoration Monarchy, they were never able to field as many candidates in elections for deputies as there were seats available (the most normal thing is that they did not even field one-fifth). In Andalusia, of some seventy seats available in each election, only on one occasion were they able to win four and their normal level was only two or three. Their strength was decreasing, in part because having originally had relatively extensive rural support, they were gradually losing it and in part also through the exhaustion of their own program and their inner divisions. When the dictatorship was proclaimed, no one thought that the coming of the Republic would be soon: In the 1923 elections the Republicans had fielded in Andalusia only five candidates, none of whom were elected. Another obstacle for the Republicans was that, as has already been noted, their methods were little different from those of the established parties. In 1891 the Republican candidate for Puerto de Santa María (Cádiz) campaigned with Mazzantini who promised to fight the bulls for the voters if his friend won. In this instance one can speak of a lack of ideological motivation, but in other instances there are clear cases of an agreement with the monarchical government to which they were theoretically opposed. In 1914 as a compensation for his actions in Barcelona, the Republican Lerroux received as an encasillado his home district of Posadas (Córdoba). More frequent than a pact with demagogic Republicans was one with moderate Republicans, ultimately innocuous because of its limited scope: The Sevillan Republican Montes Sierra was elected deputy for the capital from 1907 to 1918 with governmental collaboration and something similar occurred in Málaga.

It may not be properly said that the weakness of Andalusian Republicanism was due to its replacement by workers' groups for the simple reason that this replacement did not happen. It is certain, as Ortega said, that the votes for the Socialist party were acts of virtue, in the sense that they supposed the independence of the proletarian electorate, but it is also certain, as Díaz del Moral noted in referring to Andalusia, that the blossoming of the Socialist seed depended "not so much on its quality, as on its adaptation to the soil and the climate." Until 1917, with the sole exceptions of the elections of 1905 and 1910, the Socialists did not obtain even 1,000 votes in Andalusia from each contest that they entered (votes which, on the other hand, came almost exclusively from the urban environment). After this date the situation changed somewhat: In 1919 their votes reached some 55,000, of which half came from the rural districts of Jaén and Córdoba (which explains the Socialist influence in this region during the Second Republic). At any rate, as also happened with Republicanism, the mobilization that the Socialists obtained was characterized by inconstancy. The Socialist trade unions (UGT) had 39,000 members in Andalusia in 1920, but in 1922 the membership had decreased to 21,000; the decline in membership in the Socialist party (PSOE) between these two dates was even more startling (from some 26,000 in 1920 it diminished in 1923 to scarcely 1,300). The only electoral success of the Socialist party in Andalusia (apart from the possibility of fraudulent proceedings being used against it) was the victory of Professor De los Ríos in the circumscription of Granada in 1918. However, this victory was obtained in the bosom of an anti-cacique alliance and, therefore, it is very possible that De los Ríos' votes are not all computable as Socialist votes. In the next election (1919) the Socialist trade unions refused to participate in the electoral contest. This fact is good evidence of the anarchist tendency of the Andalusian proletariat to act independently of concrete trade union affiliation. Moreover, this tendency is shown in many other facts: the absence, for example, of concrete abstentionist propaganda in each election; the utilization of Socialist centers for anti-authoritarian lectures (as demonstrated by Díaz del Moral); the common acceptance by all trade union organizations of "the distribution" as the supreme revolutionary principle, and so on. The existence of the anarchist proclivity created an authentic vicious circle in Andalusian (and Spanish) politics of the period: One did not vote because the system was corrupt, but it was corrupt because one did not vote. The definitive impotence of the Socialists was the most important consequence of all this: In 1923 they obtained scarcely 1,600 votes in all Andalusia of which only 26 came from the rural area.

Another vehicle of political mobilization could have been Catholicism. The truth is that at the beginning of the period there were no Integralist or Carlist candidates anywhere in the region, but one could imagine that the appearance of religious or social problems would produce the advent of a large Catholic party. However, it did not happen and one reason is found in the fact that very probably there did not exist sufficient fear among the Catholics for them to mobilize: When the first Catholic workers' circles were founded in Granada, it is curious to note among them not only Conservative politicians but Liberal ones as well (in reality, there was no difference between the two).

On the other hand, the normal instruments of mobilization, which were used as political vehicles in other European countries, did not exist in Andalusia.

One of the leaders of Spanish Catholic trade unionism in the 1920's, Mondero, explicitly recognized that they had reached Andalusia late and Díaz del Moral, in describing the situation in Córdoba, reached the conclusion that Catholic trade unionism was condemned to impotence by the joint opposition from employers and workers. Under these conditions it is not at all strange that although after World War I there was an explosion of the Catholic press (which had at least one important daily in each provincial capital), the political activity of this sector could be practically reduced to that of the Liga Católica Sevillana that, founded in 1893, participated in elections, with some eclipses, from 1903 until 1923. Although it had a markedly anti-cacique tone and important support in the capital (or perhaps precisely for these reasons), the Liga was not able to elect any candidate of its own except in 1919 when the government was the most rightist of the period.

As far as the official political groups were concerned, it cannot be said that any of them consistently offered a renovating aspect. The Maurists and the Reformists for some time obtained a certain popular support in the cities, but the assimilating strength of the system was so strong that they became one more patronage group. Maurism only lasted as a campaign of popular agitation from 1914 to 1917 and, as for the Reformists, in spite of their monarchical possibilism, in 1923 they counted on encasillado candidates who ran as cuneros in districts without competition.

Thus no political force was capable of renovating the political system. Neither, as it was logical to expect, did the political system renovate itself. It is true that there were some changes, but they were insufficient and in general tended to make the Restoration system not viable rather than to give rise to a new one. Thus, for example, in contradiction to what is commonly said, in Andalusia competition increased somewhat: If in 1891 – 1901 only 50.2 percent of the positions for deputies in the elections were truly contested, in 1903 – 1916 58.7 percent were, and in 1918 – 1923, in spite of the retrocession of the election of this last date, 62.5 percent were true contests. In general the professional politicians who counted on an organized cacique system in the district which they represented tended to increase. At the end of the period there were in Andalusia nineteen "organized" districts with a stable cacique but only twelve "meek" districts. Moreover, since the parties were divided into patronage groups, the country was very difficult to govern. Violence had decreased (as well as the most strident corruption) and the elections were becoming less and less manageable, but this did not mean that anything fundamental (patronage, for example) to the old system had disappeared. The imposition of the dictatorship of Primo de Rivera in 1923 took advantage of this situation and of the undeniable unpopularity of the cacique system where public opinion existed.

5. The dictatorship of Primo de Rivera (1923—1930).

The new regime has been correctly described by some historians (Raymond Carr and Jesús Pabón, for example) as a Regenerationist and anti-cacique reaction against the Restoration system. That the latter was already exhausted is proved, at least with respect to the Andalusian region, by the fact that in all the press it is impossible to find even one instance of approval for the fallen regime. But there is still a fact of even greater importance: During the first months of Primo de Rivera's regime there is throughout Andalusia a true ambience of anti-cacique messianism. One has the feeling that the ills of the country are going to be definitely resolved within a very short period of time. This atmosphere is in many aspects similar to that of the *arbitrismo* of the seventeenth century: As in that period, the current proposals for the transformation of the vital heart of the country refer almost exclusively to the moral aspects of daily life (therefore it is not surprising that the military governors immediately dedicate themselves to forbidding blasphemy or to moralize public spectacles). A good indication of the aforementioned ambience is the personal archive of the dictator, in which are found thousands of letters from ordinary citizens proposing to Primo de Rivera, the "iron surgeon" imagined by Costa, reforms of the most varied kinds and frequently of an infantile nature. Even the members of the old regime share this mentality: There are municipal secretaries who denounce themselves as guilty of political corruption and senators who renounce their daily fees as such. As also occurred in the time of the Conde Duque de Olivares, the mentality is quite simplistic as may be seen not only by the endless number of proposed reforms, but also because the cacique system is pursued as an abstract evil with little or nothing to do with concrete persons or actions.[6]

This atmosphere is indispensable in order to understand the work of Primo de Rivera's government from September 1923 to April 1924, a period which the dictator dedicated almost exclusively to political reform. This is not the appropriate place to allude to the measures of a constitutional character which Primo considered. It is sufficient to indicate that his proposals in this area attempted to concretize a reform of electoral law, an increase in representation in the Senate, a new municipal statute, and so on. Nevertheless, all these measures either were no more than mere proposals or their application stopped considerably short of fulfilling the desired Regenerationist purposes. However, a series of measures did see the light and were applied.

The first of the anti-cacique measures was the dissolution of provincial municipal governments and deputations. The new ones were originally formed by the largest taxpayers, but later they were replaced, in spite of the new municipal law drawn up by Calvo Sotelo, by members appointed by the government. At the same time a true inspection force was imposed on administrative organisms. As Primo de Rivera himself made public, in no fewer than five Andalusian provinces (all of the provinces with the surprising exception of Granada and Almería where, in all probability, the situation was even worse) all the municipal governments under inspection were accused of several types of irregularities. During the investigative process there was no lack of curious anecdotes: There were at least three suicides of municipal employees and still more frequent flights to America or fires in archives before they could be consulted.

Another anti-cacique measure was a decree of incompatibilities according to which the most outstanding members of the old political regime were forbidden to serve on the board of directors of commercial concerns or to advise them as lawyers. This was a measure which only affected professional politicians, because it did not include, for example, deputies. The Andalusian politicians most impaired by this decree were precisely two of the most distinguished opponents of the Primo de Rivera regime: Sánchez Guerra and Alcalá Zamora. Many deputies, whose political promotion depended on their economic power and not vice versa, were, on the contrary, free of the decree, among them some of the most distinguished members of the local Andalusian ruling class. Finally, the Primo de Rivera dictatorship acted in a decisive manner against judicial power at all levels and especially at the municipal level. According to the inspectors sent by the dictator, there were even municipal judges who had been convicted of murder, but in all instances they were closely linked (some even by family ties) with the caciques. In certain provinces (and especially in Córdoba, a fact that could have influenced the later career of Alcalá-Zamora) the persecution was particularly violent, incited by local collaborators of the new regime who sought, and obtained, judicial posts or collaborators of their own volition.

The creation of military delegates in each judicial district can be termed both an anti-cacique and a Regenerationist measure. In fact, they were given the mission of pursuing corruption at all levels, but they also established a kind of guardianship which would make feasible the advent of new politics: Therefore, they came to be a kind of "pocket iron surgeons" such as Primo de Rivera was for all Spain. In general, one may say that they departed from undoubtedly good intentions but, perhaps precisely for that reason, their arbitrismo was even superior to that of their commander. The latter seems to have quickly realized their limited efficiency because in 1925 he began to decrease their number, in spite of the fact that in 1927 the aggregate of the Andalusian civil governors thought that the mission which had been assigned to them continued to make sense.

In order to prove the effect which these military delegates had on local Andalusian life, let us examine a concrete provincial case: that of Granada. In this province the dictator himself was forced to dismiss two delegates (the one for Loja, Montefrio y Alhama, and the one for Baza) because they had taken their mission too seriously and had pursued caciques disposed to cooperate with Primo. A third (from Motril) was dismissed due to accusations that he had created his own cacique system and received gifts from his subordinates. In general, what is certain is that the military delegates replaced the old deputies in their role as promoters before the central government of the interests of their districts, thus creating a new type of cacique system.

The fundamental Regenerationist work was to be led, according to the ideas of Primo de Rivera, by the Unión Patriótica (Patriotic Union), the first mention of which we find in April 1924. As with so many other subjects, Primo was notably contradictory with respect to this one: One never knew for sure whether the UP was a single party, an "association of men of good faith," or a "national movement." What is of no doubt is that it did not arise spontaneously, except in very exceptional cases (for example, in Sevilla the Unión Patriótica was formed from a base of Catholic elements, some of which, such as Giménez Fernández, later changed to pure opposition). It is true that in some cases Primo de Rivera managed to attract to partisan politics elements which had not participated in public life previously and which were of well-known importance. But at the provincial level in Andalusia the most common occurrence was for Primo to rely on the old caciques. In Córdoba, for example, he gained the collaboration of the former partisans of the Marqués de Cabra (who previously had been Conservatives and later Liberals) and even of a Reformist. There also appeared Cruz Conde, unknown previously, who thanks to the support of the dictatorship managed to create his own cacique system.

As had occurred at times with ministers of the interior, Primo de Rivera found that his influence, purely personal, on occasion conflicted with that of the proper governmental authorities. In Cádiz, the home province of the dictator, he managed to place in the heart of the UP old Conservatives (like the Pemán family) or Maurists (Carranza and the Conde de los Andes). This constitutes the greatest proof that at the provincial level the UP definitely did not signify anything new and Primo probably never intended it to. In Granada the

UP provincial leadership was in dispute between a Conservative and a Maurist and in Jaén elements of the same persuasion (Foronda, Saro, Yanguas) fought over the leadership. Formed primarily by former Conservative caciques, the Andalusian UP was only another patronage system controlled more by its local leaders than by Primo who, for example, had to send an inspector to Jaén to resolve personalist battles and try to form a true "Primo de Rivera" party.

In conclusion, the measures adopted by the dictator were excessively simple and inconsistent. It is true that the dictatorship broke up the cacique system, persecuting the old caciques and occasionally replacing them with new ones. The regime also established in power a Regenerationist propaganda that previously had existed only in intellectual circles, but which with respect to the transformation of local Andalusian life, as in general with respect to its political action, was a parenthesis, failing to fulfill the reformist proposals of which it had boasted upon coming to power. The best proof of this is the integration of the old caciques into the new dictatorial politics: When Romanones asked his followers (theoretically Liberals) if they accepted the dictatorial regime as a temporary expedient, he discovered that only 121 of the 737 he consulted said no (in Andalusia only in Sevilla and Granada were the answers negative). Thus derives the weakness of the old regime in opposition to Primo de Rivera: It had no other option than to turn to the army of the king to free itself of Primo.

5. Toward the Republic.

The collapse of the dictatorship brought another messianic climate equal to that of September 1923 to the Andalusian political horizon. But it was much less durable because, with freedom (or at least a "soft" dictatorship), the political situation deteriorated much more rapidly.

The UP disappeared as rapidly as it had risen. The old caciques, aware that they could expect no benefit from the government, returned to their folds. Romanones himself expressed his confidence that his old collaborators "would return, because he was not spiteful." It is true that an important sector of the UP founded the Unión Monárquica Nacional whose members defended dictatorship as a perpetual form of government, but this fact did not improve the situation of the monarchy at all; rather it contributed to its difficulties because of the monarchical idea, but they also arose as a consequence of the fall of the dictatorship. In many regions of Andalusia there were judicial prosecutions against Primo's collaborators, especially Cruz Conde. In a few instances the old parties were rebuilt (some caciques endured: such was the case of Carranza in Cádiz), but their content was pure patronage, as it had been previously. The constitutionalism which some of the old politicians opposed to Primo de Rivera had tried to convert into a regenerating design never had any support within the cacique system: Its members, many of whom were Andalusian, had to be content with only ten seats in the encasillado drawn up by Berenguer, the new prime minister. This constitutes, of course, the best proof that the monarchical leaders still operated in terms of cacique politics, because with only one or two exceptions per province, the encasillado candidates were exactly the same as before 1923. Finally not even the new Centrist party, intended to renovate the content of monarchism, achieved any change: In Andalusia it only obtained a certain foothold in some provinces (Granada, Almería, and Córdoba) on the basis of the least conservative sectors of Maurism.

To attempt to continue the old system was a hopeless anachronism, for Spain was no longer what it had been at the beginning of the century. In Andalusia the levels of greatest illiteracy among the provinces had fallen from 80 percent to 62 percent (Jaén) and the minimum from 64 percent to 41 percent (Huelva). Such social change favored the parties opposed to the system. Republicanism, which one could have judged as exhausted in 1923, acquired new strength thanks to a youth movement in its old centers as well as the creation of new ones. Though the Republican press had practically disappeared before 1930, it reappeared in at least three provinces (Cádiz, Córdoba, and Málaga), while the regional organs of independent liberalism (*El Liberal* in Sevilla or *El Defensor de Granada*) showed a genuine Republican proclivity. Among the middle and lower-middle classes, the intellectuals, young people, and professionals, Republicanism began to mean something very different from what it had meant before. Among the founders of the Autonomous Republican party (Partido Republicano Autónomo) of Granada there were 12 landowners, 21 educators, 13 professionals, and 2 journalists. The Socialist party, which in 1924 scarcely had 776 members in Andalusia and in 1929 still only some 3,000, grew prodigiously. At the national level the UGT grew at the rate of a thousand new members per week following the fall of the dictator and in October 1931 it reached some 120,000 in Andalusia alone.

It is only departing from these premises, which show us an exhausted political system (more the fault of the monarchists than of the monarch), that we see a growing political mobilization, as the result of which the elections of April 12, 1931, which toppled the monarchy, must be understood. The monarchist factions were not united for the election. Only in one of the eight Andalusian capitals (Jaén) were the monarchists able to unite, while in four others there were three candidates for every two positions. In all there were 319 candidates to fill 217 majority positions and 110 minority positions in the provincial capitals. The monarchical division was not confined only to this proliferation of candidates but also to the content of their programs: While the extreme right apologized for the dictatorship, the old parties limited themselves to proposing municipal programs.

The results of tho April 12 election have been much discussed, not only because of their immediate political consequences but also because the available data concerning them are scarce, when not erroneous, and because the interpretation of their significance has given rise to certain misunderstandings. In provincial capitals the percentage of voters was higher than in any previous election of deputies, being approximately 57 percent. With the lone exception of Cádiz, the Republican-Socialist slates triumphed completely in all the Andalusian capitals to the extent that if their total votes are compared with those of the monarchists they are almost double (as may be seen in Table 1-5; if we were to take into account only the number of councillors elected, the differences would not be so clear). Still it would be necessary to indicate other characteristics of these results: If we take into account the municipal districts of each one of the provincial capitals (with the already mentioned exception of Cádiz), the magnitude of the monarchist defeat may be verified by bearing in mind that only in 2 (out of a total of 58) did the monarchists manage to win. One of them was more rural than urban and in the other the monarchists ruined their victory through their division. This fact is important because it demonstrates the defection from the monarchy of the more well-to-do wards. On the other hand, it is interesting to note that within the general monarchist defeat the most affected are the classic parties of the turno.

While the Conservatives and Liberals obtained 47 councillors, the extreme monarchist right (Maurists, UPetistas, etc.) obtained 50 and the left (Albists, Constitutionalists, Reformists, who soon became Republicans), 17. In Sevilla, for example, the so-called monarchist coalition gained almost double the number of votes as the Liberal coalition. Finally, the case of Cádiz is an exception perhaps understandable because that city had a tradition of marked electoral corruption, but also because Republicanism was very poorly organized (it was the only provincial capital in Andalusia where the number of Socialist candidates was greater than the Republicans).

In the rural centers one observes in general a notable stability in the sense that they continued to elect those who had represented them before 1923. This is especially true in provinces with the least degree of economic growth (Almería and Granada) or in the poor and mountainous zones (Sierra de Cazorla,

Ronda, Medina Sidonia). However, as the number of inhabitants increased, a Republican victory became more and more frequent (as is shown by the results contained in Table 1−6). In almost half of the towns with more than

TABLE 1−5.

Election results of April 12, 1931, in Andalusian provincial capitals

City	Monarchist candidates		Republican-Socialist candidates	
	Votes	Councillors	Votes	Councillors
Almería	2,752	15	3,290	20
Cádiz	7,451	37	1,755	3
Córdoba	2,667	17	9,340	27
Granada	3,045	16	5,649	29
Huelva	1,851	10	4,457	23
Jaén	1,917	10	3,700	22
Málaga	4,207	16	4,397	32
Sevilla	7,593	18	14,996	32
TOTALS	31,483	139	57,584	188

Source: Local press from April 13 and 14, 1931.

TABLE 1−6.

Election results of April 12, 1931, in the rural environment

Provinces	Towns of more than 10,000 inhabitants		Towns of 5,000 to 10,000 inhabitants	
	Monarchist victory	Republican victory	Monarchist victory	Republican victory
Almería	5	1	7	0
Cádiz	7	6	9	0
Córdoba	10	9	8	13
Granada	3	1	11	0
Huelva	2	4	11	7
Jaén	5	12	15	10
Málaga	2	3	16	1
Sevilla	9	4	9	6
TOTALS	43	40	86	37
Unknown results	6		12	

Source: Local press.

10,000 inhabitants the Republicans triumph, and the same thing occurs in a little less than one-third of those that have between 5,000 and 10,000 inhabitants. Effectively, as stated by the Marqués de los Hoyos, monarchist minister of the interior, the results from the large towns were also "disastrous" for Alfonso XIII. It is true that the small towns were the stronghold of the monarchists, but this does not mean that they voted for the monarchy, rather that they continued not voting at all. As the cacique from Granada, Natalio Rivas, wrote, "those towns which voted for the monarchists bowed to the Republic three months later" because "rural Spain will always be ministerial."

In conclusion, what was risked on April 12, 1931, was not so much the content of the form of government that Spain was to have as it was the system of her political life. If the monarchy fell it was because it had identified itself, to the discredit of the monarchists, with the cacique system, and if the Republic was received with joy it was because its birth was identified with an undeniable political modernization in the country, whose defects (such as a proclivity toward radicalism) for the moment were not appreciated. There is not the slightest doubt when the election results are studied at the regional level that the King did well in suspending the exercise of his power because, as was soon demonstrated, the change had been substantial. However, it may not be said that it was total. Although during the Second Republic the ruling elites of the country were renewed in a fundamental way, the same thing did not occur at the provincial or local level. Shortly after the proclamation of the Republic, the same Natalio Rivas wrote to Lerroux protesting that his followers in the Alpujarras, the Liberal caciques, were persecuted by the new Republicans, when the latter were only former UPetistas. For a long time local Spanish life was destined to remain at this level of patronage.

NOTES

1. This article is based on the doctoral dissertation of the author which will soon be published. This is the reason for omitting the majority of the quotes. On the cacique system see J. A. Durán, *Historia de caciques, bandos e ideologías en la Galicia no urbana (Rianoxo, 1910–1914)* (Madrid: Siglo XXI, 1972); González de Seara, "Materiales para una sociología electoral de la Restauración," in *Anales de Sociología, II (Barcelona, 1966)*; Juan J. Linz, "The Party System of Spain, Past and Future," in *Party Systems and Voter Alignments*, ed., Lipset and Rokkan (1967); Linz, "Parties, Elections and Elites under the Restoration Monarchy in Spain (1875–1923)," VII World Congress International Political Science, Brussels, November 18–23, 1967; Esteban Mestre, "Los delitos electorales en España" in *REOP*, IV-VI, No. 20 (1970), pp. 125 *ff.;* Juan del Pino Artacho, "Aspectos sociológico-politicos del caciquismo español," in *REOP*, I-III, No. 15 (1969), pp. 211 *ff.;* Javier Tusell Gómez, "Para la sociología política de la España contemporánea: el impacto de la ley de 1907 en el comportamiento electoral," in *Hispania,* Madrid, XXX, No. 116 (1970), pp. 571 *ff.* and, especially, the October 1973 issue of the *Revista de Occidente* with articles by Romero Maura, Varela Ortega, and Tusell Gómez.

2. In order to comprehend the elaboration of the encasillado it is indispensable to use the private archives of the politicians of the period, the local press, and the official archives. The author has used, of the first, those of the Conde de Romanones (Madrid) and La Cierva (Murcia) and, only in part, that of Dato (Madrid) among national political figures and those of Burgos y Mazo (Moguer) and Natalio Rivas (Madrid) among Andalusian political figures. The local press may be consulted in the Hemerotecas or Archives of the provincial capitals. Of the official archives the most important is that of the Ministry of the Interior.

3. The prevailing electoral system was of small rural districts that elected a single deputy, but in provincial capitals and, exceptionally, in large towns (such as Jerez) more than one deputy was elected, giving a certain representation to the minorities.

4. For electoral behavior in the urban environment, see Javier Tusell Gómez, *Sociología electoral de Madrid, 1903–1931* (Madrid: Edicusa, 1969), and Borja de Riquer, "Les eleccions de Solidaritat Catalana a Barcelona" in *Recerques,* II, pp. 94–140.

5. The official results of the elections for deputies are found in the archive of the Spanish Cortes and in more detail in the municipal archives or in the *Boletines oficiales de la Provincia.* The data contained in the work of Miguel Martínez Cuadrado, *Elecciones y partidos políticos de España (1868–1931),* 2 vols. (Madrid: Taurus, 1969), are often erroneous, apart from the fact that the author seems to believe that corruption was not really general.

6. In order to comprehend the work of Primo de Rivera's dictatorship at a local level it is indispensable to use the records of the period from the Presidencia de Gobierno that are preserved in the Archivo Histórico Nacional.

7. The local press offers, in the days immediately following elections, quite complete results.

2

Anarchists versus Syndicalists: Conflicts within the Confederación Nacional del Trabajo, 1917 – 1923

Gerald Meaker *(not a friend of anarchosyndicalism)*

Middle-class liberalism on the nineteenth-century pattern largely dominated Spanish politics down to 1923. The absence of a threat from the left prior to 1917 was due not so much to repression as to the division and extreme weakness of modern leftist forces in Spain. Lower-middle-class Republicans had been discredited in the late nineteenth century and were sorely divided and impotent during the first three decades of the twentieth. The Spanish Socialist party, founded in 1879, remained faithful to classic Marxism at least down to 1918 and, being neither Leninist nor truly revisionist, proved incapable of generating support in the Spanish environment.

Prior to 1931 the only leftist and revolutionary force of any significance in the country was the anarchosyndicalist CNT. The reasons why Spain was the only land to produce a mass worker movement of anarchosyndicalism have long intrigued commentators and historians. The most common responses have to do with vague arguments of "national character" or the "primitive rebels" thesis. The latter is no more acceptable than the former, for in the most primitive countries of Europe—Russia and the Bal-

wrong

kans—there was no anarchosyndicalism equal to Spain's, and Leninism proved more attractive. In backward Eastern Europe, anarchosyndicalism developed strength mainly among Jewish revolutionaries and in certain areas of western Russia—the most advanced, individualist, and Westernized, not the more primitive, sectors of Russian society.

A theory of the development of anarchosyndicalism might be more effectively couched in terms of the inter-action of multiple factors in a land of structural inter-mediacy. By the beginning of the twentieth century, Spain had a long tradition of formal liberalism and individual rights but in fact little genuine democracy. It had at-tempted precociously progressive forms of government but lacked the economy and cultural development to build a fully modern society. Its working classes were propor-tionately more stimulated by this context than in most un-derdeveloped countries. If they lacked the education and the advanced skills and industrial organization to fit into social democratic trade unionism on the North European pattern, they were more autonomous and resourceful than their counterparts in Eastern Europe. Autonomous worker radicalism, free of the tutelage of a middle-class socialist intelligentsia, gravitated toward anarchosyndicalism, spreading roots among a half-educated and developing proletariat whose small-shop structure of work seemed to respond more favorably to the loose confederalism and spontaneity of individuated anarchosyndicalism. But an-archosyndicalism remained largely anarchist in its goals and tactics and was never able to seriously threaten an overthrow of the Spanish system prior to its temporary suppression by the Primo de Rivera dictatorship in 1923–1924.

The following selection describes the impact of World War I on Spanish society and the expansion of anarcho-syndicalism into a mass movement, while dissecting its internal divisions and contradictions and its failure in the early 1920's. The author is professor of history at California State College, Northridge, and has recently published The

Revolutionary Left in Spain 1914 – 1923 *(Stanford, 1974),
on which the present essay is based.*

The anarchosyndicalist Confederación Nacional del Trabajo was one of the
more peculiar mass movements of the early twentieth century, a hybrid organization in which atavism and modernism were in precarious but potent equilibrium. The assumption, made by many observers over the years, that the
CNT was essentially a monolith and that its adherents could all be satisfactorily
categorized simply as "anarchists" cannot be sustained. Rather the movement
was chronically divided between two more or less antithetical tendencies—one predominantly anarchist and the other predominantly syndicalist—which were themselves further subdivided. Much of the power and appeal
of the Confederation lay precisely in its ambiguity, in its ability to express an
essentially peasant anarchist rancor against the intruding forces of modernity
and at the same time articulate for the growing proletarian class a syndicalist
program that relied on modern organizational concepts (i.e., industrial unionism) and, in its own way, pointed toward an industrial future. Originating in a
country where anarchist ideology had deep roots, Spanish syndicalism was
unique among the syndicalist movements of the world in that it remained over
a period of nearly three decades a true *anarcho*syndicalism, an unstable but
enduring synthesis of two frequently antagonistic impulses. More than unique,
it was a tour de force and a contradiction in terms: a mass trade union organization that successfully resisted the seemingly irresistible forces of bureau-
cratization and accommodation and remained a revolutionary movement to
the end.[1]

It was the slowness of the Spanish process of modernization that made it
possible for the CNT to sustain its ideological synthesis over a long period of
time. Spain's misfortune was that as a result of the liberal reforms of the nineteenth century the crust of the traditional society was broken without the nation finding the means to generate the economic dynamism with which that society might have been more or less rapidly transformed. The sluggish pace of
Spanish industrial development, slowed by the poverty of the agrarian sector
and not aided by effective state intervention, failed to culminate in what Alexander Gershenkron has called "the great spurt"[2] and tended, indeed, to nur-
ture rather than transform the millenarian and rebellious mood of the masses
of peasant-proletarians and the anarchosyndicalist proclivities that flowed
from that mood. Although industrialization dated from about 1870, the Spanish
economy remained retarded and semi-colonial and—in contrast, for example,
to Giolittian Italy—never in this era succeeded in achieving a rate of growth

that encouraged positive expectations or reformist tendencies in the working classes. Even in Catalonia, the major industrial center of Spain, the pace of economic growth was far from remarkable; factory units remained relatively small in size and productivity low by the standards of the more advanced industrial nations.[3]

Like the newly recruited workers of the expanding Catalonian industrial zone—the main stronghold of anarchosyndicalism in Spain—the CNT was at once millenarian and materialistic, radical and reactionary, intransigent and possibilist. Beguiled by the myth of the general strike, it saw itself as the demiurge of an Iberian Revolution; but in the period under review it waged some impressively disciplined partial strikes for limited and mundane objectives. Proud of its antibureaucratic ethos and disdainful of such things as paid officials, strike funds, social insurance, and permanent secretariats, it was nevertheless moving, in the years before 1923, haltingly but unmistakably toward something resembling a permanent syndicalist bureaucracy focused, like all bureaucracies, more on means than on ends. The present essay is mainly concerned with this duality of spirit within the CNT, seeking to chronicle the struggle that went on, in the years up to 1923, between moderate and extremist tendencies in Catalonia. The stakes of this struggle, it must be added, were very high, since the victory of the extremists in the twenties more or less guaranteed that the CNT would greet the arrival of the democratic Republic in the early 1930's less as a friendly collaborator than as a dangerous rival.[4]

The dual nature of the CNT was implied by its beginnings, which saw the coming together of two principal currents: the old Bakuninist anarchism, partially disabused of its individualist tendencies and reluctantly but increasingly committed to work within the trade unions as the only way to realize libertarian objectives; and the new syndicalism, which reflected French experiences and ideas and gave expression to an organizational mystique centered on the supremacy of the workers in the factory and of the factory in society.[5] Although they sought to influence the same working-class constituency and shared certain short-run objectives, the two tendencies coexisted in less than complete harmony. Indeed, as early as 1915 some rather harsh polemics began to take place between them. The heart of the debate was the then somewhat abstract question of whether the post-revolutionary society would be run by local "communes," as the anarchists insisted, or by the *sindicatos* as the syndicalists demanded.[6]

The anarchist-syndicalist tension within the CNT was to some degree rooted in geography, in the sense that the two main Cenetista (CNT) bastions of that era—Catalonia and Andalusia—did represent diverging ideological outlooks.

The Andalusian Regional Confederation (founded in 1918) was clearly more anarchist and agrarian in mood, while the Catalonian Regional Confederation (CRT, founded in 1908) represented a more urban and syndicalist point of view. But it is important to recognize that the anarchist-syndicalist struggle went on within both major regional confederations and was not *primarily* a contest between regions. Anarchism and syndicalism are best conceptualized, rather, as two polarities between which the majority of Cenetista militants tended to fluctuate, depending on the circumstances and the prevailing mood. Anarchism embodied an austere ethic, an almost total critique of bourgeois-industrial society and a puritan longing for a return to an uncorrupted, pre-industrial age; syndicalism, by contrast, evoked the more modern vision of a worker's world, rationally organized, industrialized, and productive, but exposed to the probability that organizational power and material gain would become ends in themselves. Anarchism, again, connoted an extreme emphasis on spontaneity and localism in the revolutionary struggle; syndicalism implied a greater concern with organizational preparation, planning, and centralized direction. Anarchism, finally, was a blend of peasant negations; syndicalism, with its less categorical rejection of authority and its faith in organization, was the potentially more positive ethos of an urban proletariat, and may be viewed, in the Spanish context, as a "westernizing" and transitional creed.[7]

It was in Catalonia that the anarchist-syndicalist polarity was most evident. Here the active Cenetista militants fell into three not very clearly demarcated groups: (1) a minority who remained almost wholly anarchist in character; (2) the majority, who were essentially anarchosyndicalists, exhibiting all the ambiguities of their creed; and (3) another minority who were almost wholly syndicalist, being represented especially by the leaders of the Catalonian Regional Confederation and by the heads of some of the larger unions.

The first group were sometimes referred to as "pure" anarchists and were centered around *Tierra y Libertad,* the organ of the Catalonian Federation of Anarchist Groups. They were the least reconciled to the trade union tactic and most fearful that the purity of anarchist ideals would be compromised by an attempt to implement them through the medium of mass unionism. Invariably these purists gave priority to the preservation of anarchist values and resisted the urge to yield to revolutionary opportunism. They were, in effect, too doctrinaire to be good revolutionaries, preferring a smaller CNT made up wholly of *obreros conscientes* over a truly mass organization in which libertarian values would be lost.[8]

The second group—the anarchosyndicalists—were the mainstream of the movement, definitely concerned to preserve anarchist values and achieve a libertarian revolution but convinced that this could only be accomplished through the trade union organization, which they viewed, of course, not as an end itself but as an expendable instrumentality that they were willing to risk for the sake of achieving a revolutionary victory. They were the most authentic revolutionaries within the CNT, yet their basically anarchist character caused them to be excessively addicted to spontaneity and habitually unable to mount the coordinated, large-scale effort that alone could have offered any possibility of success. Millenarianism was part of their temper and encouraged them to see the revolution as always just over the near horizon. Still, it was precisely their ability to blend millenarian-revolutionary fervor with the modern organizational ethos of industrial unionism that made the CNT the irrepressibly vigorous organization that it was—a movement unquestionably closer to the temper of the Spanish people than any other in this era of painful social transition.[9]

The third element within the CNT—the "pure" syndicalists as they were sometimes called—consisted of those who either had never been committed anarchists (Salvador Seguí was the most prominent example) or who had transcended their anarchist origins (as was the case with Angel Pestaña). They had not consciously surrendered their revolutionary objectives, but the weight of the responsibilities of office which they bore, along with a temperamental inclination toward prudence and planning, pushed them toward moderation in practice—a moderation that they systematically, and no doubt unconsciously, obscured by means of a revolutionary-reformist rhetoric that seemed to satisfy most of their followers. The principal tension within the CNT was between these "pure" syndicalists and the anarchosyndicalists; but the struggle remained disguised and to a large extent muffled by the lack of ideological clarity among the Cenetistas, by a common loyalty to the organization, and, above all, by the intense pressures generated by their unremitting struggle against the forces of order and privilege.

In 1919–1920 a fourth tendency would emerge within the CNT, that of the communist-syndicalists, who combined an authentic revolutionary impulse with an emphasis on the need for organizational centralization and discipline that was almost Leninist in character; most of the communist-syndicalists would end up in the ranks of the small Spanish Communist party created in 1921.

Although founded in 1911, the CNT was outlawed until July 1914, and the outbreak of the war a month later would mark the real beginning of what would prove to be the first great phase of syndicalist ascendancy in the twentieth century. The effect of the war on Spanish life was paradoxical and uneven: Boom conditions and spreading impoverishment went hand in hand. A callous and opulent *nouvelle bourgeoisie* was spawned, characteristically inclined to spend its unprecedentedly large profits on various forms of consumption rather than on plant modernization, with the result that the war boom would fail to produce that qualitative transformation of the industrial base that might have been expected. [10] The size of the labor force was increased—perhaps by 20 percent—but the ranks of the unemployed were also enlarged, chiefly because of depressed conditions in certain industries whose markets or sources of raw materials were adversely affected by the war. Urban Spain profited, in general, more than rural Spain, and the tide of migration from the countryside to the cities was accelerated. From January 1914 to January 1919 Spain's larger cities grew by somewhere between 10 and 12 percent, about half of this gain being due to rural migration. [11] The industrial zones were filling up with peasant-proletarians who could not fail to add to the volatility of the labor force, especially in the postwar period. In Catalonia, the arrival of large numbers of migrants from the arid and economically troubled provinces to the south tended to radicalize the labor movement, partly because of the new arrivals' *incultura* (lack of sophistication) and willingness to act as strikebreakers and partly because of their greater susceptibility (in contrast to the native Catalan workers) to the more extreme anarchist and anarchosyndicalist proselytizers. [12] Inflation had a further radicalizing effect. Although the rate of inflation in Spain did not match that of the belligerent nations, it was severe enough, rising from 106.9 in September 1914 to 123.6 by March 1917 and 145.4 by March 1918. [13]

The impact of the war in the countryside was particularly mixed. The outbreak of hostilities cut Spanish migration to the New World by about 75 percent by 1915, thus depriving rural Spain of a historic and vital safety valve. [14] But at the same time the demands of the Allied powers for foodstuffs led to greatly increased cultivation and to something approaching full employment, the peak of agrarian prosperity being reached in late 1916. [15] The war also disrupted markets and caused a severe scarcity of shipping, resulting in soaring unemployment and a substantially increased current of migration toward the industrial zones of the peninsula (primarily Catalonia) or toward France, where both farm and factory workers were in demand. But some regions—western Andalusia would be an example—experienced little migration, and, in general, the wages of rural workers appear to have risen substantially, by perhaps 300 percent by the war's end, a fact that helps to explain the relative quiescence of the agrarian south during the urban upheavals of 1917 and down to the spring of 1918. [16]

The Confederación Nacional del Trabajo was still very small in 1914, possessing only about 15,000 members and but one regionally organized nucleus, that of the Catalonian Regional Confederation. Contact between the National Committee of the CNT and the several hundred unions—large and small—outside Catalonia was on an individual basis, making coordination very difficult. The organizational principle of the CNT continued to be craft union-ism, although the first industrial union (termed Sindicato Unico) was organized in Barcelona as early as 1915. There were three formal power centers within the Confederation, all located in Barcelona: the National Committee, the Com-mittee of the Catalonian Regional Confederation, and the Committee of the Barcelona Local Federation of Trade Unions. The most influential of these was actually the second, for the reason that nearly two-thirds of all CNT members were under its control. [17]

The tension between anarchist and syndicalist currents within the CNT was evident in the frequently somewhat strained relations between the National Committee, which tended to be dominated by anarchist or anarchosyndicalist ideologues, and the Committee of the CRT, which was composed of less doc-trinaire militants who bore an immediate responsibility for the day-to-day mate-rial welfare of thousands of trade unionists. Whereas the Committee of the CNT was preoccupied with the long-run revolutionary and sectarian objectives of the movement, the leaders of the CRT focused on short-run goals and were greatly concerned with the need to preserve and strengthen the hard-won or-ganizational structure of the CRT and not to risk it in reckless undertakings. [18] Much the same thing could be said of the men who guided the Committee of the Barcelona Local Federation. Most of these militants could probably be de-scribed as anarchosyndicalists, and they certainly viewed themselves as "rev-olutionary" labor leaders; but the responsibilities of office had inevitably a moderating effect on them, causing them to be increasingly absorbed with bread-and-butter issues and "small gains." The recurring complaint of the more extreme militants was that these leaders guided the movement far too cautiously, letting "revolutionary opportunities" pass by without taking bold action. [19]

To these three power centers should be added a fourth, namely the editorial office of Solidaridad Obrera, which, after 1916, was headed by the Leonese militant Angel Pestaña. This leader, who had only come to Barcelona in the summer of 1914 and who did not belong to any Cenetista union, exemplified in his career the extreme openness and penetrability of the CNT resulting from its lack of an entrenched paid officialdom and its addiction to the mystique of amateurism in administrative affairs. By virtue of his speaking ability, organ-izing skill, and austere charisma, he won in a few months a place of leadership in the CNT that would have required years of patient labor in another organization.[20] Starting as a quite doctrinaire anarchist, Pestaña responded to the imperatives of office by gradually moving away from his earlier intransigence. He continued for a number of years to think of himself as an anarchist and tried to maintain his contacts with the men around *Tierra y Libertad*, but the unexpected fund of <u>moderation</u> in his character steadily widened the distance between himself and those purists.[21] He had, in fact, made the transition from anarchist ideologue to syndicalist functionary without quite realizing it. *dimwit!*

Because of the lack of paid officials in the CNT, which necessitated that all committee members work long hours at their jobs, Pestaña felt that the main center of de facto power in the Confederation lay in his editorial office. Since the Leonese leader (who apparently managed to support himself by working at his watch repair business at odd hours) could be found on the premises of *Solidaridad Obrera* most of the time, workers and militants naturally gravitated there in search of advice and information. Pestaña would later boast that more decision-making took place in the editorial offices of "Soli" than in the other three committees combined.[22]

One issue on which the two major Cenetista factions did not disagree was the war, which was opposed by the vast majority of militants.[23] This was in part simply doctrinaire fidelity to anti-militarist principles, but it was also to some degree a reactive response—an instinctive rejection of the belligerently pro-Allied mood of the despised Socialists, Republicans, and Radicals.[24] To be fair to the men of the CNT it should be said that their position on the war was not, in fact, precisely pacifist but revolutionary: Even before Lenin's pronouncements at Zimmerwald their feeling was that the war should be brought to an end not by mere restoration of peace on the basis of the status quo antebellum but by a revolutionary effort of the European workers. One of the reasons they would feel so much affinity with the Russian Bolsheviks at the time of the October Revolution was the anti-war, peace-through-revolution policy with which the Bolsheviks were identified.[25]

The year 1917 was one of revolutionary or quasi-revolutionary disturbances all over Europe, among both belligerent and neutral nations. The root cause of these upheavals was of course the war and the steadily mounting burdens that it placed on civilian populations. Since Spanish governments proved unable to erect any real barriers between the war and Spain's vulnerable economic life, the working classes paid a price in the form of rising living costs and mounting unemployment. These twin burdens at length produced something that no one had expected and that shook the ruling groups badly: an alliance between the two main, and hitherto hostile, peninsular labor movements, the anti-political

CNT and the very political socialist UGT (General Union of Labor, which had about 100,000 members). This alliance, consummated in July 1916 and known as the Pact of Zaragoza, was designed to coerce a sluggish government into taking the economic measures required to protect the workers' livelihood and, failing that, looked toward a revolutionary general strike designed to replace the monarchy with a republican regime more sympathetic to the needs of the workers. [26]

The genesis of the general strike of 1917 was very complex and cannot be discussed in detail here. Suffice it to say that the strike owed far more to the economic and political effects of the war than to the March Revolution in Russia. [27] Leadership of the strike was largely in the hands of the socialists, who tried to coordinate it in the whole peninsula; by contrast the Cenetista effort was restricted almost entirely to Catalonia. Here again the duality of the CNT asserted itself. The extreme anarchosyndicalists dreamed of a thoroughgoing anarchist revolution and revealed their extreme impatience with the socialists' characteristically slow and methodical preparations. The moderate syndicalist leaders, represented by Seguí and Pestaña, saw a need for careful and systematic efforts and for alliances with the Republicans and with the army; above all, they accepted the necessity of a democratic Republic as an intermediate goal to which the Cenetistas should adhere. [28]

Chiefly because the army refused to support it, the August general strike was decisively defeated and resulted in severe repressive measures against the workers. [29] The Cenetistas were left, above all, with a renewed sense of bitterness against the Republicans who, it was felt, had encouraged the launching of the movement with their revolutionary rhetoric and had thn "betrayed" it by their failure to go into the streets alongside the workers. Most Cenetistas felt a renewed contempt for the Republican institutions which, under the urging of Seguí and Pestaña, they had for a brief moment accepted as a halfway house leading toward the desired regime of libertarian communism. [30] The alliance with the socialists lapsed, and the old hostility between the two labor movements resurged, aggravated by the socialist majoritarians' continued and very ardent support for the Allied war effort.

It was precisely at this moment of defeat, cynicism, and gloom that the first news of the Bolshevik Revolution in Russia reached Spain, like a ray of light from another world, inspiring a sudden revival of hope. The most jubilant response to the Bolshevik victory came from the "pure" anarchists of *Tierra y Libertad* who were, for a time, convinced that the Bolsheviks were actually anarchists hostile to all authority and state power and that Russia and the world were on the brink of an anarchist millennium. [31] But the Bolshevik Revolution soon engendered among Spanish anarchists a crisis of belief, calling into question their commitment to spontaneity in the revolutionary process and their hostility (at least on the theoretical level) to the use of authoritarian and coercive tactics. Torn between the high idealism and essential humanism of their libertarian creed and their intense admiration for the Russian Bolsheviks as the successful practitioners of revolutionary *Realpolitik,* many anarchists wavered between millenarian enthusiasm and critical objectivity. A surprising number, impressed by the quasi-anarchist tone of Lenin's *State and Revolution,* accepted for a time the Leninist insistence that the revolutionary process could not be left wholly to the workings of mass spontaneity but had to be "organized" and even "authoritarian." [32] Of course, the Cenetistas did not go so far as to accept the dictatorship of a Communist party, assuming that the proletarian dictatorship would be exercised by the sindicatos. "All power to the sindicatos" became a common refrain and marked an advance over their earlier reliance on the notion of a vague "class" revolution. [33]

The dichotomy within the CNT was again revealed by the more restrained enthusiasm for the Revolution that the moderate syndicalist leaders displayed in the pages of *Solidaridad Obrera.* Departing from earlier Cenetista assertions that the war could only be ended by a revolution of the masses, they expressed, in essence, the same fears that European liberals had voiced, namely, that the Bolshevik coup might actually prolong rather than shorten the war. They welcomed the Revolution and paid homage to the Bolshevik accomplishment but always more reservedly and with a shrewder recognition than the "pure" anarchists that Soviet Russia might not be a regime of perfect freedom. [34] The moderates recognized that, in Spain as elsewhere, the Bolshevik Revolution connoted revolutionary audacity and encouraged the belief that the time was ripe for a revolutionary overthrow of the old order—a belief that the "pure" syndicalists, especially in view of the August debacle, could not share. [35]

Indeed, the essential coolness of their response to the Bolshevik Revolution confirms the suspicion that the Seguí-led moderates were, unaware, moving to a de facto reformism. Their innate caution and concern for organization, their absorption with material demands, their willingness to concede a certain legitimacy to other groups in society (and even, as in the case of Seguí, to contemplate electoral liaisons with some of those groups)—all suggest that, consciously or not, their ultimate goal was essentially accommodation with the existing society. Lacking, one suspects, an authentically revolutionary temper, the moderates were moving, whether or not they would admit it, toward an integration of the working classes on the most favorable terms possible rather than toward a Sorelian apocalypse.

Thus the Bolshevik Revolution became a weapon in the struggle of the extreme anarchosyndicalists against their moderate opponents within the CNT. The former were in fact genuinely enthusiastic over the Revolution, but they also recognized that the Bolshevik myth could be utilized to help radicalize the CNT, to push it down the path toward the anarchist revolution that they believed to be possible in Spain in the near future and to convert or silence the moderates within the organization. The fact that for two years so little was known about the Revolution in Russia made it easier to align with the Bolsheviks and to convince oneself that the Russian leaders were at heart anarchists. Even after the "pure" anarchists of *Tierra y Libertad* (finally discerning the bitter truth about authoritarian tendencies in Russia) fell away,[36] the militant anarchosyndicalists closed their eyes to signs of a reemerging and dictatorial state and an increasingly omnipotent Bolshevik party and remained stubborn adherents of Bolshevism until the middle of 1921. That they clung to their illusions so determinedly owed to the fact that, of all major groups within the CNT, they were the most authentically revolutionary and to the fact that the pro-Bolshevik enthusiasm and revolutionary combativeness of the workers continued to be very great for more than two years after the ending of the war.[37]

The struggle between the extreme anarchosyndicalists and the "pure" syndicalists within the CNT was only half-acknowledged by the militants themselves and was not generally perceived by the public or the authorities, who, like most subsequent commentators, tended to lump all the Cenetistas together as "anarchists." The contest was waged not in terms of doctrines (which most Cenetistas were singularly ill-equipped to articulate) but on the basis of arguments about timing and about the wisdom or unwisdom of particular actions. Most of the leading militants saw themselves as *both* anarchists and syndicalists and certainly as revolutionaries; yet the eternal split between those committed primarily to the ideological *ends* of the movement and those increasingly absorbed in the organizational *means* to be utilized manifested itself with growing force. Both sides believed theoretically in "direct action," but the extreme anarchosyndicalists retained their faith in the efficacy of "general" as opposed to partial strikes and were adamantly opposed to diluting direct action through participation in the mixed commissions (representing government, employers, and workers), which were being set up in this period. The moderates, not unlike the Socialists of the UGT, were willing to rely occasionally on the general strike, providing it was carefully prepared, but preferred to wage partial strikes for limited demands and to terminate them when they threatened to impair the organizational structure; and they were willing to participate in the government-sponsored industrial commissions. That the differences between these two tendencies did not become apparent more *morons + deceivers then!*

quickly and rupture the organization early in its life must be attributed to the revolutionary-reformist rhetoric of the "pure" syndicalists, which hid from themselves as well as from others their essential moderation—a rhetoric whose greatest practitioner was probably Salvador Seguí.

The revival of the CNT/CRT got under way in the aftermath of the August defeat, with the formation of a new provisional National Committee headed by the ardent anarchosyndicalist and pro-Bolshevik Manuel Buenacasa. This committee launched a vigorous organizational campaign, putting itself in touch with member unions in every part of the peninsula—a laborious undertaking since the organization had no paid secretariat and no typewriters, all letters being written by the committee members personally in longhand. [38]

The biggest step toward the revival, reorganization, and expansion of the movement was the congress of the CRT held in the Barcelona district of Sans from June 28 to July 1, 1918. This was primarily a syndicalist gathering marked by a very businesslike atmosphere, free both from anarchist rhetoric and from eulogies to the Bolshevik Revolution. [39] The major step taken here was the approval given to the conversion of the CRT from craft unionism to industrial unionism. The Sindicato Unico was now made the compulsory form for all unions within the CRT, which meant, of course, the creation of larger unions embracing all the sections (i.e., trades or skills) within a particular industry such as metallurgy, construction, and electricity. This facilitated greater centralization, greater discipline, and greater striking power against employers. Whole industries could now be paralyzed, if the workers chose; and the employers were correspondingly compelled to enlarge the size of their own organizations, thus producing a general escalation of labor conflict. The ambivalence at the heart of the CNT/CRT revealed itself even here. For at the same time that this step toward greater centralization was taken, steps were taken also to preserve as much local autonomy as possible, so that the Sindicatos Unicos emerged as a curious amalgam of industrial "mass" unionism and localist "craft" unionism. Thus the Sindicato Unico was not in fact a unitary union but really a federation of *oficios,* that is, of trades or local sections. The *junta general* of the union was made up of representatives from all the sections, and when it voted to support the strike of any particular section, all sections were required to render support. But at the same time the constitution of the Sindicatos Unicos was careful not to deprive the individual sections of the right to wage isolated strikes on their own if they chose to. [40]

The new unions also continued to disdain compulsory dues, paid officials, strike funds, and coercive regimentation of members—thus making a positive virtue out of their decision to refrain from doing those things which they were in any case powerless to do. In Spain, as in France, the syndicalist creed was in many respects a "rationalization of weakness,"[41] adjusted to the realities of a labor force whose peasant origins, poverty, illiteracy, ingrained individualism, and spontaneity generally precluded the discipline and authority in trade union affairs that was possible elsewhere. At the same time, though the Cenetistas lauded the "non-coercive" aspects of their unionism, frequently contrasting it with the "authoritarian" and "bureaucratic" practices of the Socialists, it must be said that they were capable, at least on occasion, of imposing an impressive and even severe discipline on union members. Certainly the emerging dictatorship of the anarchist action groups over the sindicatos, discussed below, frequently resulted in rather blatant acts of coercion.

In any case, the Sindicato Unico now exerted a mythic appeal, leading masses of workers to believe that the way to the Promised Land had at last been found. From about the middle of 1918 workers began pouring into the new unions, so that the CRT rose from a little more than 100,000 members late in 1918 to 433,746 by December 1919.

There is little question that during the period immediately following the Armistice Spain was in a more perilously revolutionary situation than had been the case even in the summer of 1917. The monarchy and the ruling groups had been pro-German during the war and inevitably suffered a serious loss of face as a result of the Allied victory. As the war came to a close, Republican and anti-monarchical feeling swept over Spain and the expectation of some sort of revolutionary movement was very widespread. [42] This feeling was especially encouraged by the rising wave of disturbances in Andalusia and the south, where workers and peasants, galvanized by news of the peasant land seizures in Russia, had begun a phase of intense agitation, organizational growth, and rebelliousness (involving even the attempted expropriation of land and the proclamation of "Bolshevik" republics in a number of towns) that would last through 1920 and be known as the Trienio Bolchevista. [43]

Although it seems clear that the regime was more vulnerable than in 1917, the workers more numerous, more aggressive, and better organized than ever before, and the international atmosphere filled with portents of change and upheaval, no move was made against the monarchy. This was largely because the Socialists—who in the nature of things were best prepared to lead and coordinate a revolutionary movement—had been both sobered by the post-August repressions and, ironically, heartened as well by the unexpected electoral gains that their martyr-role in the August strike had won them in the elections of 1918, when their parliamentary contingent soared from one deputy to six. More and more the Socialist leaders were convinced that they could win what they wanted by continuing to adhere to the tactic of unceasing electoral struggle. Hence, though the Socialists shared in the republican euphoria that followed the victory of the Allied powers and often spoke in rather violent language, they had clearly lost their taste for revolution. ✓

The Cenetistas were as usual divided over the whole issue of revolution. The febrile anarchosyndicalists (led by militants such as Buenacasa, Boal, and Eusebio Carbo) were excited by the Russian events, by the agitations in Andalusia, and by the bread riots in Madrid early in 1919, and were certain that Spain was on the verge of a momentous uprising. Confirmed in their intransigence by the radicalized hordes of workers who poured into the Sindicatos Unicos after mid-1918, they wanted to use the Confederation aggressively and were willing to risk ruining it in order to bring down the regime. Every strike would seem to them an opportunity to push things beyond mere material demands and to move toward revolution.

By contrast, the moderate syndicalists, led by such men as Salvador Seguí, Salvador Quemades, Angel Pestaña, Simón Piera, and José Molins, were far more cautious and even pessimistic about the possibility of a successful revolution in Spain. They were greatly encouraged by the rapid growth of the sindicatos but frankly doubted that a revolutionary coordination of the labor forces of the peninsula could be achieved or that agrarian and urban forces could be successfully harnessed at that time. Their desire, despite the postwar instability and ferment, was to continue recruiting efforts, organizational work, proselytizing among the peasants, and the waging of strikes for essentially limited objectives. Yet despite their revolutionary skepticism, it was they, ironically, far more than the revolutionary anarchosyndicalists, who recognized the need for allies in the struggle and who persistently urged liaison with the Socialists and the Republicans—against the extremists who imagined that the CNT could go it alone and were inclined to treat potential allies with contempt.

The year 1919 was the CNT's great year—a year of triumph and of unprecedented growth, which would carry the Confederation to a membership of more than 765,000. [44] Salvador Seguí, the clever and charismatic, albeit cautious, leader of the CRT, launched a grandiose strike against the Anglo-Canadian power company, known colloquially as La Canadiense, which fed power produced by the Ebro River to the homes and factories of Barcelona and whose closure could paralyze the whole industrial complex. This strike grew out of a dispute involving the attempt of the company to reduce the wages of certain workers, probably as part of their postwar retrenchment. Seguí and the syndicalists seized upon this episode to launch an industrial struggle that was neither revolutionary in purpose nor merely aimed at material gains. It was essentially political, seeking to win from both employers and government full recognition of the Confederation's right to exist and to carry out its organizational labors in an atmosphere free of coercion and intimidation. [45]

The details of the La Canadiense strike need not concern us here. Suffice it to say that it lasted for forty-four days, virtually paralyzed for a time the life of Barcelona, and was, in fact, the greatest strike ever waged in Spain. What impressed most observers, however, was the remarkable order, discipline, and resoluteness with which the strike was conducted, under Seguí's leadership, and the awesome power that the new Sindicatos Unicos manifested. This was a syndicalist strike par excellence, and the anarchist groups, with their propensity for individual acts of violence, were kept wholly under control and in the background. In the end, under the prodding of the Romanones government, the employers opened talks with the syndicalist leaders, and an agreement was finally reached that fell little short of complete victory for the workers: All imprisoned workers were to be released, excepting a few who were to be tried on criminal charges; all strikers were to be rehired without penalties; wage raises were granted; the eight-hour day was instituted; and the strikers were to be paid for the time they had been on strike. Implicit in the settlement was an acknowledgment by the forces of order in Catalonia that the CNT/CRT had the right to exist and to act as a bargaining agent for the region's industrial workers. The settlement was, then, a triumph for the Seguí-led syndicalists and for the whole concept of an industrial unionism looking not toward an immediate social revolution but toward the more limited and attainable objectives of organizational power, material gain, and (in the broad sense of the word) political influence within a pluralistic society. [46]

Here, one must say, was a crucial moment in the history of twentieth-century Spain. The moderate syndicalists had won a tremendous victory and were on the verge of consolidating their hold over the Catalonian working classes and turning the CNT/CRT into a powerful and, above all, constructive force in the national life. This was a force which, in alliance with other progressive forces in Spain (and it should be noted that Seguí was always ready for such alliances), might have imposed fundamental reforms on the regime or even, perhaps, have helped bring in the republic a full decade before it actually made its appearance. [47]

The moderate syndicalists were trapped, however, between the revolutionary intransigence of the more extreme anarchosyndicalists, the obduracy and incomprehension of the ministries in Madrid, and the radicalism of the masses of newly recruited Cenetistas. In a massive meeting, attended by some 25,000 excited and bellicose workers, held in the Plaza de Toros in Barcelona on

March 20, Salvador Seguí, heckled by armed anarchists in the stands, spoke persuasively and at length, finally convincing the workers—and this was an authentic tour de force—that they should accept the settlement they had won from the employers and return to work. [48] This was Seguí's greatest hour, and it looked as though the brilliant Catalan leader had saved the victory of La Canadiense and his own place in the history of the Spanish labor movement. One writer spoke of the "miracle" of Seguí's convincing 25,000 men to return to work who did not wish to do so. [49] *not a democrat then!*

But only a few days later, in the face of the civil governor's refusal to release the few remaining jailed workers, the militant anarchosyndicalists were able to seize the initiative from the moderates. Even as Seguí was negotiating for the release of the remaining prisoners, the anarchists of the action groups were exhorting the workers to launch a general strike in Barcelona with the aim of winning not a partial but a total victory over their social enemies. Many of the workers were, indeed, in an exalted frame of mind and believed they glimpsed millennium over the horizon. But the anarchist action groups exerted something more than mere moral suasion. They were, in fact, armed visionaries who were prepared to impose the strike on the Cenetista masses whether they wished it or not. [50] *not possible* ?

Thus, despite the objections of the moderates, the CRT declared a general strike on March 24. This was, indeed, an impressive movement, remarkably coordinated and thoroughly organized, which once again, for the second time in less than two months, virtually brought the life of Barcelona to a halt. Not all workers understood why a new strike had been called so soon after the previous one, but the discipline of the Sindicatos Unicos—enhanced by pressure from the anarchist groups—was so great that the mass of workers obediently and unhesitatingly laid down their tools. [51]

This time, however, the forces of order in Barcelona were better prepared. Martial law was immediately proclaimed, thousands of troops were brought into the city, and the ancient Somatén, a kind of bourgeois militia, carried out a systematic intimidation of workers in the streets. The Somatén also forced shops and businesses to stay open and at the same time worked out a system for keeping the city supplied with necessary foodstuffs. Hundreds of labor leaders were arrested, and on April 2 all unions in the city were closed down and their records seized. The strike held up well for about a week and a half, but after that point it began to lose its cohesion and more and more workers began returning to the factories. By April 14 it was over and the Cenetistas had been completely defeated. [52]

This disastrous strike was decisive for the development of the CRT and for the struggle between extremist and moderate tendencies within the organization. For hard on the heels of the repressive measures associated with the La Canadiense strike there followed another and longer phase of repression that did not end, it should be noted, with the termination of the general strike but went on for another four months under a decree of martial law proclaimed by the military governor Milans del Bosch. Even the militant anarchosyndicalist Manuel Buenacasa, who approved of it at the time, would later acknowledge that the general strike had been "the greatest tactical error" the Cenetistas could have committed. [53]

The CRT by no means crumbled under the blows leveled at it (closing of the unions, arrest of many leaders, a ban on the collection of dues, etc.) and, indeed, the unions continued to flourish underground and even to expand their membership. New, clandestine committees were created, and tens of thousands of pesetas continued to be collected from the workers. But clandestinity inevitably meant a displacement of the more moderate, "pure" syndicalist leaders, who were increasingly elbowed aside in the juntas of the unions by the militant anarchosyndicalists affiliated with the anarchist action groups that were proliferating in this period. The interest of the groups, of course, centered less on organizational work and the winning of small gains than on clandestine struggle and the utilization of terrorist tactics on behalf of a dimly perceived revolutionary goal. [54]

The severity of governmental repression at this time, which made little or no distinction between moderate and extremist leaders, would seem to have reversed, in effect, the natural if incipient development of the CRT toward bureaucratism and accommodation and helped to throw power into the hands of the more revolutionary and doctrinaire elements—those who saw the syndical structure of the CRT not as inherently valuable but as an expendable weapon in the conquest of an always-impending anarchist revolution. Besides their chronic tendency to underestimate the toughness and survival power of their opponents, the extreme anarchosyndicalists were also more prone than the Seguí-led forces to rely on authoritarian methods. While paying lip service to the anarchist ideals of nonviolence, the sanctity of human life, and the inviolability of the individual, they were, as authentic revolutionaries, fatally attracted by dictatorial methods. It was precisely for this reason that of the major Cenetista factions they were the ones most drawn to the Bolshevik Revolution, to the dictatorship of the proletariat, and to the use of violence for revolutionary ends. [55]

This leads us to one of the more controversial issues connected with Spanish anarchosyndicalism, namely, the genesis of the terrorism that blighted the industrial life of Barcelona in the years 1918 – 1921 and resulted in the deaths by shooting of hundreds of workers and employers. The question has been little studied and nearly always treated tendentiously. Most writers favorably disposed to the workers' cause have laid responsibility on the shoulders of the employers, describing the *atentados* carried out by the Cenetistas as merely defensive and retaliatory. [56]

The truth, however, would seem to be that the terror was initiated by the workers—more precisely by the anarchists of the action groups—as a tactic in the industrial struggle. [57] That this reliance on terror helped produce a severe reaction on the part of the conservative forces and contributed greatly to the defeat and destruction of the CNT/CRT in this era is a truth that many, indeed most, students of the subject have been unwilling to acknowledge. Yet terrorism had always been a part of the anarchist *modus operandi,* rarely eulogized in theory but frequently resorted to in practice despite its incompatibility with the idealistic and pacifist side of anarchist consciousness. [58]

The background to the anarchosyndicalist terror of 1918 – 1921 was the migration to Barcelona of large numbers of peasant-proletarians from the "dry" provinces to the south. Many of these new workers, or *murcianos,* as they were generically called, were attracted by anarchist proselytizers, converted into obreros conscientes, and drawn into the action groups that began to form as early as 1916 and that became much more numerous after 1918. [59] These groups—made up, for the most part, of extremely young militants averaging about twenty-one years of age—began as early as 1916 to carry out assassinations of employers whom they regarded as especially intransigent or unregenerate. The original motive was not, in fact, precisely revolutionary; the slayings seem to have been viewed as a technique of labor relations designed to break down the resistance employers displayed in granting the wage concessions that their high wartime profits in many cases justified. The tendency of many employers to yield precipitately to force what they would not yield to equity only encouraged the use of this peculiar labor tactic. [60]

Although the use of assassination in labor disputes should probably be regarded as an extreme form of the "rationalization of weakness," the irony of this period is that precisely at a time when the Catalonian workers, by means of the Sindicatos Unicos, were creating an unprecedentedly strong and disciplined organization, able by means of peaceful coercion to win them the material gains and social power they desired, there was being fastened on the CRT a terrorist apparatus—a kind of anarchist Mafia—whose domination would prove almost impossible to break and would help carry the organization to disaster. Yet it needs to be acknowledged that the assassinations, at least in the earlier period, were often instigated by union leaders who designated the employers to be liquidated and supplied the funds to pay the young anarchist *pistoleros* who carried out their orders. In this way—by collusion between labor leaders and anarchist gunmen—"propaganda of the deed," as the anarchists called it, was translated into an industrial context. [61]

Angel Pestaña, who knew many of the anarchist gunmen and who only belatedly took an open stand against the terrorist tactic, says that in the beginning the young terrorists of the anarchist action groups were motivated by the highest ideals, being in the grip of an "apocalyptic" consciousness. [62] Many of these youths doubtless retained their purity of purpose to the end, but it was almost inevitable that unsavory and opportunistic types would be drawn into the action groups in increasing numbers and that a certain corruption should result. Violence, as always, fed on itself, and a somewhat mindless, self-sustaining system of murder-for-pay was initiated, financed by the dues paid by the rank-and-file union members who did not participate in the assassinations and certainly gained no benefit from them. This ability of the anarchist action groups to draw on the treasuries of the unions and to coerce workers who hesitated to pay dues was crucial to the whole terrorist phenomenon in Barcelona in this era and helped explain not only its scope but its stubborn persistence. [63]

There is no question that many of the youthful pistoleros came from that marginal sector of society best described as the proletarian *bas fond*—men on the fringes of industrial life, hovering between the working class and the criminal class. The action groups contained a growing minority of men who were little more than ideological desperadoes who, under cover of ill-assimilated libertarian slogans found an outlet for antisocial and even homicidal impulses, and who were willing to do almost anything rather than return to the ill-paid drudgery of factory work. Nothing less than a praetorian class had sprung up within the CNT, finding its way of life in the practice of terror.

Thus Buenacasa (who did not oppose the use of terror at the time) complained a few years later about "the newcomers, those without ideas . . . , the ambitious ones, the hotheads . . . , the roving youths [who] saw their hour approaching." The leaders of the CNT, he said, found themselves "enveloped in a dirty vortex and unable to struggle against the gigantic wave of bullies and spongers who dominated in that ambience." It was in this context, as Buenacasa acknowledges, that the assassination of employers and others began "on a large scale," without the CNT being able to do anything about it. Even Buenacasa had to admit that of the thousands of terrorist attacks carried out in that era "very few could qualify as revolutionary deeds. [64]

Angel Pestaña also complained in later years about the "avalanche" of marginal or lumpen elements that inundated the CNT, beginning in the latter part of 1918. He noted the entry of many young workers of "that class of men who live on the indefinite frontier between labor and common crime." Many of them, he noted, had absorbed a superficial anarchist ideology and had been "inflamed" by the Bolshevik Revolution, which in their minds seemed to sanction all violent tactics, including the *atentado personal*.[65] But worse, perhaps, than assassination inspired by ideological passion was the inhuman system or "industry," as Buenacasa called it,[66] of organized and dispassionate killing-for-profit that virtually took over the CNT in these years of clandestine struggle between Cenetistas and the patronal-governmental forces.[67] Government repression, by displacing the moderate leaders, paved the way for this phenomenon, which, once established, proved impossible to dislodge. Terrorism became rooted in the CNT and endemic in the city of Barcelona. It would be suppressed, in the end, only by *force majeure* and at the cost of the decimation of the labor movement.

At the time, Cenetista leaders disclaimed all responsibility for the terrorist attacks.[68] Yet in his memoirs, some thirteen years later, Pestaña candidly acknowledged that the terrorists were in fact sheltered and protected by the sindicatos and that the Cenetistas shared a "collective complicity."[69]

Inevitably, the use of terrorist methods by the Cenetistas led to the adoption of a counter-terror by the employers of Barcelona, which was embodied in the de Koening band, headed by a German adventurer, and which reportedly received some 50,000 pesetas per month from the Employers' Federation. With this money, and aided by the services of a certain Manuel Bravo Portillo (who had been police chief of Barcelona until exposed by Angel Pestaña in *Solidaridad Obrera* for his pro-German espionage activities), the de Koening band hired gunmen from basically the same *bas fond* stratum as the pistoleros of the CNT and began to carry out the assassination of Cenetista pistoleros and labor leaders. All too frequently, it must be noted, the moderate (and highly visible) leaders of the CNT would be shot in retaliation for deeds carried out by the anarchist gunmen who remained anonymous and hidden. The de Koening band underwent somewhat the same evolution as the anarchist action groups, getting out of hand and turning the killing into a depersonalized "industry" which fed upon itself. Baron de Koening was banished from Spain early in 1920 and his band was dissolved; but its role in the anti-Cenetista struggle would be quickly taken over by the gunmen of a newly formed movement known as the Sindicatos Libres, a rival labor organization, against whom the men of the CNT found themselves waging a war of extermination.[70]

fascista !

who ?

Limitations of space do not permit a full discussion of the Libres, but it must be stressed that, in contrast to the ritual assertions of pro-Cenetista publicists, they were far from being mere tools of the employers and were not invented by the then military (later civil) governor of Barcelona, Martínez Anido. The Libres arose, rather, as a natural reaction on the part of the more traditional and conservative workers *outside* within the CNT against the increasing domination of that organization by those committed to anarchist principles and tactics. Not all of the workers who enrolled in the CNT/CRT during 1918 – 1919 were revolutionary or even anti-monarchical; nor were all of them anti-clerical, and the growing influence of the anarchists within the organization, which culminated (in December 1919) in the commitment of the CNT officially to Bakuninist principles and also to entry into the Comintern, was irritating to a sizable minority of Cenetistas who saw the CNT as a purely syndicalist, apolitical organization not committed to any party or sectarian ideology—or to social revolution as a goal. Most galling to such workers was the increasing domination of the CNT by the anarchist action groups, which were now assessing heavy compulsory levies on the members of the sindicatos in order to finance their ever-escalating terrorist campaign and who were exerting a growing intimidation of those workers reluctant to pay their dues. [71]

Discontent over these procedures reached a climax in October 1919 when, in a meeting in the Ateneo Obrero Legitimista of Barcelona, the Sindicatos Libres (known nationally as the Confederación General del Trabajo) was formed under the leadership of the alleged Carlist Ramon Sales. Most of the delegates gathered here were refugees from the CNT, and many of them had been factory delegates. The new organization published a manifesto aimed at all workers who were "sick of the tyranny and slavery to which we have been subjected by our so-called redeemers." While the men of the Libres asserted their opposition to the "tyranny" of the employers, they proclaimed themselves to be even more opposed to the dictatorship of the "spongers" of the Sindicatos Unicos, who were exerting "the most abject, hateful, and criminal despotism." In the harshest terms they denounced "the bullies, the gamblers, the union rowdies—in short, all those who until now have lived at the expense of our honest work." The manifesto also demanded a purely trade-union organization, free of any political or religious affiliation and open to all workers, who would be united on the basis of "respect for the particular and private ideas and convictions of each individual." The appeal ended with the cry: "Enough of tyranny! Enough of [dues payments] that are robberies! . . . Enough of slavery, despotism, and servitude!" [72]

The Libres began a recruitment campaign, winning over a surprising num-

ber of workers in a variety of industries and starting a small but growing current of desertion from the ranks of the CRT. [73] It should be stressed, too, that
no small effort was made by the Libres to avoid a confrontation with the Cenetistas and to maintain a liaison for syndical purposes. On the ground of purely
trade union (as opposed to revolutionary) struggle they insisted that they
would "never, never be an obstruction to the endeavors of the workers on behalf of just demands." They insisted that the Libres were not a "yellow" organization, but they also made it clear that they were adamantly opposed to any
"revolutionary action" intended to paralyze the country, create starvation, and
turn the hungry masses against "the existing order of the world," since this
would only lead to "a tyranny similar to that of Russia." At the same time, one
sees in the literature of the Libres traces of that popular xenophobia which the
internationalist creed of the CNT had usually kept submerged in the mass of
Cenetistas, but which now flared up. Thus the Libres were sure that the CNT
was being backed by "Jewish and German" bankers who were actively trying
to destroy the sources of the country's wealth and set up anarchist schools
"without God and without law." [74]

The Cenetistas—especially the men of the action groups—regarded the defection of the Libres with sectarian anger, viewing it as "betrayal" and "treason," to be stamped out by force. Thus it was, in reality, the Cenetistas who
declared war on the Libres, launching a campaign of extermination against the
leaders and organizers of the new labor body which resulted in a proletarian
civil war that would not really be extinguished until the coming of the dictatorship of Primo de Rivera in September 1923. Since the Libres had already
warned that they would kill three Cenetistas for every one of their own who fell
in battle, the stage was set for a bloody and wholly tragic internecine struggle
within the ranks of Catalonian labor. [75]

The easing of repressive measures by the Sánchez de Toca government,
beginning in August 1919, enabled the sindicatos to return to a legal existence
and permitted the reemergence of the moderate syndicalists as the dominant
figures within the juntas and commitees of the organization. Terrorist activity
also subsided, and the period from August to November 1919 was, in fact, the
last phase of unquestioned supremacy for the "pure" syndicalists in the postwar era.[76] The hopes of the moderate syndicalists were pinned, above all, on
the Mixed Commission set up under the auspices of civil governor Julio Amado
in the early autumn of 1919, which they believed could resolve the large number of industrial disputes then in progress and permit the return to work of all
Catalan workers. The more extreme anarchosyndicalists were deeply opposed
to the commission on the grounds that it smacked of "governmentalism" and

"collaboration." [77] They accepted it only with the utmost reluctance as the price they had to pay for Amado's agreement to free them from jail (where most of them were languishing) and permit the CRT to resume its legal functioning. Revolutionary and intensely sectarian in outlook, they became increasingly frustrated and angry during Amado's governorship, as moderate Cenetistas succeeded in regaining positions of influence within the CRT and swung the workers over to their compromising policies. [78]

In retrospect, one must say that the civil governorship of Amado was perhaps the last chance for moderate syndicalism in Spain in this era, an interlude when it appeared that labor peace might be secured in Catalonia, the moderate forces within the CNT strengthened, and the terrorist phenomenon permanently suppressed. Relations between employers' representatives and syndicalist leaders within the Mixed Commission were surprisingly good, and on November 12, 1919, a formula was agreed to by which the vast majority of labor disputes in the region could be settled and the workers return to their jobs. [79]

This time the hopes of the moderates were spoiled not by the extremists within their own ranks but by the Employers' Federation. The radicalization of the working classes had—by an inevitable dialectic—radicalized a certain portion of the employers to an intense degree, engendering in them an intransigent class-war spirit that perfectly matched that of the militant anarcho-syndicalists. [80] Thus in the October 20 congress of the Employers' Federation, the moderates were shoved to one side and a more or less calculated decision was made to pursue not peace but social and industrial war. The means chosen was a massive lockout designed to close down virtually all industries in Catalonia and, later, in all of Spain.

On November 14, the day on which the workers, with virtual unanimity, had agreed to return to work, the employers challenged the very existence of the syndicalist organization by stationing guards at the gates of some of the major factories with instructions to single out all those recognized as syndicalist leaders or factory delegates and turn them away. This produced an explosion among the Cenetistas that gave the extreme anarchosyndicalists an opportunity to denounce the Mixed Commission and terminate Cenetista participation. [81] The commission was never revived; with it, there perished the last opportunity to achieve a negotiated settlement of the postwar industrial struggle.

A formidable coalition of interests was forming against the Cenetistas, composed of employers, Regionalists (who now shelved their autonomist ambitions in favor of a united front with the conservative forces in Spain and with the army), military juntas, Madrid ministers, and Sindicatos Libres. Shocked by anarchist terrorism, the force of public opinion was swinging against the Cenetistas who, as Pestaña later affirmed, were falling into disrepute with elements that were once sympathetic to them.[82] On November 25 the employers went over to the offensive, finally launching their vast and coordinated lockout, throwing some 200,000 workers into the streets jobless and hungry and closing down all but the most essential industries.[83]

The rising tension between moderates and extremists within the CNT revealed itself in a sharp disagreement as to how this challenge was to be handled. The militant anarchosyndicalists believed that the employers' attack should be met head on and that instead of honoring the lockout and passively letting themselves be starved the workers should boldly occupy the factories of Catalonia and resume the offensive. The National Committee of the CNT, still dominated by Buenacasa and Boal, was, as usual, more intransigent and revolutionary, feeling certain that any attempt by the government to evict 200,000 workers from the factories would fail and in failing would precipitate the revolutionary upheaval that they so eagerly awaited.[84]

The Seguí-led moderates of the CRT committee believed, however, that a proletarian revolution in Catalonia, not to mention the rest of Spain, was not a realistic possibility at that time, and they refused to order the factory occupation. They hoped in this way to avoid disaster and to preserve the CRT to fight another day. Yet it was questionable whether disaster could be avoided, whatever policy was pursued. A factory occupation would doubtless have resulted in massive repression against the Cenetistas and in the probable destruction of the unions; but the decision to wait out the lockout meant slow strangulation for the sindicatos, whose members would be unemployed, increasingly hungry, and unable to pay rent, food bills, or union dues. The lockout proved, indeed, to be the most crippling of the postwar period, idling the great majority of Barcelona workers and lasting about ten weeks. The CRT would never really recover, in this era, from its effects.[85]

The anti-Seguí anarchist journal *Espártaco*, long critical of reformist tendencies within the CRT and especially of the Mixed Commission, angrily denounced the failure to counter the lockout with a revolutionary general strike and lamented that syndicalist leaders in Spain were falling into the same bureaucratism and egoistic self-importance that characterized the leaders of North European and North American labor movements; they were even traveling in sleeping cars and letting themselves be driven around in automobiles.[86] The unpopularity of Seguí and Pestaña with the men of the anarchist groups probably reached its peak in this period. There were angry outbursts in the union halls of Barcelona, fistfights, the firing of weapons, and even attempted atentados against the moderate leaders.[87]

The background to the great Madrid congress of the CNT, held in the Teatro de la Comedia in December 1919, was thus a year and a half of tumultuous growth, severe industrial conflict, and mounting tension between revolutionary anarchosyndicalists and more moderate "pure" syndicalists. The extremists were eager to hold a congress at this time because the extraordinarily rapid growth of the Sindicatos Unicos in Spain, along with the triumph of the Bolsheviks in Russia and the agrarian agitations in Andalusia, filled them with what can only be described as hubris and an apocalyptic sense of impending revolution. They wanted, above all, to use the congress as a means to quash reformist tendencies within the CNT and to commit the organization, for the first time, to an explicitly anarchist creed.

The atmosphere of the congress was entirely pro-Bolshevik.[88] The anarchosyndicalist leaders were not in fact unaware of authoritarian policies in Russia—these being discussed in the congress by Segui and Eleuterio Quintanilla[89]—but they imperatively needed the myth of the Bolshevik Revolution both for their struggle against the moderates and in their effort to rouse the Spanish masses and lead them toward revolution in Spain. They also relished the opportunity to "dump" the Socialists (who were approaching the Bolshevik Revolution much more cautiously) and make it clear to everyone just who were the real revolutionaries.[90]

In the debates on the Comintern question the militant anarchosyndicalists sought unconditional adherence to Moscow, while the moderates wanted no adherence at all. The result was a compromise: the CNT's provisional adherence was voted, but this was to last only until a truly syndicalist world congress could be held in Spain.[91] The congress then voted by acclamation that the final goal of the CNT was "libertarian communism," that is, anarchism.[92] This declaration greatly distressed the moderates, for they feared that it was tantamount to a declaration of war against other leftist parties and would prevent alliances with other groups necessary for the broadening of civil liberties which were essential to the survival and growth of the trade unions.[93]

The debate on the Comintern revealed not merely the split between moderates and extremists but also the profound ambiguity under which the militant anarchosyndicalists themselves labored—torn by the conflict between anarchist ideals, which stressed nonviolence, opposition to authority, and individual liberty, and the demands of revolutionary action, which seemed to require coercive dictatorship and systematic violence similar to that in Russia.

Other victories for the extremists within the Congress of the Comedia included the decision to condemn the Mixed Commission, to reject national federations of industries, and to repudiate efforts to achieve a fusion with the Socialist workers of the UGT. The debate on this last issue was one of the most impassioned and revealing of the whole congress. Against the efforts of moderates such as Seguí, Pestaña, and Quintanilla to push through a reasonable and conciliatory unification proposal, the congress overwhelmingly gave its approval instead to an arrogant and somewhat imperialistic resolution (put forward by the Catalan anarchosyndicalist Valero) declaring unification with the "political" Ugetistas impossible and demanding instead the "absorption" of the Socialist workers who were given three months to join the CNT or be declared "yellow."[94] The puerility of this motion was a clear reflection of the exalted mood of the new proletarians and of their millenarian conviction—stimulated by the Bolshevik victory and by the CNT's own fantastic growth over the previous eighteen months—that Spain was on the eve of a social revolution in which the Cenetistas would play the major role.

But the irony of this congress is that even as the delegates were proposing the absorption of their Socialist rivals and confidently prophesying an early revolutionary victory, the CNT's situation in the country was unmistakably beginning to deteriorate. Not only in Catalonia but in Andalusia as well, the tide was turning against the Cenetistas, mainly as the result of the repressive measures being taken against them. The remarkable momentum they had gained during the course of 1919 was already starting to slacken, and 1920 would bring them not the awaited revolution but, in the end, defeat and demoralization.

In Catalonia this retardation resulted initially from the lockout, which lasted for ten weeks (not ending until January 26) and left the Cenetistas materially weakened and with their enthusiasm somewhat diminished. The lockout coincided, moreover, with a change in the political climate in Madrid, where the conciliatory Sánchez de Toca government (which had backed Amado's efforts to bring workers and employers together) gave way to the ministry of Manuel Allendesalazar, who, as a "hard" conservative, was committed—especially since the failure of the Mixed Commission—to a policy of renewed repression as the only means of pacifying the industrial scene in Catalonia.[95]

Thus the sterile alternation between harshness and conciliation, so characteristic of Spanish governments in this period, was continued, and a formidable new governor, the tough-minded Count Salvatierra, was appointed. This official took advantage of a terrorist attack on the head of the Barcelona Employers' Federation and commenced the new year by dissolving the Catalonian

Regional Confederation and closing down the workers' centers. As always, such a policy tended to displace the moderate syndicalists and to lodge power in the hands of the more extreme militants, who were better prepared to carry on clandestine struggle and more prone to use the terrorist tactics that such a struggle encouraged. This repressive phase lasted until May 1920 and was followed by a final attempt at conciliation (May to November), during which the CRT—encouraged by a new governor, Carlos Bas—once more rose to the surface of Catalonian life, giving the moderates a last opportunity to regain their positions of influence. [96]

If this interlude of détente had lasted longer, the moderate syndicalists might have been given a greater opportunity to entrench themselves. But the forces of order in Spain were greatly alarmed by the threat of Bolshevism in Europe (they knew that Spaniards were attending the Second Comintern Congress in Moscow) and by the rising strike wave in Spain, which they viewed as a revolutionary movement. [97] Above all, this brief era of attempted reconciliation was marred by a mounting number of terrorist incidents. In the face of these developments, the prime minister, Dato, became increasingly skeptical that conciliation would work, and, finally, in November he removed the amiable Carlos Bas from the governorship and replaced him with a man of iron, General Severiano Martínez Anido, who had formerly been the military governor of the region and who was now given carte blanche to take whatever measures he deemed necessary to end the renewed wave of terrorism in Barcelona. [98]

Terrorism had, in fact, become endemic in the city, rooted like a cancer in the very fibers of the labor movement and nourished by the ever-growing control that the anarchist action groups exerted over the treasuries of the unions—a control greatly enhanced, of course, whenever clandestine conditions were imposed. The moderate syndicalists tried to warn their *correligionarios* that terrible reprisals might be visited on the CNT/CRT unless this tactic were abandoned. As early as January 1920 the moderates had held a secret plenum of the Confederation in Barcelona at which a large majority agreed that terrorist methods should be abandoned. Such orders were sent out via the Barcelona Local Federation, [99] but the hard fact was that the sindicatos were no longer under the control of their moderate elements, and these orders proved to be utterly without effect. As though nothing had transpired, the pistoleros of the action groups serenely continued to plan and to execute their atentados on the same scale as before—oblivious to all warnings of the disaster that necessarily lay down that road. The problem, as Pestaña later recognized, was that terrorism had created its own vested interest—a whole class of men had come to the fore who found in terrorism a way of life, dreading more than anything a return to normalcy. [100]

Martínez Anido—the prototype of the authoritarian and implacable policeman—evolved a ruthlessly simple strategy for extirpating terrorism. Knowing that the terrorist apparatus was sustained, in the last analysis, by the thousands of pesetas paid into union treasuries (for non-terrorist purposes) by the rank-and-file union membership and sequestered by the action groups, Martínez Anido resolved to liquidate the whole syndical structure in Catalonia, imprisoning or exiling all leaders of any prominence (November 20, 1920) and absolutely forbidding the collection of dues. Disturbed by the fact that the manpower of the action groups was, despite all attrition, continually replenished by a flow of youths into Barcelona from other parts of Spain, he began systematic deportations of these outsiders, sending them back in long columns to their places of origin, under guard and in chains. His most drastic and controversial recourse was the imposition of the *ley de fugas*, under which scores of militants—not all of them pistoleros—were systematically shot after being taken prisoner by the police. [101]

About the only thing that may be said on behalf of these brutal tactics is that they worked—gradually bringing the Hobbesian civil war in Barcelona to an end—and that there is no certainty that any other methods would have been successful. These measures, reinforced, to be sure, by the economic collapse that came at the end of 1920, finally broke the back of the Catalonian Regional Confederation and of the terrorist incubus that had fastened itself upon it. Beginning in the winter of 1920–1921 the Sindicatos Unicos—only a short time before the focus of millenarian expectations—began to experience a growing exodus of workers that became especially marked after the middle of 1921. By 1922 the sindicatos had lost about 90 percent of their membership, and the CRT was to all intents and purposes destroyed. [102]

An ironic consequence of Martínez Anido's reign of terror was that by imprisoning so many regular labor leaders—both anarchosyndicalists and "pure" syndicalists—he helped throw power into the hands of a small and rather unrepresentative group of communist-syndicalists. They were headed by two fiery middle-class intellectuals neither of whom was from an anarchist background and both of whom were relative newcomers to the CNT: Andrés Nin and Joaquín Maurín. These visionaries (temporarily dominating the committees of both the CNT and the CRT) sought to transform the Confederation into a truly effective revolutionary organization by suppressing its anarchist-inspired spontaneity and stressing centralized organization and discipline. [103] Traveling to Moscow in the summer of 1921, they underwent a conversion from revolutionary syndicalism to Leninism and committed the CNT to membership in the Red International of Labor Unions (Profintern). But the "organic link" resolution that they signed in Moscow, which sought to subordinate European trade unions to communist political control, had not the least chance of being accepted by the mass of Cenetistas and, indeed, had no other consequence in Spain than to cause an angry reaction against the Comintern-Profintern and to touch off an anarchist revival within the CNT. [104]

It was at this time—mid-1921—that hitherto ardently pro-Bolshevik militants such as Manuel Buenacasa and Eusebio Carbó, along with all those who thought like them, suffered severe disillusionment with the Russian Bolsheviks and finally turned against Bolshevism altogether, regretting that they had half-succumbed to its statist and authoritarian heresies. They now reverted to a more pristine but, it should be noted, more sobered anarchist ideology, which repudiated not only the proletarian dictatorship but also the idea of immediate revolution, insisting upon the need to instill an anarchist "consciousness" in the masses—through a long process of propaganda and education—before those masses could make a revolution worth having. Disenchantment with the masses—mainly because of their materialism and "statism"—was very pronounced among both "pure" anarchists and anarchosyndicalists in this period. [105]

The last major confrontation between the more extreme anarchosyndicalists and the moderate or "pure" syndicalists occurred in the midst of this period of defeat and dissolution. It came at the Zaragoza Conference, a plenum of all Cenetista leaders held in 1922 for the purpose of resurrecting and reorganizing the shattered organization in response to the restoration of constitutional guarantees by the Sánchez Guerra government (April 1) and the release of all imprisoned Cenetista leaders. The mood of most Cenetistas—even of those who were now reverting to the anarchist rhetoric of the pre-Bolshevik era—was one of chastened sobriety. There was general recognition that the Cenetistas' own excesses, and especially their reliance on terrorist tactics, had a great deal to do with the disaster that had befallen the organization. Control of the CNT now lay, for the moment at least, in the hands of the "pure" syndicalists, who were able to win several victories. [106]

Both major factions agreed on the need for the CNT to withdraw from the Comintern-Profintern, and this was voted (over the opposition of the communist-syndicalists) without difficulty, the conference agreeing to send representatives to the anarchosyndicalist International then being founded in Berlin. The supremacy of the moderates was more clearly demonstrated by the election of a new (acting) National Committee dominated by "pure" syndicalists or moderate anarchosyndicalists. Moderation was also revealed by the delegates' decision to approve the participation of Salvador Seguí in the Mixed Commission and to "absolve" both him and Pestaña of various charges that the more extreme militants had brought against them. The moderates were also able to push through a resolution calling for regular salaries for members of the various Cenetista committees—a departure from anarchosyndicalist orthodoxy that greatly aroused the ire of the purists.[107]

But perhaps the main testimony to the supremacy of the moderates at Zaragoza was the passage of the "political" resolution, an ill-drafted, obscurely phrased, and at some points almost impenetrable statement—obviously the result of much haggling and compromise—that nevertheless conveyed an unmistakable message of conciliation. The resolution endeavored, in effect, to say that the CNT was now prepared to recognize the ineluctable pluralism of Spanish society and to concede a certain legitimacy to other social groups and even, under some circumstances, to work with those groups. With Delphic circumlocution it seemed to hint that the CNT might even be prepared to enter into electoral understandings in order to preserve those basic civil freedoms that the moderates rightly recognized as indispensable to the revival and continued growth of the CNT. That this was its meaning is suggested by the fact that Seguí, its chief sponsor, had moved quickly (after his return from exile) to reestablish his contacts with the Republicans and even with the dynastic parties. He was obviously tempted by the possibility of an electoral role for the CNT, however often he was forced by the orthodox anarchosyndicalists to issue earnest denials on this score.[108]

Following the Zaragoza Conference the CNT began a gradual revival under the auspices of the "pure" syndicalists, slowly repairing its shattered syndical structure, reestablishing its journals, and regaining some of its lost membership. But the supremacy of these elements did not long endure, lasting only about ten months. Unfortunately for the hopes of the moderates, the reestablishment of constitutional guarantees in the spring of 1922 did not result in a prolonged era of social peace but rather in a gradual resurgence of terrorism in Barcelona, which the ouster of Martínez Anido on October 25 [109] failed to arrest and may even have encouraged. The pistoleros of the action groups and of the Libres resurrected their old quarrels and gradually reescalated their war of mutual extermination. From December 1922 to May 1923 there were no fewer than 34 deaths and 76 injuries as a result of atentados carried out by both sides.[110]

No longer able to rely on the funds of the sindicatos, the gunmen of the action groups inaugurated a new method of money raising, that of social brigandage—the carrying out of armed robberies for the purpose of financing the activities of the groups. The most dramatic of these was a train robbery that netted them some 500,000 pesetas. Angel Pestaña, doubtless regretting his earlier acquiescence in the use of terrorist methods, was quick to denounce the new tactic, and thereby incurred the bitter animosity of the more extreme anarchosyndicalists. The atmosphere of hostility that formed against him within the CNT became, he said, "unbreathable," and only the arrival of the dictatorship in September 1923 kept the tension between moderates and extremists from reaching "the point of explosion." [111]

Pestaña himself fell victim to the pistoleros of the Libres on August 25, 1922, being badly wounded and laid up for several months. A short time later the National Committee of the CNT was moved from Barcelona, where it was controlled by syndicalist influences, to Zaragoza, where the extreme anarchosyndicalists were stronger.[112]   But the severest blow to hopes for reversing the trend to terrorism came on a Sunday evening in March 1923 when the leading moderate of the CNT, the incomparable Salvador Seguí was shot down by gunmen of the Libres on the crowded Calle de la Cadena in Barcelona.[113] Whether even the gifted Seguí could have withstood the increasingly anarchist and extremist tide within the CNT will never, of course, be known with certainty. What is certain is that no other Cenetista leader possessed the charismatic appeal, political talent, and moderation needed to guide the CNT out of the terrorist blind-alley into which the "cave-anarchists" (as Oscar Pérez Solís called them) had led it and into a positive and constructive role in the national life of Spain.[114]   Relations between Seguí and the extreme anarchosyndicalists, it should be noted, were very bad in the months preceding his death. Only after his death would the extremists compose eulogies to his memory and seek to claim him as an authentic "anarchist."[115]

The anarchist revival within the CNT was also encouraged by the greater cohesion achieved by the Catalonian Federation of Anarchist Groups. The core around which the anarchist forces were increasingly united was the notorious Los Solidarios group, headed by Buenaventura Durruti, Francisco Ascaso, Juan García Oliver, Rafael Escartín, and Ricardo Sanz. These men, inflexible anarchists by nature and terrorists by profession, were the spearhead of the anarchist resurgence within the CNT and would later, in 1927, be the founders of the Federación Anarquista Ibérica (FAI), which became more or less the politburo of the anarchosyndicalist movement in Spain.[116]

The final blow to the hopes of the moderates came in the aftermath of the military coup d'état carried out by Primo de Rivera in September 1923, which liquidated the parliamentary system and created the conditions under which terrorism would at last be brought under control. The CNT was permitted to function above ground for some eight months after Primo came to power, and it was the extreme anarchosyndicalists who urged that it be dissolved as a pro-test against the dictatorship, while the moderates sought to maintain the legal functioning of the sindicatos and continue the process of rebuilding. Pestaña especially urged this course and evidently hoped to play a collaborative role similar to that played on the UGT side by the Socialist leader Largo Caballero, going so far as to urge Cenetista participation in Primo's mixed commis-sions.[117]

Had the CNT been able to stay above ground during the dictatorship, there is little question that the process of rebuilding would have been greatly ad-vanced and the role of the moderate syndicalists considerably strengthened. But the very coming of the Primo de Rivera regime seems to have encouraged the resurgence of the more extreme anarchosyndicalist elements within the CNT. A change in the balance of forces was evident in the meeting of the Cata-lonian Regional Confederation held at Granollers on December 30, which in contrast to the Zaragoza Conference eighteen months earlier, was distinctly anarchist in character. Against only token opposition, the conference defiantly reaffirmed the Bakuninist principles of the Congress of the Comedia.[118] Another Cenetista plenum held in Sabadell on May 4, 1924, was even more completely dominated by the anarchosyndicalists than that of Granollers, with the result that only one communist-syndicalist dared make an appear-ance—and was unanimously denied the right to speak. Only a few days after this the issue of clandestine activity versus legality was taken out of the hands of the Cenetistas as the result of the assassination of a Barcelona official by one of the anarchist action groups. In retaliation, the governor ordered the closing down of the still-reviving sindicatos and the suspension of Solidaridad Obrera, with the result that the CRT would remain underground for the rest of the dictatorship. Thus for the final time in this era the government—provoked by a terrorist attack—intervened in such a way as to undermine the moderate Cenetistas and strengthen the hand of the extremist elements.[119]

Whether the defeat of moderate tendencies within the CNT flowed mainly from structural causes inherent in the Catalonian labor milieu or was signifi-cantly affected by the play of contingent factors is difficult to say. Certainly there were many structural elements working against the emergence of the kind of moderate trade unionism of which Salvador Seguí seemed to be the harbinger: the slowness of economic growth, the continuing small scale of in-dustrial units, the unremitting pressure of rural migration, the high rate of illit-eracy, the intransigence of a petty-bourgeois employer class, the caste structure of Catalonian society, the unusual strength of the anarchist infrastructure in Barcelona, perhaps even certain psychological traits—such as "individualism" and "spontaneity"—of the Catalonian proletariat. The precise order of causal efficacy in which these factors should be arranged is not a matter easily decided and probably depends to a large extent on one's underlying philosophical assumptions.[120] *Much work remains to be done on this question,* [not by you hope!] and there is needed, above all, much more comparative study focused on comparable industrial regions in other parts of Europe and Latin America, so that the more significant variables in the Spanish situation may be isolated. For the curious fact remains that, although a number of areas displayed in the early twentieth century many or most of the "causal" factors cited above, Spain is the only country that ever produced truly mass anarchist and anarchosyndicalist movements.[121] *Italy, Portugal, Argentine etc etc.* [wrong]

Structural determinants apart, the question remains as to the role of contingency in the defeat of the Seguí-led syndicalists. Given all the forces making for labor *extremism* in Catalonia, one may well ask whether there was ever a real possibility in this era that the *moderates* could have gained a secure ascendancy within the CNT/CRT and guided it toward integration and accommodation. The possibility of such a development must, I believe, be acknowledged. The thrust of the present essay has been that moderate leaders existed within the CNT/CRT and that under the protective cover of revolutionary-reformist rhetoric they were attempting to build a CNT more syndicalist than anarchist and, one must say, more reformist than revolutionary—a movement committed increasingly, that is, to long-range organizational power, to bureaucratic professionalism, and to something less than a total overthrow of the existing order. The *prudence* of the "pure" syndicalists, their relative coolness toward the Bolshevik Revolution, their acceptance of mixed commissions and paid secretariats, their willingness to link up with the socialists, and their concern to maintain contacts with the Republican and dynastic parties—these all suggest the possibility that the CNT might have evolved in a different manner than it did. The masses themselves, as we have seen, were fundamentally ambivalent—chronically torn between *millenarianism and materialism,* capable [are these actually incompatible] of being led by their chiefs down the path either of revolution or reform.

Various contingencies worked against a moderate evolution: the war itself, which accelerated the flow of rural migrants into Catalonia, swamping the CNT with too many raw recruits of a millenarian cast of mind; the Bolshevik Revolution, which engendered both an *extremist mood among the workers* and excessive fears among the ruling classes, thereby encouraging a social polarization that could only bode ill for *moderate* syndicalism; terrorist assaults that on

but, elsewhere?

several crucial occasions shattered an existing détente and propelled the government into repressive actions that inevitably displaced and weakened the moderate forces.

The assassination of Seguí was clearly one of the most crucial contingencies of this era. The biography of this great leader remains to be written and his role fully assessed, but it is difficult not to believe that his death made a substantial difference. One need not subscribe to the great man theory of history to recognize Seguí's unique talents and his central role as the catalyst of a moderate syndicalism committed to renovating rather than revolutionizing Spanish society. It seems almost certain that if Seguí had lived he would have collaborated with the dictatorship of Primo de Rivera, exerting every effort to keep the CNT above ground and attempting, like Largo Caballero on the Socialist side, to pursue the patient organizational labors for which he was so well fitted. Such labors, carried out during the 1920's, might well have solidified the forces of moderation within the CNT/CRT and, by weakening the role of the anarchist groups, have led to a fruitful collaboration with the Republic launched in 1931.

But the might-have-beens of history are legion, and the crucial fact is that the working out of structural and contingent forces in the Spanish context fatally weakened the "pure" syndicalists and preserved the CNT as an authentically anarchist movement—a peculiar kind of mass trade union organization that somehow managed to retain its anti-bureaucratic and revolutionary character, its obsession with spontaneity, and its quasi-millenarian conviction that a great redemptive revolution was ever imminent.

This is to say that Spanish syndicalism was to some degree retarded in its development, running on a different time track from similar movements in other parts of Europe. In France, for example, the syndicalists had long since—in 1906—proclaimed their independence from all political and sectarian influences, including that of the anarchists. [122] More than that, the failure of the great strikes of 1909 – 1913, the collapse of proletarian solidarity during the war, the growth of large-scale industry—all of these things sapped the faith of French syndicalists in the myth of an essentially spontaneous "class" revolution and had at the same time eroded their conviction that the state could only be an implacable enemy. The calling into question of these vital and sustaining myths meant that by 1914 there existed at the heart of French syndicalism a "malaise" (to use Robert Wohl's term) that had not yet afflicted the Spanish movement.

In Spain, by contrast, the syndicalists emerged morally unscathed from the war period, uncompromised by collaboration with bourgeois governments, and untouched by economic transformations that had not yet affected the Iberian peninsula. Only founded in 1911 (the CRT in 1908) and not really launched until 1914, the CNT was still in its adolescent phase, unbroken, idealistic, and filled with optimism about the future. The war boom had not undermined its economic base of small factory units nor (save for the "pure" syndicalists) called into question its revolutionary anti-statist and "direct action" proclivities. Its temporary defeat at the hands of Martínez Anido was material rather than moral, and there was, in the 1920's, no widespread feeling that the CNT's hybrid ideology or raison d'être had been rendered obsolescent. The strength, finally, of the anarchist infrastructure in Catalonia and the south helped ensure that the reigning faith of the CNT would continue to be *anarcho*syndicalism —an anachronistic but immensely vigorous creed that harmonized remarkably well with the angry mood of the "new masses" of the industrial zones and which clearly reflected something very basic in the temper of the Spanish people in an era of transition.

The CNT, then, would not go down the path traveled by most mass labor organizations, toward de facto reformism and bureaucratic caution, but would continue instead into the thirties as a revolutionary movement committed to "spontaneity" and to the creation of a regime of anarchist communism. "Pure" syndicalist and communist-syndicalist tendencies would be effectively contained, and the organizational power of the Sindicatos Unicos would remain harnessed to anarchist aspirations that would prove, in the early 1930's, as antithetical to republican as to monarchial institutions.

Very poor 3/10

Too emotive, incoherent, inconsistent biased and shows a poor understanding of what syndicalism is.

Bloody wanker, I bet you're a flaming Tory MP or something now, you pseudo-revolutionary.

NOTES

1. On the uniqueness of the CNT see Angel Marvaud, *La question sociale en Espagne* (Paris, 1910), p. 57, *ff.* For the flavor of the movement the best interpretive account is still Gerald Brenan, *The Spanish Labyrinth* (Cambridge, England, 1962), Ch. 8. The CNT during the era of the World War and the Russian Revolution is discussed in my book, *The Revolutionary Left in Spain, 1914 – 1923* (Stanford, 1974). For the early 1930's see John Brademas, *Revolution and Social Revolution: A Contribution to the History of The Anarchosyndicalist Movement in Spain, 1930 – 1937* (Oxford dissertation, 1956), and for the Civil War period see César M. Lorenzo, *Les anarchistes espagnols et le pouvoir, 1868 – 1969* (Paris, 1969). The urban milieu in which the anarchosyndicalist movement arose is best evoked in Joan Connelly Ullman, *The Tragic Week: Anticlericalism in Spain 1876 – 1912* (Cambridge, Mass., 1968). An excellent survey of the Spanish labor movement in the nineteenth and twentieth centuries—well integrated with the economic history of Spain—is found in M. Tuñón de Lara, *Introducció a la història del moviment obrer* (Barcelona, 1966).

2. *Economic Backwardness in Historical Perspective* (Cambridge, Mass., 1962), p. 43. As Gershenkron notes, long delays in the industrialization of backward countries permit too much time for social tensions to accumulate and to assume serious proportions. The more delayed industrialization is, the more traumatic it will be. Ideally, the "great spurt" ought to precede the maturation of the social question (pp. 28, 44).

3. The Spanish and Italian industrial milieus bore a certain similarity to each other in this era. Both countries fell into the "moderately" backward category, Spain being nearer the bottom of this division, and both suffered from capital shortages, invertebrate social structures, caste barriers, illiteracy, repressive anti-labor policies by the state, and extensive peasant migration into the industrial zones. The difference was the higher growth rate and relatively greater prosperity experienced by the Italians. Relative to such great industrial states as Britain, the United States, and Germany, the Italian record seems unimpressive; relative to Spain it appears more respectable. Daniel C. Horowitz has written that around the turn of the century the Italian economy was "expanding rapidly and unprecedented prosperity made wage demands seem natural to the workers and relatively easy to concede for the employers. . . . The enthusiasm and immediate success of the trade unions during 1901 created an atmosphere which did more to turn the trade unions toward moderate objectives than all the preachings of the Reformists." *The Italian Labor Movement* (Cambridge, Mass., 1963), p. 60. See also Shepard B. Clough, *The Economic History of Modern Italy* (New York, 1964), pp. 132, 170.

4. On the troubled relations between the resurgent CNT and the Second Republic see Carlos M. Rama, *La Crisis española del siglo XX,* 2nd ed. (Mexico, 1962), pp. 147 – 151.

5. Juan Díaz del Moral, *Historia de las agitaciones campesinas andaluzas: Córdoba* (Madrid, 1929), pp. 168 – 171.

6. Max Nettlau, "Die Jahre 1915 . . . bis 1923," p. 231A (unpublished manuscript in the International Institute for Social History, Amsterdam, hereafter referred to as Nettlau MS.).

7. Anarchists and syndicalists disagreed on a variety of matters, among them the question of craft versus industrial unionism (many anarchists wanted to keep—or return to—small-scale craft unions, which they felt were more easily penetrated by anarchist

ideas than the large industrial unions); and the question of whether the post-revolutionary society would be governed by a plurality of local groups, most especially by the local
commune, or by the sindicatos (anarchists feared that the structure of federated sindicatos would lead to new statism). The contrast between anarchist and syndicalist attitudes is analyzed in Hubert Lagardelle, "Anarchisme et syndicalisme," in *Syndicalisme
et Socialisme* (Paris, 1908), and in Victor Griffuelhes, *L'action syndicaliste* (Paris,
1908). See also Edouard Berth, *Les derniers aspects du socialisme* (Paris, 1923).

8. For the views of the "pure" anarchists see especially: José Antonio Birlán, ed.,
"Dionysios", *Almanaque de Tierra y Libertad para 1921* (Barcelona, 1920); Francisco
Jordán, *La dictadura del proletariado* (Madrid, 1920); José Prat, *¿ Herejías?* (Barcelona,
1922).

9. Gerald Brenan, *The Spanish Labyrinth* (Cambridge, 1962), p. 188.

10. Ramón Tamames, *Estructura económica de España* (Madrid, 1960), Ch. 28;
Jaime Vicens Vives, *Historia económica y social de España y America* (Barcelona,
1958), Tome IV, Vol. II, p. 163.

11. Instituto Nacional de Estadistica, *Principales actividades de la vida española en
la primera mitad del siglo xx* (Madrid, 1952), p. 10. It is estimated that about 40 percent
of the rural population increase in this period made its way to the cities, and that on the
eve of the war about half of the population of the larger cities was made up of recent migrants, of whom an estimated 70 percent had been agricultural laborers. Raymond Carr,
Spain 1808 – 1939 (Oxford, 1966), pp. 413 – 414.

12. *Informes de los inspectores del trabajo sobre la influencia de la guerra europea
en las industrias españolas* (Madrid, 1918). Ricardo Sanz, *El sindicalismo y la política*
(Toulouse, 1966), p. 20.

13. Instituto de Reformas Sociales, *Encarecimiento de la vida durante la guerra: Pre-
cios de las subsistencias en España y en el extranjero, 1914 – 1918* (Madrid, 1918), p.
82.

14. Jean Baelen, *Principaux traits du développement économique de l'Espagne de
1914 a l'avènement du Directoire Militaire* (Paris, 1924), p. 20.

15. Fernando de los Ríos, "The Agrarian Problem in Spain," *International Labor Review* (June 1925), p. 832. Jules Laborde, *Il y a toujours des Pyrénées* (Paris, 1918), p.
163, *ff.*

16. Juan Antonio Lacomba, *Crisi i revolució al país Valencià* (n.p., 1968), p. 191, *ff.*
Laborde, *ibid.,* pp. 164 – 165. Instituto de Reformas Sociales, *Información sobre emi-
gración española a los países de Europa durante la guerra* (Madrid, 1919), pp. 37, 51.
Jean Costedoat-Lamarque, *La question agraire en Andalousie* (Paris, 1923), p. 85.

17. Manuel Buenacasa, *El movimiento obrero español, historia y critica, 1886 – 1926,*
2nd ed, (Paris, 1966), pp. 54, 127. Nettlau MS., p. 251. By 1919 the proportion of Cenetista militants under the control of the CRT dropped to approximately 57 percent. *Memoria del congreso celebrado en el teatro de la Comedia de Madrid los días 10 al 18 de
diciembre de 1919* (Barcelona, 1932), pp. 9 – 34.

18. Nettlau MS., p. 251.

19. *Ibid.,* pp. 231A, 231B.

20. Angel Pestaña, *Lo que aprendí en la vida* (Madrid, 1933), pp. 46 – 47. Pestaña
discusses the "openness" of the CNT in his *Normas orgánicas* (Barcelona, 1930).

21. Nettlau MS., p. 264.

22. Pestaña, *Lo que aprendí, op. cit.,* p. 161.

23. José Negre reflected the views of most Cenetistas when he wrote, "Let Germany win, let France win, it is all the same to the workers, who will continue to be exploited and tyrannized just as before the war, and probably more than before." *Solidaridad Obrera*, September 5, 1914.

24. Eduardo Comín Colomer, *Historia del anarquismo*, (Madrid, 1965), I, pp. 291-292.

25. See, for example, *Solidaridad Obrera*, January 6, 1917.

26. Andrés Saborit, *Julián Besteiro* (Mexico City, 1961), p. 125; and *La huelga de agosto de 1917* (Mexico, 1967), p. 50.

27. Nettlau MS., p. 241.

28. Saborit, *Julián Besteiro, op. cit.*, p. 261.

29. The best and most thorough study of the August general strike is found in Juan Antonio Lacomba, *La crisis española de 1917* (Madrid, 1970), Ch. 6. Saborit, *La huelga, op. cit.*, expresses the viewpoint of a major socialist participant. For journalistic but informative works on the August strike see José Buxadé, *España en crisis: La bullanga misteriosa de 1917* (Barcelona, 1917); Augusto de Castro, *O que eu vi e ouvi em Hespanha, Junho a agosto de 1917* (Lisbon, 1917); and Fernando Soldevilla, *Tres revoluciones* (Madrid, 1917).

30. On the anti-Republican theme see *Solidaridad Obrera*, November 5, 1917; and *Tierra y Libertad*, November 28, 1917.

31. *Tierra y Libertad*, November 14, November 21, and December 26, 1917.

32. *Ibid.*

33. *Solidaridad Obrera* (Bilbao), December 3, 1920.

34. *Solidaridad Obrera*, November 11, 1917; January 11 and July 11, 1918.

35. José Viadiu, *Salvador Seguí* (Valencia, 1930), pp. 64-67. In October 1919 Seguí spoke to a gathering of Madrid workers: "What would happen right now, comrades and friends, if the revolution, triumphant all over Europe . . . should come knocking on our door? You answer for me. We are not prepared; we have no organization. We would . . . have to say to the bourgeoisie: 'No, we do not wish to accept that responsibility; wait a minute; wait for us to orient ourselves; we do not know what to do.'" Angel Pestaña and Salvador Seguí, *El sindicalismo libertario en Cataluña* (Madrid, n.d.), p. 23.

36. The first anarchist criticism of the Bolshevik Revolution came in September 1918 from Federico Urales, who criticized Lenin for dissolving the Constituent Assembly (*Solidaridad Obrera*, September 21, 1918). The anarchosyndicalist Manuel Buenacasa defended Lenin, saying that Urales failed to recognize that the Russians, next to the Spaniards, were the most "apolitical" people in Europe, and that the Constituent Assembly, therefore, did not represent a true majority. *Ibid.* A more "official" anarchist critique of Boshevism came a year later when José Prat published his *¿Dictadura o Libertad?* (Barcelona, 1919). The most forceful Spanish anarchist attacks on the new Soviet state appeared in "Dionysios," José Antonio Birlán, *op. cit.*

37. See, for example, Manuel Buenacasa's defense of the Russian Bolsheviks against the attack made on them by the Russian anarchist Peter Kropotkin in his "Message to the workers of the West European countries," *Solidaridad Obrera* (Bilbao), August 27, 1920.

38. Buenacasa, *El movimiento . . .* , *op. cit.*, pp. 64-65, 253-254.

39. *Memoria del congreso celebrado en Barcelona los días 28, 29, 30 de junio y el I de julio del año 1918.* (Barcelona, 1918).

40. Rafael Vidiella, "Causas del desarrollo, apogeo y decadencia de la CNT," *Leviatán,* No. 10 (February 1935), pp. 29 – 30. The decisions of the congress regarding the structure and functioning of the Sindicatos Unicos are summarized in *Memoria del congreso . . . del año 1918, ibid.,* pp. 71 – 79. The complete *reglamento* of the new industrial unions is reproduced in F. Solá Cañizares, *Luchas sociales en Cataluna 1812 – 1934* (Madrid, 1970), pp. 33 – 36.

41. See John Bowditch, "The Concept of Elan Vital: A Rationalization of Weakness" in Edward Meade Earle, ed., *Modern France* (Princeton, 1951), pp. 32 – 43.

42. Jaime Brossa, "The Domestic and Foreign Policy of Spain," *The Nation,* April 5, 1919, p. 519.

43. The best source for the Trienio Bolchevista is Díaz del Moral's *Historia de las agitaciones . . . , op. cit.* See also Constancio Bernaldo de Quirós y Pérez, *El espartaquismo agrario andaluz* (Madrid, 1919) and Instituto de Reformas Sociales, *Información sobre el problema agrario en la provincia de Córdoba* (Madrid, 1919).

44. *Memoria del congreso de . . . 1919, op. cit.,* p. 34.

45. An excellent summary of the strike is found in Alberto Balcells, *El sindicalismo en Barcelona, 1916 – 1923,* 2nd ed. (Barcelona, 1968), pp. 73 – 99. See also Pestaña's account of the strike in Francisco Madrid, *Ocho meses y un día en el gobierno civil de Barcelona* (Barcelona, 1932), pp. 14 – 20.

46. Balcells, *ibid.,* p. 82.

47. See "Una magnífica visión constructiva de Salvador Seguí," in Madrid, *Ocho meses, op. cit.,* pp. 93 – 98. On the theme of Seguí's moderation see also César Lorenzo, *Les anarchistes espagnols . . . , op. cit.,* pp. 55 – 58; and Juan Gómez Casas, *Historia del anarcosindicalismo español* (Madrid, 1968), pp. 141 – 142.

48. F. Baratech Alfaro, *Los sindicatos libres en España: Su origen, su actuación, su ideario* (Barcelona, 1927), p. 57. Julio Alvarez del Vayo, *The Last Optimist* (New York, 1950), p. 188.

49. José Maria Francés, *Memorias de un cero a la izquierda* (Mexico City, 1962), p. 429.

50. Guillén Salaya, *Historia del sindicalismo español,* 2nd ed. (Madrid, 1943), p. 24.

51. Alfaro, *op. cit.,* pp. 57 – 58.

52. Balcells, *op. cit.,* p. 88. The best source on the general strike is Pla y Armengol, *Impresiones de la huelga general* (Barcelona, 1930). Some documentary material is provided in E. G. Solano, *El sindicalismo en la teoría y en la práctica* (Barcelona, 1920?), pp. 84 – 113.

53. Buenacasa, *El movimiento . . . , op. cit.,* p. 216.

54. See the article from the *Nieuwe Rotterdamsche Courant* quoted in *Kommunisticheskii Internatsional,* No. 5 (1919), col. 764.

55. The intransigence of the militant anarchosyndicalists is most clearly reflected in Buenacasa, *El movimiento . . . , op. cit.,* and in Sanz, *op. cit.*

56. See, for example, José Peirats, *Los anarquistas en la crisis política española* (Buenos Aires, 1964), pp. 18 – 19.

57. D. Quintiliano Saldaña in the Prologue to José M. Farré Moregó, *Los atentados sociales en España* (Madrid, 1922), pp. x – xii; Alfaro, *op. cit.,* p. 63.

58. On the terrorist theme see J. Romero Maura, "Terrorism in Barcelona and its impact on Spanish politics 1904 – 1909," *Past and Present,* No. 41 (December 1968), pp. 130 – 183.

59. The nature, composition, and activities of the anarchist "action groups" in this period remain a matter of considerable obscurity, on which much more research needs to be done. The role of the *murcianos* in the Barcelona labor movement and in the action groups especially needs to be clarified. My admittedly subjective impression is that the non-Catalan migrants from the "dry" provinces played a disproportionately large role in the terrorist movement, but this should be investigated.

60. Pestaña, *Lo que aprendí, op. cit.*, p. 170. On the youthfulness of the pistoleros, see J. Oller Piñol, *Martínez Anido* (Madrid, 1943), p. 106 and Sanz, *op. cit.*, pp. 97 – 98, 103 – 104.

61. Pestaña, *Lo que aprendí, op. cit.*, p. 174; Alfaro, *op. cit.*, p. 61.

62. Pestaña, *ibid.*, p. 180.

63. Sanz, *op. cit.*, p. 58. See also the interview of Martínez Anido in *El Sol*, February 15, 1922.

64. Buenacasa, *El movimiento . . . , op. cit.*, p. 68.

65. Pestaña, *Lo que aprendí, op. cit.*, pp. 92, 165 – 167; Sanz, *op. cit.*, p. 99.

66. Buenacasa, *El movimiento . . . , op. cit.*, p. 68.

67. Barcelona led all other cities in this period with 809 *atentados* (Bilbao, 152; Valencia, 151; Zaragoza, 129; Seville, 104). The number of such "social crimes" in Catalonia rose steadily after 1916: 43 in 1917; 93 in 1918; 107 in 1919; 304 in 1920; and 254 in 1921. Of these attacks the number against workers (many of these by other workers) was 440; against employers and foremen, 218; against the police and the Somatén, 88. The total of those actually killed in Barcelona (1917 – 1921) was 255, with 733 wounded. Maximiano García Venero, *Historia de los movimientos sindicalistas españoles (1840 – 1933)* (Madrid, 1961), pp. 365 – 366.

68. Pestaña, *El terrorismo en Barcelona* (Barcelona, 1920), p. 15.

69. Pestaña, *Lo que aprendí, op. cit.*, p. 175.

70. That it was the workers' terror that produced the patronal terror has been acknowledged by both Pestaña (*Lo que aprendí*, p. 176) and Buenacasa (*El movimiento . . .*, p. 68). On the counterterror, see Balcells, *op. cit.*, p. 114.

71. Alfaro, *op. cit.*, p. 65. Angel Pestaña acknowledged that the majority of the workers in the Sindicatos Unicos were more concerned with economic than with ideological issues. His estimate was that only 30 percent were ideological syndicalists. *El Sol*, January 19, 1921.

72. García Venero, *op. cit.*, pp. 382 – 383; Salaya, *op. cit.*, p. 28; Alfaro, *op. cit.*, pp. 68 – 70.

73. The Libres appear to have made significant gains among cooks and waiters, metalworkers from the Hispano-Suiza plants, rubber workers, bank workers, and employees of the waterworks. Alfaro, *op. cit.*, pp. 71, 74 – 77.

74. *Ibid.*, pp. 77 – 80.

75. *Ibid.*, p. 74; J. Oller Piñol, *Martínez Anido*, (Madrid, 1943) p. 38.

76. Manuel Burgos y Mazo, *El verano de 1919 en Gobernación* (Cuenca, 1921), pp. 354-355; Melchor Fernández Almagro, *Historia del reinado de Don Alfonso XIII* (Barcelona, 1936), pp. 360 – 361.

77. Buenacasa, *El movimiento . . . , op. cit.*, pp. 70 – 72.

78. Madrid, *op. cit.*, p. 41.

79. Madrid, *op. cit.*, pp. 39 – 40; Balcells, *op. cit.*, p. 122.

80. Burgos y Mazo, *op. cit.*, p. 451.

81. Madrid, *op. cit.*, pp. 34 – 35.

82. Pestaña, *Lo que aprendí, op. cit.*, p. 186.

83. The intransigence of the employers was remarked by Governor Amado, who referred to them as "stubborn men, of profoundly retrograde opinions . . . who wished to smash the Syndicalist organization and remold it to their desire and caprice." Madrid, *op. cit.*, p. 42.

84. Buenacasa, *El movimiento . . . , op. cit.*, p. 72.

85. The anarchist journal *Espartaco* (February 23, 1920) complained bitterly about the failure of the moderate syndicalist leaders to meet the lockout with a revolutionary strike: "If the general strike had been declared against the lockout, even supposing that it had not taken on a revolutionary aspect, [with] shooting, fires, assaults, barricades, [in view of the then-existing cohesion] of the workers' forces, the bourgeoisie would have had to yield through hunger before us, since we are used to hunger and the bourgeoisie are not; but since bread was available [because of the failure to strike], those who could buy [bread] ate it, and there was left to the locked-out workers no way to avoid starving to death other than to be shot or to surrender."

86. *Ibid.*

87. Madrid, *op. cit.*, p. 41

88. See the discussion by Angel Samblancat in *El Comunista* (Zaragoza), January 2, 1920. Buenacasa later wrote that the "immense majority" of the delegates considered themselves "true Bolsheviks," seeing in Bolshevism "the revolution we dreamed of." *El movimiento . . . , op. cit.*, p. 89.

89. *Memoria del congreso . . . de 1919, op. cit.*, pp. 357, 359 – 362, 368 – 371.

90. *Ibid.*, p. 367.

91. *Ibid.*, p. 373. Following the Congress of the Comedia, the Committee of the CRT selected three militants to go to Russia and investigate the new Soviet order. Of these, only Angel Pestaña was able to reach Moscow and attend the Second Congress of the Comintern, held in the summer of 1920. I have dealt at length with the Pestaña mission in my *Revolutionary Left in Spain, op. cit.*, Ch. 10.

92. *Memoria del congreso . . . de 1919, op. cit.*, p. 373.

93. Vidiella, *op. cit.*

94. *Memoria del congreso . . . de 1919, op. cit.*, p. 167.

95. Salaya, *op. cit.*, pp. 26 – 27.

96. Balcells, *op. cit.*, pp. 138 – 139, 143.

97. Carlos Seco Serrano, *Alfonso XIII y la crisis de la Restauracion* (Barcelona, 1969), pp. 131, 133.

98. Madrid, *op. cit.*, pp. 79 – 93; Piñol, *op. cit.*, Ch. 4.

99. Pestaña, *Lo que aprendí, op. cit.*, pp. 187 – 188.

100. *Ibid.*

101. Sanz, *op. cit.*, p. 59; Gaston Leval, *Ni Franco ni Stalin* (Milan, n.d.), pp. 50 – 51.

102. Andrés Nin, "Pourquoi Dato fut assassiné," *La Lutte de Classes*, July 5, 1922; "La terreur blanche en Espagne," *L'International Communiste*, No. 16 (March 1921), cols. 3717 – 3720; Venero, *op. cit.*, p. 413; Piñol, *op. cit.*, p. 111; *El Sol*, August 13, 1922.

103. See the biographical essay on Nin by Wilebaldo Solano in Andrés Nin, *Els moviments d'emancipació nacional* (Paris, 1970), pp. 9 – 65; and also Nin's Foreword to Joaquin Maurin, *Anarkhosindikalizm v Ispanii* (Moscow, 1925). The organ of the communist-syndicalists was *Lucha Social* of Lérida.

104. On the Profintern Congress of 1921 see George Williams; *The First Congress of the Red Trade Union International at Moscow, 1921* (Chicago, 1922). The anarchist revival was reflected in the pages of the journal *Nueva Senda:* See, for example, the issues of November 10, 1921, and April 8, 1922.

105. *Lucha Social,* November 12, 1921. For the elitist and "educationist" theme see Prat, *¿Herejías?, op. cit.*

106. Nettlau MS., p. 277; *Lucha Social,* November 26, 1921. Thus the leaders of the now-shrunken Barcelona Federation of Sindicatos Unicos acknowledged publicly that the "unanimous desire" of the syndicalists was for an "era of peace," that is, a "respite." *Lucha Social,* April 8, 1922.

107. *Lucha Social,* June 24, 1922; *El Sol,* June 13, 1922. The text of the Zaragoza resolution on the Comintern will be found in *La Lutte de Classes,* July 5, 1922.

108. The text of the "political" resolution will be found in *El Sol,* June 16, 1922. Regarding Seguí's electoralism, a socialist writer observed that Seguí had a "very outstanding political spirit," and that he "wished to evolve, might have accepted going to parliament, and in his speeches did not renounce the [discussion of] political themes." Seguí, according to this writer, had an "understanding" with Lerroux and was on "speaking terms" with the Republican Rodrigo Soriano, who had ties with García Prieto. Partido Socialista Obrero Español, *Convocatoria y orden del día para el XII congreso ordinario del partido* (Madrid, 1927), p. 62.

109. Peirats, *op. cit.,* pp. 35 – 36.

110. José García, *Diktadura Primo de Rivera* (Moscow, 1963), p. 98.

111. Pestaña, *Lo que aprendí, op. cit.,* pp. 100-101.

112. *Cultura y acción,* October 7, 1922.

113. *La Antorcha,* March 23, 1923.

114. Oscar Pérez Solís wrote that Seguí had seen "better than anyone the extremely grave dangers hovering over the Catalan labor organization because of the possessed and visionary men who had carried it into the blind alley of terrorism. Seguí, who perhaps had very little faith in the chimerical theories of anarchism, which earned him violent attacks . . . from the cave-anarchists . . . confronted with presence of mind the tragic situation that [Anarchist] experiments created in Catalonia; and in the end, having been the only syndical leader who sustained opposition to a suicidal tactic with exemplary firmness, he ended as a victim of the barbarous struggle he had tried to stop. Those who killed him . . . surely saw in Seguí the only balanced man who might have been able to give the [Catalonian proletariat] a serious, disciplined organization without revolutionary deliriums or criminal violence . . . ." *Memoria de mi amigo Oscar Perea* (Madrid, 1929), p. 236.

115. See, for example, Salvador Seguí: *Su vida, su obra* (Paris, 1960).

116. Sanz, *op. cit.,* pp. 111, 124.

117. Tuñón de Lara, *op. cit.,* p. 325.

118. Joaquín Maurín, *L'Anarchosyndicalisme en Espagne* (Paris, 1924), p. 40.

119. *Ibid.,* pp. 36 – 37.

120. Explanations of the mass character of anarchism and anarchosyndicalism in Spain seem to fall within two main schools of thought: the "idealist" school of Brenan *(The Spanish Labyrinth)* and Borkenau *(The Spanish Cockpit)* stresses the stubbornly "Iberian" and "preindustrial" character of the Spanish masses and doubts that the transition to a modern industrial character will ever be complete; the Marxist school, represented by such writers as Ramos Oliveira *(Politics, Economics and Men of Modern Spain)* and Jesús Hernández *(Negro y Roja: Los Anarquistas en la revolución española),* plays down the notion of unique "Hispanic" character traits and emphasizes instead the effect of economic backwardness, seeing anarchism and anarchosyndicalism merely as manifestations of an early phase of economic development inevitably destined to pass away under the impact of industrial modernization and the coming of large-scale factories.

121. Southern Italy, in particular, seems to reveal most of the causal factors usually regarded as producing anarchism in Spain: economic retardation, agrarian inequality, the pressure of an "alien" state, illiteracy, anti-clericalism, social banditry, millenarianism, and so forth. But anarchism never became a mass movement in Italy. On millenarianism in both the Italian and Spanish contexts see Erik Hobsbawn, *Primitive Rebels: Studies in Archaic Forms of Social Movement in the Nineteenth and Twentieth Centuries* (New York, 1959), Chs. 5, 6.

122. Jean Maitron, *Histoire du mouvement anarchiste en France, 1880 – 1914.* (Paris, 1952), pp. 288, *ff.*

3

The Azaña Regime in Perspective (Spain, 1931 – 1933)

Gabriel Jackson

Inauguration of the Second Spanish Republic in 1931 was in some respects the most creative political development in Europe during the early 1930's. It reversed the dominant trend in underveloped countries toward rightist and authoritarian systems, making a sharp break with the elitist, semi-oligarchic regime that preceded it. Indeed, the break may have been too sharp to be enduring, for in its effort to accommodate the upsurge of popular leftist forces through democratic means, the new Spanish political system was suddenly called upon to cope with a wide range of extremely acute problems.

The following selection presents the goals and ideals of the leaders of the new regime, describes their achievements, and analyzes some of their limitations. Gabriel Jackson is professor of history at the University of California, San Diego, and author of the prize-winning The Spanish Republic and Civil War, 1931 – 1939 *(Princeton, 1965). This article was originally published in the* American Historical Review, *Vol. 64, No. 2 (1959), pp. 282 – 300, and is reprinted by permission of the author.*

In April, 1931, Alfonso XIII, vacating his throne peaceably, handed the reins of power to a provisional government composed of the several republican parties and the Socialists. In June the freely elected Constituent Cortes met to write a republican constitution. As the general lines of division within the chamber gradually became clear during the summer, a coalition of liberal republicans and Socialists emerged as the dominant bloc; and from October, 1931, to September, 1933, Manuel Azaña, whom friends and enemies alike referred to as the soul of the Republic, served as Prime Minister of successive coalition cabinets. Despite a world depression, several military uprisings, and the restlessness of workers and peasants, the stability of the government was not seriously threatened until the fall of 1933. The Azaña regime thus presented a unique political opportunity to those forces that were seeking a democratic, reformist, laic solution for the multiple problems of Spain. The leaders of the republican-Socialist coalition had matured during the vigorous economic and cultural renaissance of late nineteenth- and twentieth-century Spain. Their republic was intended simultaneously to fulfill that renaissance and to give Spain a constitution embodying the most advanced European democratic features. The formation of the constitution has been amply dealt with elsewhere.[1] It is the purpose of the present article to explore the relationship between the policies and accomplishments of the Azaña regime and the main economic, political, and cultural currents of late nineteenth- and twentieth-century Spain.

The seventy-odd years preceeding 1931 constituted a period of substantial economic growth, though progress was significantly slower after 1918 than up to that time. Neither reliable statistics nor thorough analyses of the Spanish economy are available, but it is possible to discern the major trends.[2]

Agricultural and industrial production were rising steadily in Spain from the 1860's through 1914, although there were temporary downturns during periods such as the two years following the Spanish-American War. World War I created boom conditions in the big industries, particularly steel and textiles. But after 1918 Spain was unable to hold her wartime markets, and in the 1920's neither agricultural nor industrial production maintained the pre-1914 expansion except in certain agricultural exports and a few newer industries, notably chemicals and hydroelectric development.[3] Spain's population increased steadily through the nineteenth and twentieth centuries. Both new businesses and the creation of public services in the cities contributed to raise the urban standard of living. The cost of living as well rose steadily, though it was not so high in the 1920's as at the peak of war prosperity. Emigration relieved the population pressure somewhat in both prewar and postwar periods but came to a virtual end with the depression of 1930.[4]

Spain's industrial development took place behind increasingly high tariff walls from 1888 onward, and was largely dependent upon foreign capital, raw materials, and technical guidance.[5] Both circumstances made for high costs of production and high prices, while dependence on foreign capital had increasingly irritated the pride of Spaniards of all political persuasions. Spain's international trade developed steadily in value until the world depression of 1930.[6] But her unfavorable balance of trade, her dependence on foreign capital, and her political instability made the peseta one of the weakest of European currencies, a fact that in good times concerned only statisticians, but which was always likely to become an important consideration of prestige for ministries whose general political position was weak.

The progress and the problems of the economy highlighted for thinking Spaniards their unsolved political problems. In 1873 Spain's First Republic had been torn to pieces by cantonalist revolts on the Left and the recrudescence of Carlist war on the Right.[7] In 1875 the Restoration, by ending the Carlist wars and establishing a constitutional monarchy of mildly liberal tendency, had encouraged the beginnings of Spain's economic and cultural recovery. But elections were thoroughly controlled. The Conservatives and Liberals alternated in power by gentlemen's agreement. The Parliament was only a forum for oratory. In the countryside the *caciques* ruled the masses, combining ordinary machine political methods with more powerful pressures such as control of seasonal employment, water rights, and grazing grounds. They reinforced these economic pressures when necessary by the brute force of the *Guardia Civil*. Beneath the veneer of parliamentary government Spain was dividing along class and regional lines.

Not only was the monarchy bankrupt, but large sectors of the Spanish people were being alienated from their traditional Catholic faith. The rural workers of Andalusia and the Levant coast turned in large segments to Bakuninist anarchism, the urban workers of the central and northern provinces tended toward Marxian socialism, and the industrial proletariat of Catalonia toward syndicalism. Among the educated classes various forms of neo-Kantian philosophy, of positivism, of utopian and Marxian socialism eroded the traditional faith. Increasingly secular thought was of course characteristic of the whole European world, but the explosive potential was perhaps greater in Spain because of the always ardent Spanish desire to govern life according to a transcendent ideal. New ideas tended to be important not so much for their practical consequences in some limited sphere of activity as for their ability to satisfy the Spanish thirst for spiritual unity and inspiration.

During the period 1875–1931 there was a steady and growing republican movement. It was always more significant for the quality and prestige of its adherents than for numbers, and it lacked substantial political organization until the last years of the Primo de Rivera dictatorship. In general the republican program asked for constitutional, representative government complete with universal suffrage, honest elections, and the civil liberties characteristic of the United States and the advanced European states; elimination of the army from the political life of the nation; curbs on the economic power of the Church as well as secularization of education and the passage of civil laws governing marriage, divorce, and burial. The Republicans also favored, but never consistently fought for, land reform, irrigation works, road and harbor improvements—in general such economic measures as would strengthen the urban middle class and help to create a class of small independent farmers. They tended to sympathize with federalist rather than centralist solutions for the ever-recurring problem of regionalism.

Most important throughout both the Restoration and the reign of Alfonso XIII was the broad educational and philosophical influence of the Spanish disciples of the early nineteenth-century German philosopher Krause. The spiritual center of the Krausist movement was the Institución Libre de Enseñanza, a private school founded in Madrid in 1876 and startlingly similar in outlook and method to contemporary American progressive institutions such as the Dalton or the Putney schools. Neither the founder, Francisco Giner de los Ríos, nor his chief collaborators, Joaquín Costa, Manuel B. Cossío, and Gumersindo de Azcárate, were associated with political parties. But their ideas on such diverse subjects as primary education, law, art, Spanish economic problems, and cultural history decisively influenced the program of the Republic of 1931. Their lofty humanism appealed to many educated Spaniards as an ideal Catholicism purged of the institutional shortcomings of the Church.[8] Krausism represented, for its partisans and enemies alike, the modern embodiment of the humanist, heterodox Catholicism of Erasmus, of Luis Vives, of Giodano Bruno. A high proportion of the deputies and ministers of the Second Republic were at once graduates of the Institución, ardent admirers of Giner, and conscious partisans of the Erasmist tradition.[9] Krausist and republican thought achieved its most concrete expression in the years 1931 – 1933.

Full understanding of those years requires some knowledge of the nature of the Constituent Cortes. In the chamber of 470 deputies the largest parties were the Socialists, with about 120 deputies, and the Radicals with some 90. The Cortes did not operate, however, on party principles in the British or American sense. Thus many individual deputies seated themselves at different times with the government's supporters or with the opposition, according to individual conviction rather than party directive. Leading figures in the government frequently did not represent the largest parties. Both Alcalá-Zamora, first Prime Minister and later President of the Republic, and Manuel Azaña, leading figure of the whole period, belonged to a party with less than thirty deputies. [10] The fluidity of party lines was further emphasized by factional divisions. Thus such intellectual Socialists as Jiménez de Asúa and Fernando de los Ríos were closer to the several small republican parties than to the working-class followers of Largo Caballero. Similarly the Radical party, though it constituted the nucleus of the conservative republican opposition, contained a minority that frequently supported the Azaña government. Early in 1934, after the electoral victory of a conservative coalition, Martínez Barrios, formerly second only to Lerroux in the Radical party, joined Azaña.

An important transitional role was played by leaders such as Alcalá-Zamora and Dr. Marañón who had only declared themselves republicans after the fall of the Primo de Rivera dictatorship. [11] These men were concerned with constitutional rather than republican government, and with assuring a peaceful transition to the new regime once they had become convinced that it was impossible to achieve constitutional government within the framework of the monarchy. Alcalá-Zamora had been a royal official and a protégé of the Count of Romanones. Dr. Marañón numbered the royal family among his patients. In 1926 he had been fined for his part in the Night of St. John plot. The leading figure in that conspiracy had been the Count of Romanones and his presumed purpose had been to remove the dictator and restore the constitutional monarchy. [12] Marañón, Alcalá-Zamora, and many other prominent politicians who had had no quarrel with the monarchy rallied to the Repulic in the hope of exercising a restraining influence on the anticipated revolution. The choice of Alcalá-Zamora as provisional Prime Minister did much to calm the initial fears of Catholics and monarchists at the moment of the change. Months later, as such men became increasingly estranged from the republican-Socialist majority, they nevertheless continued to support the Republic against the opposition of the minuscule Communist party [13] and against the sporadic outbreaks of anarchist and military violence.

Despite the multiplicity of party labels and shifting loyalties, a working majority of the Cortes had accepted the leadership of Manuel Azaña by the fall of 1931. The Azaña coalition consisted of about 250 deputies of the Socialist party; two liberal republican groups: the Radical Socialists, led by Alvaro de Albornoz, and Republican Action, which was the party of Azaña himself; and two other republican groups similar in general outlook to the above parties, but committed to regional autonomy—the Galician Federalists of Casares Quiroga and the Catalan *Esquerra* (Left). Until mid-1933 this coalition showed in practice, if not in theory, much the same degree of unity as one finds in the British Labour party or a Scandinavian Social Democratic party. There was friendly discussion of a possible merger between Republican Action and the Radical Socialists,[14] and the Galician and Catalan deputies found in Azaña a premier fully sympathetic to their regional aims. For Azaña in turn it was axiomatic that he could not govern without the active cooperation of the Socialists. There was a long tradition of friendly relations between Socialist and republican leaders under the monarchy, and an assumption on the part of men like Albornoz and Azaña in the late 1920's that under the Republic, which they were confident would come, republicans and Socialists would naturally share power.[15]

Ideological differences were by no means insuperable, as the Marxism of the Socialist intellectuals was scarcely more radical than the liberalism of the almost contemporary New Deal in the United States. Writing in the spring of 1932, the Socialist Jiménez de Asúa defined, in the order of their importance, the following tasks for the young Republic: to determine the responsibilities of the old regime and to write a constitution; to reform the army; to regulate the relation of the Church to the laic state, and of the regions to the central government; to build schools, improve the system of justice, and proceed with agrarian reform.[16] To determine the "responsibilities" meant to expose the role of the army, the King, and the corrupt politicians in the Primo de Rivera coup of 1923. The parliamentary investigation and ultimate condemnation of the former King provided those conservatives who had recently rallied to the Republic with an opportunity to dissociate themselves from el Rey Chico. It provided liberals and Socialists with an opportunity to educate public opinion concerning the evils of military intervention in politics. It provided everyone with an opportunity to blame Spain's historic ills on the King and to create a temporary feeling of unity and virtue among the diverse republican forces. The remainder of Sr. Jiménez de Asúa's program was bound to arouse conservative opposition, but nothing in his program would have frightened any of the members of the republican parties in the Azaña coalition. Moreover, much of it was in accord with Krausist idealism.

The combination of the Krausist heritage with European socialism is perhaps best epitomized in the person of Fernando de los Ríos, professor of law, Socialist deputy, Minister of Justice, and later of Education, under Azaña. From Krause and from his uncle Francisco Giner, the young man imbibed the ideal of human perfectibility through improvements in education and through fuller social justice. From Kant and from followers of Kant including Krause, he gained his concern for "Man" as an end. The study of Marx had convinced him that capitalism had liberated things while enslaving men, and that socialism would be necessary to correct the evils of a society in which profits and property had more rights than men. A visit to Russia in 1920, however, had shown him the dangers of any dictatorship, no matter how praiseworthy the ends sought by that dictatorship. By 1926 he had defined for himself his "humanist socialism," of which the economic reorganization of society would be only a part. Humanist socialism must work by persuasion only, must defend existing liberty, and assimilate to its whole political outlook the ethical teachings of Kant and the Krausists. Such a socialism would be the true successor in spirit to the Erasmist and humanist traditions of sixteenth-century Spain. [17]

The ideals of the republican and Socialist leaders were to be quickly tested in action after the flight of the King. Inheriting both a world depression and the problems of the bankrupt monarchy, the government was obliged to act rapidly on many long-standing issues. Here we can but analyze the most important currents of republican policy without attempting to recapitulate in detail the political history of the period. [18] Most obvious of the government's early difficulties was the immediate financial crisis caused by the fall of the peseta and the flight abroad of about one-fifth billion pesetas during the first eight months of the Republic's existence. [19] The depreciation of the peseta was a long-term development against which the Primo de Rivera government had struggled unsuccessfully through the twenties, but the depreciation following the proclamation of the Republic was much more rapid than that of the past, and the flight of capital abroad clearly reflected the fears of the wealthy. The republican government attempted to end speculation within Spain and to impose strict control on all gold and foreign exchange transactions. It required government licenses for all purchases of foreign equipment, the maintenance of foreign bank accounts, and the use of capital for businesses outside Spain. Through the *Centro Oficial de Contratación de Moneda* it managed all foreign exchange operations and slowed down the export of capital, sometimes delaying even licensed payments abroad by as much as six months. Through these measures the downward trend was arrested early in 1932, and the peseta stabilized by 1934, though at the sacrifice of a portion of Spain's foreign trade. The government did not attempt to "peg" the peseta, and it did not use its gold reserves to prevent depreciation. [20]

Opinions in Spain varied, as they do elsewhere, as to the significance of depreciation and the wisdom of manipulating the currency. The important point for the present discussion is that the republican finance ministers, the Socialist Prieto, and the Catalan republican Jaime Carner practiced policies which Spanish financiers had recommended in 1928, whereas the Primo government had ignored this advice in favor of a costly effort to revalue the peseta for prestige reasons, with a resulting loss of gold reserves and an increasing market speculation in pesetas. [21] The coalition government indicated its conservative economic character also by retaining Spain's ultra-protective tariff, by applying strict import quotas to both manufactured goods and foods, and by extending to new industries the "consortium" policy of Primo de Rivera, a form of management-labor-marketing control imitative of Mussolini's corporate state.

Of decisive importance among the early actions of the new government was its reform of the army. In the nineteenth century the army had made and unmade governments, and from 1923 to 1930 Spain had been ruled by a military dictator. Primo de Rivera had, however, laid the basis for a later diminution of the army by his popular termination of the Moroccan war. The Republic, whose legitimacy was acknowledged at the time even by its avowed enemies, [22] was determined to eliminate the army from the political life of the nation. As the first republican Minister of War, Azaña offered all Spanish officers the opportunity to retire on full pay and formulated the following plans: to cut the size of the army by about half, to reorganize the remaining divisions with modern equipment, and to recruit officers in the future from the noncommissioned ranks. He hoped thus to save money, increase efficiency, and democratize the army, while building an officer corps loyal to the Republic. [23] Given time, he might well have succeeded, but the immediate results boded ill for the future. The majority of republican-minded officers took the opportunity to retire, and the leading generals, seeing their caste position and their political influence clearly threatened, became more monarchist in sentiment than they had been in the twenties. The government in the period 1931 – 1933 was able easily to suppress the several military risings against it, notably that of General Sanjurjo in 1932. The public pronouncements and the private conduct of the generals, however, showed their almost pathological hatred of Azaña and their conviction that the Republic intended to destroy the honor and the substance of the Spanish army. [24] Within five years they were to seize the opportunity to destroy quickly the Republic which had humiliated them but not deprived them of power.

The considerable economies achieved by army reform, coupled with the paring of padded departmental budgets, made funds available for all kinds of public works. Ever since the days of Joaquín Costa irrigation and hydroelectric development had held an important place in all plans for the economic recovery of Spain. [25] During the prosperous twenties Primo de Rivera had spent an average of 60 to 80 million pesetas annually on what Costa had dubbed *política hidráulica.* But the Republic appropriated 80 million in 1932, 175 million in 1933, [26] and undertook coordinated planning of the whole development under the nonpolitical chairmanship of Manuel Lorenzo Pardo, leading Spanish hydraulic engineer and a disciple of Costa.[27] During these years, also, the government spent large sums on parks, clinics, and tuberculosis sanatoria.[28] Primo de Rivera had built a number of arterial highways in the 1920's. Azaña's Minister of Public Works, Indalecio Prieto (a Socialist and a successful "self-made" businessman), followed this with the building of secondary rural roads and with electrification and centralized direction of the railways. He also planned a railroad tunnel under Madrid which would for the first time connect the trunk lines to the eastern, northern, and southern provinces, each of which had (and still has) its own terminus.[29] As the building of schools was another immediate concern of the Republic, a 400 million peseta loan was floated for such construction in 1932.[30] When in October of that year thousands of peasants were granted temporary occupation rights on uncultivated land, the government paid their rent to the legal owners.[31]

Although the Azaña coalition demonstrated in its expenditures a broad concern for human welfare, it failed to meet energetically the gravest economic-social issue of the times, agrarian reform. In the government's policy on this thorny problem may be seen simultaneously its generosity, its timidity, its concern for legality, its fear of the masses, and its uncertainty of direction. Recognizing the immediacy of the problem, it proceeded by decree in May and June of 1931 to protect peasants against arbitrary dispossession by absentee landlords, to make loans to small proprietors, to authorize the renting to peasants of state and municipal lands, and to give regional labor union representatives a voice in the arbitration of local disputes.[32] When the Constituent Cortes met in July, both republicans and moderate Socialists were anxious that fair compensation be paid for all expropriated land and that all legal titles to the land be clear before expropriation became final. Decades of litigation would have been necessary to comply with the full terms of the statute finally voted in September, 1932.[33] And its adoption, even in inadequate form, was delayed for over a year by the impassioned struggle in the Cortes over the Church and the orders, by numerous *jacqueries* which frightened the government, and by the inability to decide whether individual farming (the preferred solution of the republicans) or collective farming (the preferred solution of the socialist masses) should be encouraged.[34] All that the government could claim was that 12,260 peasants had been settled on 116,838 hectares of land by December 31, 1934, in a nation whose landless peasantry numbered in the millions and where the fourteen largest estates totaled 383,065 hectares.[35]

The most troublesome problems facing the Cortes concerned the position of the Church and the nature of the educational system of the new Republic.

These two questions were intertwined. Teaching orders administered a large proportion of the existing primary and secondary schools, and Church and state had long struggled over the religious curriculum at all levels of education. [36] In the Cortes and the press Spaniards had engaged in a prolonged controversy over the political and economic power of the Church. The Republic, in the course of more than a year of highly emotional debate, separated Church and state, decreed the end of state subsidies to the Church after a transition period of two years, dissolved the Jesuits, required all orders to submit to the government an annual accounting of their income and expenditures, and forbade them to engage in industry, trade, or teaching.

We have noted already the decline of Catholic belief in the late nineteenth- and twentieth-century Spain and the intimate connection between republicanism and the heterodox tradition. The Church was itself aware, however unhappily, that the majority of adult Spaniards, except perhaps in Navarre and the Basque country, were not active communicants. [37] Likewise a high proportion of thinking Spaniards were convinced that the wealthier bishoprics and orders possessed huge hidden economic resources, and that their refusal to acknowledge and account for these, taken together with the obvious poverty of the rural clergy, was in a profound sense immoral. [38] Many of the faithful thought that the Church itself might benefit from the separation; [39] and the effort to account for the numbers, activities, and income of the orders had been a major objective of several Spanish governments ever since the passage of the first registration law, the "Law of Association," in 1887. [40] With regard to teaching, it was evident from the beginning that the Republic would be unable in so short a time to replace the services of the teaching orders and that vindictiveness motivated the effort totally to expel the orders from the field of education. [41]

But consideration of practical questions of economic power and teacher availability do not begin to plumb the emotional depths of the Cortes debate over the Church. The impassioned and carefully thought-out speeches of Fernando de los Ríos (Socialist) and Alvaro de Albornoz (Radical Socialist) on one side, and those of Gil Robles (Catholic) and Antonio de Pildain (lectoral canon of Vitoria and a Basque deputy) on the other, ranged over the history of the Spanish Church from Visigothic days to the present. [42] The Republic was identified with the struggle against the Inquisition, with the *erasmistas* of the sixteenth century, the *afrancesados* of the eighteenth, the *krausistas* of the nineteenth and the twentieth. The defense of the Church was identified with the national mission of Spain in the *Reconquista,* with the defense of contemporary Spain against the sins of liberalism and materialism. Once the floodgates had been opened, no one could consider calmly the real need for a new relationship between Church and state or a solution of Spain's basic educational problems. The deputies applauded, interpolated, courteously eulogized their opponents' sincerity, and poured salt on the wounds that would soon make further cooperation impossible. With the bitterly contested Article 26 of the Constitution, defining the new position of the Church, was voted, barely more than half the deputies were present. Sr. Albornoz himself was among the absentees.[43]

The grievous debate did not, however, prevent the Republic from enacting specific educational measures, and these indicate clearly the direction it would have followed extensively had time permitted. It established in Madrid and Barcelona model public schools that featured manual as well as intellectual training, student government, a minimum of imposed discipline and memory work, parent-teacher meetings, free lunches, and field trips. The benefits of the Institución Libre were to be extended to the Spanish masses.[44] The desire to bring Spain's cultural heritage to the most neglected rural areas (a dream of the great teacher and art historian Manuel B. Cossío as early as 1882) took shape in the organization of the *Patronato de misiones pedagógicas*. Cossío, too old and ill to participate actively, became the honorary chairman. Small libraries were founded in the villages, and groups of university students volunteered their services for traveling medical units and theater companies.[45] Figures on the government's school-building program vary considerably, but even hostile writers grant that the Azaña government spent far more than any of its predecessors. Every ministry from the turn of the century to 1931 had proclaimed the need for more schools, but since they neither wished to encourage Church-dominated schools nor to spread the influence of the Institución Libre they did very little to advance primary education of any sort in Spain.[46] But when the Church schools were closed in 1933 the Republic deprived itself of far more classrooms and teachers than it could adequately replace.[47]

In the midst of its difficulties over land reform and religious policy the Azaña ministry achieved one notable success, which under more auspicious circumstances might have opened a new era for Spain. Ever since the middle of the nineteenth century the province of Catalonia had been demanding political and cultural autonomy. Primo de Rivera had promised satisfaction for this demand, but once in power had suppressed both local government and the several cultural and artistic manifestations of Catalanism. One of the fortunate circumstances of Spanish politics in 1931 was that the ascendancy of the Azaña coalition in Madrid coincided with the victory in Catalonia of the *Esquerra*, a party devoted as much to social reform as to regional autonomy. With several prominent Catalans serving in the cabinet, and with conservatives such as Miguel Maura and Alejandro Lerroux expressing a willingness to grant a measure of autonomy, Azaña seized the opportunity to press for a statute. Passed in September, 1932, it granted linguistic autonomy, a regional parliament (the *Generalitat*), and considerable local control of taxation. Azaña, his colleagues in Madrid, and Luis Companys, leading figure in the Barcelona government, hoped that generosity on the part of the central government, taken together with the emphasis placed by both governments on social legislation, would reduce the historic antagonism between Castile and Catalonia. [48]

Yet despite its many positive achievements, the coalition disintegrated during 1933. Its loss of confident purpose and unity were clear well in advance of its defeat at the polls in November of that year. Such rapid disillusionment with a government that was fulfilling many of the humanitarian and secularly oriented ideals of the growing middle classes cannot be explained without examining the inner limitations of the republican leadership.

The liberal newspaper *El Sol,* analyzing the composition of the Cortes of 1931, noted that among 470 deputies there were 123 lawyers, 65 professors and teachers, 41 doctors, about 60 others in business and the liberal professions, and 25 workers. [49] It is important to realize also that most of these intellectuals came from comfortable backgrounds and that class lines are much more pronounced in Spain than in the United States. Many future deputies, joyously anticipating the end of the monarchy, had in 1929 and 1930 published books on the tasks of the time in which optimism, knowledge of special areas, eagerness to serve the people, and a faint note of condescension were intermingled. [50] Much that they said later in the Cortes would have been more appropriate to the *Ateneo,* the Madrid literary society which had been the center of intellectual opposition to the regime from 1875 to 1931. They seem not to have realized that while they debated the virtues of the Weimar and the Mexican constitutions, and while they delivered impassioned and well-prepared orations on the historic role of the Spanish Church, the peasants were waiting for land.

In point of fact Spanish working people as well as the middle classes had experienced the economic and cultural renaissance of the decades since 1868. An articulate, politically conscious industrial working class had grown up in the cities, and the countryside was alive with utopian hopes. Typographers and machinists, vine growers and wheat farmers, as well as lawyers and professors, felt the influence of positivism, of socialism, of the pervading nineteenth-century notion of progress. Socialist and anarchist labor groups espoused the causes of education, humanitarian reform, public works, and so-cial legislation. [51] In the struggle to raise standards of living, to educate the masses, and to reduce military, clerical, and landowner influence in the na-tional life, republican and working-class organizations sought many similar ends. But the leadership and program of the Republic remained entirely middle-class, and those Socialists who participated in the Azaña government were professional men and intellectuals who, despite Marxist overtones in their thought, were fundamentally closer to the liberal republican groups than to the Socialist workers.

The absence of enthusiastic support from the Socialist masses was all the more unfortunate because the other principal ideological and political force among the Spanish working class, the anarchists, refused from the start to co-operate with the bourgeois Republic. In Barcelona Colonel Macià, President of the new Catalan government, spent the night of April 14 trying vainly to per-suade the moderate anarchist Angel Pestaña to accept a portfolio in the gov-ernment; and on the same day Luis Companys, mayor of the city, averted a general strike only by declaring a national holiday. [52] In June, at the conven-tion of the *Confederatión Nacional del Trabajo,* a moderate minority hinted that the advent of a liberal republic might suggest some revision of the tradi-tional anarchist attitude toward political action, but the majority saw no reason to anticipate anything good from the Constituent Cortes. [53] During the summer and fall many of the moderates were expelled. At this critical moment anarch-ism, in some respects a highly ethical and idealistic movement, [54] became dominated by the more fanatical and disorderly elements within it. Ever since the revolutionary strikes of 1917, and especially since the thoroughgoing re-pression of the anarchists by the Primo de Rivera dictatorship, the *pistoleros* had increased their relative power in the movement. The younger political leaders in 1931 (the expelled moderates were mostly of a generation that had matured before 1917) saw in the Republic an opportunity to extend revolution-ary agitation, and were especially concerned to maintain their leadership of the Spanish workers in the face of rapid growth of the Socialist unions. In both rural and industrial areas they continually fomented strikes in order to prove that they had not, like their rivals, sold out to a bourgeois government. [55]

Opponents of the Azaña regime teamed with ignorant or racketeering an-archists to embarrass the government. In an impassioned defense before the Cortes of his efforts as Minister of Public Works, Prieto expounded this situ-ation in detail. He described as an instance of provocation the situation at the port authority of Huelva, where officials who belonged to the most con-servative organizations had placed the leading anarchists on the government payroll. Though listed as "commissaries," they did no discoverable work.[56] The worst of many rural clashes between the anarchists and the government occurred at Casas Viejas in early 1933. At this time the government had been trying for more than a year to replace the royalist Civil Guard with the republican, and more humane, Assault Guard. But in response to a declaration of *comunismo libertario* by a handful of armed peasants in a tiny Andalusian village, which had been impatiently awaiting land reform, the exasperated Assault Guards executed a brutal repression in the worst tradition of the Civil Guard. During the following months of investigation and bitter discussion Azaña's majority steadily declined as liberals and Socialists of his own coalition passed to the opposition. Just as in the investigation of *responsibilidades* in 1931 the accumulated evils of Spanish political life had been heaped upon the King's head, so in the investigation following Casas Viejas, the historic violence of both the anarchists and the police was laid at the door of Azaña.[57]

The sporadic military and anarchist risings against the Republic came as a bitter surprise to the Krausist and Socialist intellectuals who formed the core of the Azaña coalition. Their capacity to meet such difficulties was not increased by the absence in Spanish history of a strong republican faith. It is a striking fact that in Spain republican doctrine never truly flourished except as an angry reaction to the incompetence of monarchs—of Isabella II before 1868, of Alfonso XIII before 1931. While the great advocates of reform were closely associated with the republicans and certainly provided the inspiration for most of the legislation of the Azaña period, none of them made a dogma of republicanism. Thus when Joaquín Costa, at the height of his fame in 1901, delivered an ardent philippic demanding the political renovation of Spain, he did not analyze the successful republics or progressive constitutional monarchies of his time. Rather he invoked the *Gobierno de Cristo,* an ideal theocratic state based on his interpretation of the political ideas of Fray Luis de León, Luis Vives, and Francisco de Quevedo![58] When one considers such men as Costa and Giner, let alone more conservative intellectuals such as Unamuno, it is clear that the one transcendent ideal that had ever bound the mass of Spaniards together despite regional and class differences was the Catholicism of the Spanish Renaissance and pre-Reform. The possibility of a republic carried no such inspirational quality as the memory of the sixteenth century, and the writings of these men are filled with nostalgia for a purified Catholicism and for exalted royal leadership.[59] Here indeed was a terrible unsolved dilemma for the children of the Krausists. They loved their country's artistic and spiritual heritage, yearned to educate the Spanish masses, and wished to bring to Spain the best fruits of European science and political liberty. But they lacked both the political experience and a vital democratic tradition on which to base action. Given the fact that they, as much as the traditionalists, often found their most inspiring ideal in the past of the Spanish Church, it is not diffi-cult to understand that the protracted religious struggle had undermined their morale. Azaña personally had long been anticlerical, and the republican-Socialist majority supported anticlerical legislation repeatedly in the two-year period. But the dominant heritage of the deputies supporting the government was Erasmist, heterodox, Krausist rather than anti-Catholic. Giner and Azcárate had always avoided anticlericalism. Had not Joaquín Costa, most practical of the republican precursors, cried repeatedly that hydraulic works and improved fertilizers were neither clerical nor anticlerical?

Reviewing the work of two years, it may be said that whatever the failings of the Republic, few parliamentary governments have initiated so many important reforms as did the republican-Socialist coalition of 1931 – 1933. In finance, economics, and beneficial public works it had moved rapidly and skillfully. It began a potentially fruitful reorganization of the army. Its administration was less corrupt than that of any of its predecessors. Its idealism and good faith were manifest in its school-building program, in the pedagogic missions, in the Catalan Statute. If it was slow to produce a major land reform and if it need-lessly offended Catholic opinion in its attack on the orders, the critic must rec-ognize how complex and explosive were the problems involved. Moreover, the Agrarian Statute, the separation of Church and state, and the school-building program all initiated, however inadequately, reforms that had baffled the best-intentioned royal ministries from 1875 to 1931. At the same time it may be said that the Azaña coalition disintegrated because of its internal division over land reform, its inability to provide respected leadership for the awakened working classes, the ambiguities of its own democratic faith, and the moral attrition de-veloping out of its war with the Church.[60] In its initial optimism about the Spanish future, its educational policies, its concern for all phases of law, and its thoroughly middle-class outlook reflected the influence of Krausism and of the Institución Libre. The Catalan Statute, the public works policy, the army re-form, and the separation of Church and state fulfilled major historic aims of re-publican and reformist groups in Spain since the Revolution of 1868. Its consti-tutional thought reflected both historic Spanish republican aims and an eagerness to adopt the best features of other recent republican constitutions. Its fiscal policies were conservative, while its expenditures indicated a broad and consistent concern for human welfare. Its struggle with the Church re-leased pent-up anticlerical emotions of half a century and, in the particular conjunction of circumstances, delayed at least for many years the possibility of the democratic, reformist, laic state the Constituent Cortes had hoped to build.

NOTES

1. See Luis Jiménez de Asúa, *Proceso histórico de la constitución de la República española* (Madrid, 1932) and Rhea Marsh Smith, *The Day of the Liberals in Spain* (Philadelphia, 1938). Jiménez de Asúa was the chairman of the constitutional commission of the Cortes.

2. All sources hereafter cited depend for their statistics principally on the publications of the Instituto Geográfico y Estadístico; these in turn are not subject to any scientific check, but numerous technical shortcomings as well as motives of genial deception force the student to allow a wide margin of error. It is well known, for example, that evasion of customs regulations renders export and import figures too low, and that much landed wealth is never declared in the census. Nevertheless, a careful study of these sources, in particular of the *Anuario Estadístico de España* (Madrid, 1914 – 34) and the *Boletín del Ministerio de Trabajo y Previsión* (Madrid, 1929 – 36), could provide a much fuller account than any now available on the Spanish economy in the present century.

3. On general economic development see Conde de Romanones, *Las responsabilidades políticas del antiguo régimen de 1875 a 1923* (Madrid, 192[?]) and Miguel de Antonio, *El potencial económico de España* (Madrid, 1935) for intelligent analysis supported by statistics. The best recent volume of facts and figures on the economy is M. Fuentes Irurozqui, *Síntesis de la economía española* (Madrid, 1946).

4. On emigration see, for the pre-1914 period, Angel Marvaud, *L'Espagne au xx siècle* (Paris, 1913), pp. 379 – 382; for the postwar period, Juan Fábregas, *La crisis mundial y sus repercusiones en España* (Barcelona, 1933), pp. 154 – 155.

5. An excellent nontechnical analysis of the role of foreign capital is given in Arturo and Ilsa Barea, *Spain in the Postwar World* (London, 1945), pp. 8 – 13. Sr. Barea was a patent official whose profession gave him a wide knowledge of the methods of foreign capital in Spain.

6. Spanish tariff policies and international trade have been studied more intensively abroad than at home. See Jean Baelen, *Principaux traits du développement economique de l'Espagne* (Paris, 1924); and Georg Ackermann, *Spanien Wirtschaftlich Gesehen* (Berlin, 1939). The latter volume illustrates the important German concern with Spain's mines and industries, and the effect on them of both tariffs and political considerations.

7. The history of the Revolution of 1868 and the First Republic has been ably told in English in Joseph Brandt, *Towards a New Spain* (Chicago, 1933).

8. The Abbé Pierre Jobit, whose *Les éducateurs de l'Espagne moderne* (Paris, 1936) is the indispensable work on the Krausist philosophy, calls Krausism in Spain "premodernism."

9. J. B. Trend, *The Origins of Modern Spain* (Cambridge, Eng. 1934), discusses the intellectual temper of Spain in the late nineteenth century, dwelling particularly on university circles. The spirit of the Krausists can best be sampled in a periodical of great philosophical and educational interest, the *Boletín de la Institución Libre de Enseñanza* (Madrid, 1877 – 1936). The whole Erasmist tradition, which has no real counterpart in Western European thought, may be studied in Marcel Bataillon, *L'Erasme et l'Espagne* (Paris, 1937; available also in a Spanish edition, *Erasmo y España* [2 vols., Mexico, D.F., and Buenos Aires, 1950]).

10. The difficulty of labeling both parties and individuals will be appreciated by any reader who compares the efforts of various scholars to analyze the composition of the

Cortes. Even the numbers assigned to each party vary because each analyst must make an educated guess about the actual affiliation of many a deputy. See for example Smith, *The Day of the Liberals in Spain*, pp. 116–117; E. Allison Peers, *The Spanish Tragedy, 1930–36* (New York, 1936), p. 61; Frank E. Manuel, *The Politics of Modern Spain* (New York, 1938), p. 66; and Gerald Brenan, *The Spanish Labyrinth* (Cambridge, Eng., 1943), pp. 232–234.

11. See, for example, the interview with Alcalá-Zamora reported by the French Socialist Jules Moch in Germaine Picard-Moch and Jules Moch, *L'Espagne républicaine* (Paris, 1933), p. 41. Questioned about his recent conversion, he stated simply that his first loyalty was to the constitution and that he had resigned his royal post when the King had violated the constitution. In 1930 Dr. Marañón wrote a thoroughly laudatory introduction to a book which advocated a British-type limited monarchy rather than a republic as the solution to Spain's political problems. See Francisco Villanueva, *Obstáculos tradicionales*, 2 vols. (Madrid, 1930), prologue by Dr. Marañón.

12. Gabriel Maura Gamazo, *Bosquejo histórico de la dictadura*, 2 vols. (Madrid, 1930), I, pp. 171–172.

13. See David T. Cattell, *Communism and the Spanish Civil War* (Berkeley, Calif., 1955), pp 20–22. The party numbered at most one thousand in the spring of 1931. It could elect no one to the Constituent Cortes, and was split the following year by the defection of its principal leaders, Joaquín Maurín and Andrés Nin.

14. See the interviews with Albornoz and Azaña in Moch, *L'Espagne républicaine*, pp. 71–72.

15. This idea is clearly developed in the prologue written by Albornoz to the short volume by the young Socialist Gabriel Morón, *El partido socialista ante la realidad política de Espana* (Madrid, 1929).

16. Luis Jiménez de Asúa, "The First Year of the Spanish Republic," *Foreign Affairs*, X, (July, 1932), pp. 659–676. Sr. Jiménez, a Socialist and a well-known specialist in constitutional law, was the leading member of the Comisión Parlamentaria de Constitución chosen by the Cortes to draft the republican constitution.

17. Dardo Cuneo, "Fernando de los Ríos y el socialismo humanista," *Cuadernos Americanos*, LXXVIII (Nov.-Dec., 1954), pp. 85–113. A very similar course of intellectual development is indicated by the autobiographical passages in Rodolfo Llopis, *Hacia una escuela más humana* (Madrid, 1934). Llopis was Director of Primary Education and a Socialist. Interesting to note in the present connection is the following passage of the great Spanish scholar Américo Castro: "The Hieronymites, conversos, and humanists of the fifteenth century are called Erasmists . . . in the sixteenth; rationalists . . . in the eighteenth; francophiles, Krausists, and Europeanizers in the nineteenth. Today they are called émigrés." A. Castro, *Aspectos del vivir hispánico* (Santiago de Chile, 1949), pp. 121–122.

18. See Manuel, *The Politics of Modern Spain*, for a brief, clear political history of the Republic.

19. The figures are those of the Banco Soler y Torra Hermanos de Barcelona, quoted in Elli Linder, *El derecho arancelario español* (Barcelona, 1934), p. 137 *ff.*

20. Charles Lefaucheux, *La peseta et l'économie espagnole depuis 1928* (Paris, 1935), pp. 50–60. Lefaucheux gives the clearest available account of the complex financial policies of the Primo, Berenguer, and republican governments.

21. *Ibid.,* pp. 27 – 34.

22. Conde de Romanones, *Las últimas horas de una monarquía* (Madrid, 1931), p. 81. After pointing out that the Revolution of 1868, the Restoration of 1875, and the dictatorship of 1923 had all resulted from military action, the one acknowledged monarchist in the new Cortes wrote: "This time, the Second Republic did not triumph through military sedition, but through the manifestation of the popular will of the nation at the polls, honorably respected by the supreme powers of the country."

23. See Manuel Azaña, *Una política* (Madrid, 1932), pp. 141 – 172. Azaña made his reputation as Minister of War before becoming Premier. He explained the army reform December 2, 1931, on the occasion of a speech to the Cortes.

24. For concentrated hatred of Azaña and general feelings of persecution, see Emilio Mola Vidal, *El pasado, Azaña, y el porvenir* (Madrid, 1934), especially pp. 155 – 168. For the attitude of professional officers partisan to Sanjurjo, see Emilio Esteban-Infantes, *La sublevación del General Sanjurjo* (Madrid, 1933).

25. Gabriel Jackson, "Joaquín Costa, Prophet of Spanish National Recovery," *South Atlantic Quarterly* (April, 1954), pp. 181 – 192.

26. *Exposición gráfica del plan nacional de obras hidráulicas. Guía* (Madrid, 1933), p. 5. The author owes possession of this material to the kindness of Sr. Lorenzo Pardo.

27. For an authoritative exposition of the *Plan Nacional,* see Pedro González-Blanco, *Ordenación y prosperidad de España* (Madrid, 1934), pp. 81 – 142.

28. A. Ramos Oliveira, *Politics, Ecnomics, and Men of Modern Spain, 1808 – 1946* (London, 1946), pp. 458 – 459.

29. *Ibid.,* pp. 459 – 461. See also Moch, *L'Espagne républicaine,* pp. 231 – 242, and Juan Guixé, *Le vrai visage de la république espagnole* (Paris, 1938), pp. 129 – 138. The political conflicts of the time and then the tragic civil war have completely overshadowed the wide variety of beneficial economic and social undertakings of the Azaña ministry. Sr. Prieto has published much about his role in the civil war, but not about his work in the years 1931 – 1933. We are dependent for a written record on sympathetic journalists of the time, such as M. and Mme. Moch, French Socialists; Ramos Oliveria, editor of *El Socialista;* and J. Guixé, a disciple of Joaquín Costa.

30. Moch, *L'Espagne républicaine, p. 194.*

31. Spain. Instituto de Reforma Agraria. *Agrarian Reform in Spain* (London, 1937), p. 30.

32. *Ibid.,* pp. 25 – 27 and Moch, *L'Espagne républicaine,* pp. 255 – 256.

33. Spain. Laws, Statutes, etc. *Ley de Reforma Agraria* (Madrid, 1932). See in particular Art. 5, para. 12, and Art. 9 for the extraordinary legal complexity of the reform.

34. Both political and economic aspects of this question are treated objectively in Pascual Carrión, *Los latifundios en España* (Madrid, 1932).

35. *Agrarian Reform in Spain,* pp. 29 – 32.

36. Rodolfo Llopis, *Hacia una escuela más humana* (Madrid, 1934), p. 26 *ff.*

37. The survey of Father P. Francisco Peiró, *El problema religioso-social de España* (Madrid, 1936), which indicates extremely low church attendance among all classes, both in urban and rural areas, is quoted on the educational problem by Franco publicists as well as by republicans.

38. Estimates of the income of the larger bishoprics and orders vary widely, and no subject in recent Spanish history is more laden wih emotional overtones. Remembering always that numerical accuracy is impossible to achieve on this question, the author believes that considerable understanding of the nature of the problem can be gained from the reading of J. Torrubianó Ripoll, *Beatería y religión* (Madrid, 1930). This volume brings together a series of articles originally published in *El Liberal* during the twenties. The discussion is much more specific than is usual in such writings. Republican orators more than once referred to the factual material of Torrubianó in their discussions in the Constituent Cortes of the religious question. During the period of the Constituent Cortes the author was a member of the conservative republican party of Alcalá-Zamora.

39. Representative of this viewpoint was the Catholic law professor Alfred Mendizábal, whose book *Aux origines d'une tragédie* (Paris, 1937) was published under the auspices of Jacques Maritain. Without offering figures as does Peiró, Mendizábal refers repeatedly to the alienation of the masses from the Church.

40. See Melchor Fernández Almagro, *Historia del reinado de Alfonso XIII* (Barcelona, 1933), pp. 21 – 22, 100 – 110, and 171 – 172 for the efforts of Liberal governments in 1902, 1906, and 1910 to obtain the compliance of the orders to the Law of Associations.

41. An able and sympathetic analysis of the role of the teaching orders is given in E. Allison Peers, *Spain, the Church, and the Orders* (London, 1939).

42. For the major addresses of De los Ríos and Gil Robles in the October, 1931, debate, see Arturo Mori, *Crónica de las Cortes Constituyentes de la segunda república española* (Madrid, 1932 – 1933), III, pp. 13 – 37; Alvaro de Albornoz, *La política religiosa de la república* (Madrid, 1935); Antonio de Pildain y Zapiain, *En defensa de la Iglesia y la libertad de enseñanza* (Madrid, 1935).

43. Peers, *The Spanish Tragedy,* p. 73.

44. The program of the Republic in elementary education is the principal subject of the previously cited work of Rodolfo Llopis, *Hacia una escuela más humana.* The author discusses not only the heritage of Francisco Giner, but the American "progressive" schools and the pedagogic experiments of the Soviet Union in the 1920's. Descriptions of the functioning of the model schools are given in Moch, *L'Espagne républicaine,* pp. 186 *ff.*

45. G. Somolinos D'Ardois, "Las misiones pedagógicas de España, 1931 – 1936," *Cuadernos Americanos* (September-October, 1953), pp. 206 – 224; Luis A. Santullano, *El pensamiento vivo de Manuel B. Cossío* (Buenos Aires, 1946), a biographical sketch and selection of Cossío's writings by the actual director of the missions; Alexander Casona, *Una misión pedagógica-social en Sanabria* (Buenos Aires, 1941) for the personal testimony of a participant.

46. Marie R. Madden, "The Church and Catholic Action in Spain," *Catholic Historical Review,* XVIII (April, 1932), p. 41.

47. See Mendizábal, *Aux origines,* pp. 170 – 171, for an analysis of the purely material obstacles. Peers, in his *Spain, the Church, and the Orders,* pp. 150 – 152, makes the same criticisms as does Mendizábal, but also credits the government with vigorous accomplishment in comparison with its predecessors, and considers that "little real progress" was made in the period 1934 – 1935.

48. See three major speeches of Azaña in the Cortes, *Una política,* pp. 409 – 514; also his brief address and triumphal reception in Barcelona, September 26, 1932, *En el poder y en la oposición* (Madrid, 1934), I, pp. 1 – 5. For a scholarly analysis of the statute see the French law thesis, Henri Barrail, *L'autonomie régionale en Espagne* (Lyon, 1933). An excellent short history of Catalan regionalism, placing it in the perspective of contemporary Spanish problems generally, is Anton Sieberer, *Katalonien gegen Kastilien* (Vienna, 1936), available also in a French translation as *Espagne contre Espagne* (Geneva, 1937).

49. Cited in Smith, *The Day of the Liberals in Spain,* pp. 155 – 156.

50. See the series of short books published by Javier Morata during the last few years preceding 1931, with titles beginning *Al servicio de . . . ,* written by leading republican and Socialist personalities such as Marcelino Domingo, Jiménez de Asúa, and Julián Besteiro. One small group in the new Cortes (among whom were José Ortega y Gasset and Gregorio Maranon) appropriated to themselves the sobriquet "Al servicio de la República."

51. Both the political and the humanitarian-cultural awakening of the working classes can be studied in Juan José Morato, *El partido socialista* (Madrid, 1931) and in Anselmo Lorenzo, *El proletariado militante* (Mexico D.F., 1941[?]). The latter was the revered leader of the (nonviolent) anarchists till his death in 1914. A unique book for understanding the role of both socialism and anarchism among the rural masses is J. Díaz del Moral, *Historia de las agitaciones campesinas Andaluzas Córdoba* (Madrid, 1929).

52. See Francisco Madrid, *Ocho meses y un día en el gobierno civil de Barcelona* (Barcelona, 1932), pp. 133 – 135. Sr. Madrid served as private secretary to the first three civil governors of republican Barcelona.

53. José Peirats, *La C. N. T. en la revolución española* (Toulouse, 1951), pp. 34 – 44. This book, published by the anarchists at their exile headquarters in France, is intended as the first volume of an official history. It contains no scholarly apparatus, but does include many important documents and follows a roughly chronological sequence.

54. See Gabriel Jackson, "The Origins of Spanish Anarchism," *Southwestern Social Science Quarterly,* XXXVI (September, 1955), pp. 135 – 147.

55. Periodical literature and memoirs of the era justify the general statements concerning contradictory elements within the anarchist movement and anarchist-socialist rivalries. But no scholarly study has yet evaluated the relative strengths of anarchist and socialist groups in specific areas and for specific dates. Nor do we know the extent to which the policies of the leadership reflected the sentiments of the rank and file.

56. See Mori, *Crónica . . . ,* X, pp. 558-582 and *passim.*

57. See Ramon J. Sender, *Viaje a la aldea del crimen* (Madrid, 1934) for an account of the events and of conditions underlying this and similar outbreaks. The course of the bitter debate in the Cortes may be followed in Mori, *Crónica . . . ,* XI, pp. 426 – 652, and XII, *passim.*

58. Joaquín Costa, *Crisis política de España* (Madrid, 1914), pp. 68 – 75. Costa, as *mantenedor* of the traditional floral games of Salamanca, delivered the original speech.

59. See Francisco Giner, "La Iglesia Española," *Estudios filosóficos y religiosos* (Madrid, 1922), pp. 287 – 327; Joaquín Costa, *Tutela de pueblos en la historia* (Madrid, 1916 [?]). For a brief analysis of the underlying beliefs of more conservative men such as Unamuno and Baroja see Ramón Iglesia, "El reaccionarismo de la generación del 98," *Cuadernos Americanos,* LX (November-December, 1951), pp. 53 – 76. For the authoritarian tendencies of Costa, see my article "Costa et sa 'révolution par le haut,' " *Estudios de Historia Moderna,* III, 1953, pp. 287 – 300.

60. For an accurate and moving portrait of the ultimate pessimism of the republicans, see Manuel Azaña, *La velada en Benicarló* (Buenos Aires, 1939). Its topical reference is primarily to the civil war, but it reflects in depth the whole spiritual struggle of the republicans.

4

The Popular Front Elections in Spain, 1936*

Xavier Tusell Gómez

(Translated by Ann Kaenig Fleming and Shannon E. Fleming)

The Second Republic brought the politicization of Spanish society to a climax in 1936, culminating in the most fully mobilized and thoroughly contested election in Spanish history. The tendency toward polarization which this revealed was produced by three years of political conflict and stalemate from 1933 to 1936. Breakdown of the original Azaña coalition enabled resurgent forces of the center and moderate right to win the second Republican election in 1933. Chief representative of the center was the Radical party of Alejandro Lerroux, somewhat analogous to the French Radicals of the French Third Republic, while the main force of Spanish conservatism was the new rightist confederation, CEDA, led by José Ma. Gil Robles. The CEDA was a broad middle-class Catholic party rather similar to the Christian Social party in Austria.

With their eyes on developments in central Europe in

* Author's Note: This article is a summary of my book *Las elecciones del Frente Popular en España,* 2 vols. (Madrid: Edicusa, 1971): The only modifications that have been made are in accordance with the criticism offered by certain specialists. I have therefore omitted the bibliography and source material.

In editing the book I counted on the collaboration of Octavio Ruiz Manjón, Genoveva García Queipo de Llano, Manual Angel Coma, and Manuela Díez de Grado.

1933 – 1934, the Spanish left denounced the CEDA as "fascist" and insisted that, even though it had become the largest party in Spain, its representatives must never be allowed to enter a coalition government. When that finally occurred in October 1934, it became the signal for an abortive revolutionary insurrection in the mining province of Asturias, accompanied by lesser outbreaks in Catalonia, the Basque country, and Madrid. The insurrection of 1934 was put down by the army and more than 15,000 rebels and leftis activists were arrested. Altogether, it was a revolt without precedent in Western Europe since the Paris Commune of 1871. The left was temporarily repressed, and the following year, from October 1934 to December 1935, was a period of center-right dominance, devoted to a partial dismantling of the earlier reforms of 1931 – 1933. The two years 1934 – 1935 were polemically dubbed by the left as the "black biennium."

At the close of 1935 the center-right coalition also broke down, and the Republican President, Niceto Alcalá Zamora, refused to allow the CEDA to form a government of its own, even though it was the largest party in Spain and had a plurality in Parliament. Instead, Alcalá Zamora, a moderate Catholic liberal, appointed a personal crony, Manuel Portela Valladares, as prime minister, to hold new elections and use government pressure to try to create a new center coalition. This time the left had learned its lesson and prepared a unified Popular Front electoral alliance, while the effort to build a new centrist force failed completely.

The following article explores the manifold ambiguities of the electoral campaign and its results. This analysis demonstrates that the majority of Spanish voters by no means endorsed the extremes of either side. Nevertheless, the general tendency toward polarization in mutually exclusive blocs made constitutional cooperation difficult and presaged the breakdown that soon occurred, in a sense just as the international alliance system helped to precipitate otherwise rational statesmen into general war in 1914.

For some time Spanish political history has been employing procedures borrowed from French electoral sociology as a method of obtaining an objective study of the influence of different political groupings and voter behavior. In this regard an examination of the crucial 1936 elections which witnessed the triumph of the Popular Front holds great importance, since from a historical point of view these elections brought face to face the two Spains which, in general lines, were the same as those who only a few months later would fight not before the ballot box but with weapons in hand.

Yet there is an even more important aspect which derives from the fact that to the extent that it is possible to classify a Spanish election as a scientific model of political behavior the one of 1936 was. In effect, it is impossible to take seriously the election results during the Restoration monarchy, since only in certain urban centers do they express the will of the voters in an objective manner. Concerning elections under the Second Republic it may be said that they fulfill standards of honesty which the previous ones did not. In spite of this, the 1931 elections are little representative because the proclamation of the new regime was too near, the right was disorganized, and the left voted in a narrow alliance. Concerning those of 1933, the fragmentation of the left, divided as a consequence of their years in power, as well as of the right, makes them at times difficult to interpret. On the other hand, in the 1936 elections, as Carlos Rama pointed out some time ago: "Four fundamental elements are found in the most complete state in which they are known in contemporary Spain: a) an effective regime of public liberties; b) a sufficiently developed system of public opinion; c) a concurrence of diverse sectors in considering the electoral act as decisive for the future of the country, so that it takes on a truly plebiscitary character and d) minimum voter abstention." This explains why any proposed study concerning Spanish political behavior, in the hypothetical case of free elections, must take into account the results of the 1936 contest, even though much time has passed, political conditions favored the left and, in many instances, the electoral system made the results difficult to interpret.

1. General considerations.

Before referring concretely to our subject, it is necessary to allude, at least briefly, to the political and legislative coordinates under which these elections occurred and, as has been said, although this is the best possible model of political behavior among the Spanish people in a democratic system, there are specific factors which do not give it a timeless validity.

The February 1936 elections were held following the failure of the second parliamentary experience of the Second Republic. As is known, this second experience had as fundamental protagonists the Radicals and the CEDA, and although it has been called, in pejorative terms, the *Bienio Negro,* it probably does not totally deserve this designation. What characterizes, first and foremost, this second two-year period is not, in effect, its reactionary tone (although on occasions it did have one) but rather its instability. The latter arose, in the first place, from the incongruence of an alliance between an essentially Catholic party such as the CEDA, which grouped together the conservative masses of the country with a party of prior anticlericalism, such as the Radicals. In the second place, another important source of this instability is that the electoral triumph of the right in 1933, probably much less massive than is usually affirmed, had been achieved as a consequence of a rebuke on the part of the country to the first two years of republican government. The program of the right was, in effect, essentially negative and, therefore, too narrow to achieve consensus. There were rightists who wanted, above all, to defend Catholicism and who, therefore, were not opposed to accepting certain social reforms; for others the essential factor was the defense of economic interests. We find equal inconsistencies on subjects such as regionalism. This situation was aggravated, in the third place, by the fact that circumstances did not at all favor the ability of the right to govern tranquilly. Provocation by the extreme right made collaboration between the Radicals and the CEDA still more difficult, provoking the republican sentiments of the former and exciting the conservative feelings of the majority of the members of the latter. As for the extreme left, they also contributed, through the October 1934 Revolution, to making impossible the coalition of Radicals and the CEDA. There was only a moment in 1935 when it seemed that a program could be carried out, but then the Radicals, who had already lost a good percentage of their support, demonstrated both an ideological vacuity and an absolute administrative bohemianism. Since, on the other hand, Alcalá Zamora had not been able to overcome his prejudices against Gil Robles and the latter demanded the effective political direction of the new alliance of the center-right, the situation became increasingly tense. A coalition was still attempted under the presidency of two politicians (Chapaprieta and Portela Valladares) who in previous ministerial positions had earned prestige, but again the center-right showed its own programmatic incoherence.

The prevailing electoral law would be that of July 1933, which had modified a previous disposition of May 1931. While it is not possible, of course, to blame the tragic dénouement of the Republic on this law, one may say that neither did it favor its stability. This law had been intended by the left for their own benefit, but in 1933 the result had been the opposite of what was expected. The reason is very simple. The electoral law was based on the existence of provincial and urban circumscriptions, in the case of provincial capitals of more than 150,000 inhabitants (Ceuta and Melilla were also non-provincial circumscriptions, each one electing one deputy). Each circumscription was entitled to one deputy for each 50,000 inhabitants. In the conferring of seats a clear majority system was followed, although giving some representation to the minority: In a circumscription in which there were twenty deputies to elect, for example, the slate which won would obtain sixteen seats (the maximum number of candidates for whom the voter could vote), and the proportion was similar in the rest of the cases. Evidently, under these conditions, the large coalitions benefited. In order for the proclamation of the deputies to be legal it was also necessary for at least one member of the winning slate to have obtained at least 40 percent of the valid votes, which, doubtlessly, also favored the large coalitions (in case of not obtaining the above mentioned percentage it was necessary to resort to a second election).

At the time of selecting the candidates, everything previously mentioned had considerable importance. Naturally the right as well as the left was conscious that the broadest alliance possible was necessary because of the peculiarities of the electoral law. On the other hand, the right and the center-right faced an undeniable disadvantage: Their discord was great and good evidence of this is found in the fact that the mutual accusations which they hurled at each other are much more bitter than those aimed at the left. The latter, to the contrary, seemed to have learned the lesson of their 1933 defeat. Its fundamental consequence was, in effect, the formation of the Popular Front.

Although it has been common until recently to consider the Spanish Popular Front a product of communist influence, the truth is that such an affirmation lacks any basis, not only because Spanish Communism was not sufficiently strong as to have such an initiative in Spanish politics, but because it is very probable that the instructions of the Third International were never followed with excessive fidelity by the Spanish Communist party (as in fact, they had never been on previous occasions). Moreover, the initiative could not have come from the communists for the simple reason that we know who it was that suggested it: Azaña and Prieto. The former already in 1933 had pointed out the dangers that the left ran when they went to the polls divided, dangers which reality confirmed. Azaña, moreover, suffered in February 1936 from a special predicament, not because his conduct in office was remembered with particular enthusiasm, but, especially, because he had been the object of a persecution as continuous as it was lacking in basis by the right as a result of the revolution of October 1934. Now he counted on the Izquierda Republicana (Republican Left), a party which brought together all the groups which during the first two years had constituted the backbone of the cabinets over which he presided. Farther to the right the Unión Republicana grouped together the followers of Martínez Barrios and the right sector of the old Radical-Socialist party. In the Socialist party Prieto had defended in 1933 the alliance with the Republican Left and he also did now. His position was in reality not based on any ideological question but on something much more simple: His tactical ability told him that an electoral victory would be impossible without the support of the Republican Left. As he also gained revolutionary prestige for having participated in the October Revolution, it was not unusual for his position to win majority support in his party.

2. Candidates and candidacies.

Not only was the situation before the elections favorable to the left, but they knew how to act in a much more united manner at the time of the concrete elaboration of the slates of candidates. On an early date the Popular Front began this organization, determining in Madrid the number of seats that corresponded to each party and, in short, succeeding in having the lists sponsored by it accepted at the provincial level. Instances of indiscipline were almost nonexistent, and before the end of January 1936 a list of Popular Front candidates had already been drawn up. In accordance with the proposal of Indalecio Prieto and against the opinion of the ultra-revolutionary Largo Caballero, they endeavored to insure a dominant role for the Republican Left. On February 5 (that is, eleven days before the elections) the press published the definitive list of the left candidates, which was generally accepted without difficulty. The only objections arose from newly formed parties, as, for example, the Unión Republicana, which on its own had never had an opportunity to test its electoral might and demanded, in all probability, a number of seats superior to its strength.

In the case of the right and the center-right the situation was very different, in the first place because it was related to the elaboration of an electoral program, a subject which we shall speak of below. First, the indignation shown by Gil Robles toward Alcalá Zamora could make one think that on this occasion, as opposed to what occurred in 1933, the CEDA would opt for exclusively rightist alliances (Monarchists and Traditionalists). However, this did not occur, for it was explicitly announced that the CEDA would go to the polls with a moderate alliance of conservative Republicans (Maura), Agrarians (Martínez de Velasco), Radicals (Alba), etc.

The greatest conflict developed with the caretaker centrist prime minister, Portela Valladares. The President of the Council of Ministers tried to create a center-right political group that would represent something very similar to what the Radical party had signified during the previous two-year period. For this purpose, undoubtedly well-intentioned, he nevertheless used some clearly abusive procedures. Portela was a man of the old politics for whom elections were not something which a prime minister could stand aside from. From the beginning he tried to intervene in the elections, provoking in many provinces the creation of governmental groups which counted on former *caciques* from the monarchy for support. On the other hand, as may be seen in the memoirs of Chapaprieta and Gil Robles, his attitude with respect to the parties of the right was one of "true political blackmail." Aware that by his own means he could not obtain an electoral victory, from January 25 Portela offered to ally himself with any other group which was not extremist. In reality this request only had an effect on the Popular Front in one case (in the province of Lugo), so it may be considered that it was directed principally against the right. On February 4, when the Popular Front slates were already complete, Portela held a conversation with Gil Robles and, in order to avoid a three-way battle in many provinces, obtained from the latter an electoral alliance for which Gil Robles could not have felt much enthusiasm but which was indispensable to him. Moreover, by this move, the power of the state, so important in every Spanish election, would be on his side. The alliance, however, was not only tardy, but also filled with mistrust, which was clear even in the electoral propaganda. Concerning the fascistic Spanish Falange, Gil Robles did not reach an electoral agreement, the most important reason probably being, in contrast to what happened with Portela's group, that it could not attract an important number of votes to the right and center-right alliance.

The compilation of the rightist slates has not yet been fully described. In spite of the fact that with the passage of time the number of candidacies from the right was slowly decreasing, the union was no more harmonious, and it may be said that each province was a distinct case. At the provincial level the discussions were especially bitter, the slates were completed late, and there were frequent cases of insubordination, such as, for example, that of local groupings who refused to accept what was decided at a national level or others in which the union was simply impossible and three-way candidacies existed (Popular Front, the right, and the center).

The final result of the elaboration of the lists of candidates is easily seen in the following table. While the number of Popular Front candidates was 342, which is exactly the number of majority seats (that is, the total of those for

TABLE 4-1.

Total number of candidates by parties

Right:		
Monarchists	39	(7)
Traditionalists	31	(6)
Falangists	37	(37)
CEDA	179	(1)
Others	2	
Center-Right:		
Radicals	69	(45)
Centristas (Portela)	74	(55)
Progresistas (Alcalá Zamora)	13	(7)
Liberal Democrats (Álvarez)	8	(2)
Conservatives (Maura)	16	(13)
Agrarios	28	(12)
Lliga Catalana	22	
Basque Nationalists	14	(14)
Rightist Independents	37	(15)
TOTAL	569	
Popular Front:		
Esquerra Catalana	22	
Acció Catalana	5	
POUM	1	
Sindicalista	1	
Independent Sindicalista	1	
Communist Party	20	
Left Catalanistas	4	
Unión Republicana	42	
Izquierda Republicana	108	
PSOE	124	
Unió Socialista de Catalunya	3	
Federales	2	
Leftist Independents	5	
Galleguistas	4	
Esquerra Valenciana	1	
TOTAL	343	

The numbers in parenthesis represent the right or center-right candidates who fought in an open candidacy or who formed a complete candidacy in opposition to another of the same persuasion.

which a voter in each province could vote), the number of candidates from the center and the center-right is 569 (we have considered as real candidates those who on election day obtained at least 500 votes). In some provinces (Segovia, Navarra, or Álava) the fact that there was more than one candidate from the right and the center-right for the majority seat signifies that the right conceived the possibility of winning not only the majority representation, but also the minority. However, in other provinces what happened was simply a failure to achieve a complete union. This occurred in three of the four Galician provinces, in the Basque provinces, in two of the three provinces in Valencia, in Soria, Burgos, Córdoba, and Cuenca. If in all these provinces an alliance was not reached between the center and the right it was because there existed (or there was believed to exist) a sufficiently relevant portion of the electorate capable of supporting the former: The followers of Portela had their principal support in Galicia, the Nationalists in the Basque provinces, the Autonomous Republicans in the Levant, and so on.

A provincial study of the composition of the lists of candidates may be of interest to the extent that it provides us a view of the party system in each province. For the right it is fitting to reiterate the preponderant role of the CEDA at the national level: Only in Gerona, Vizcaya, Ceuta, and Melilla were there no CEDA candidates, while, on the other hand, in seven provinces this party presented as many candidates as there were majority seats. This fact may demonstrate that the CEDA was the party with the broadest diffusion during the Second Republic. Nevertheless, their greatest influence was found in Old Castile; in the remaining regions their importance derived from the existence of center-right groups who had allied themselves with them. As is natural, it was difficult for the CEDA to penetrate Catalonia with the competition from the Catalan Lliga or in the Basque provinces from the Nationalists, but it was also difficult in Asturias, because of the influence of Melquiades Alvarez. This reinforces the impression that the CEDA tended to become the clearly hegemonic organization of the right during the Second Republic.

Perhaps if one had to mention other right groups which counted on national support, it would be necessary to mention the Monarchists and the Traditionalists. Only in seventeen circumscriptions were they absent (the majority on the periphery), but frequently their representation in the heart of the right and center-right slates was extremely limited. They only managed more than three candidates in two cities (Bilbao and Madrid) and five provinces with a conservative tradition (Guipúzcoa and Navarra) or in those in which a local influential Monarchist personality existed (as occurred in Orense with Calvo Sotelo) or, finally, in those where the old Acción Nacional rebelled in a monarchical sense and did not join the CEDA.

As far as the center Republicans are concerned, the distribution of the candidates of the Radical party still shows an area of national influence, but later such influence will not correspond to the votes obtained. On the other hand, Portelismo was quite concentrated in regions which in earlier periods had been marked by frequent electoral corruption, such as Galicia and Granada (we find Portela's greatest personal influence in Galicia), or where it gained the collaboration of influential political groups or personages (the Balearic Islands where their representative was the millionaire Juan March, and in Valencia, Murcia, and Alicante). The rest of the center Republican groups had an exclusively provincial influence: Maura's Conservatives in Soria, the Liberal Democrats of Álvarez in Asturias, the Progresistas in Córdoba, the Agrarios in the upper Meseta, who were the heirs of the former Conservative and Liberal caciques, and so on.

Among the leftist candidacies the Republican grouping which seems to have had a radius of influence comparable to the CEDA was the Izquierda Republicana, which was only missing from the slate in eight circumscriptions. Their least influence was found in regions of autonomous proclivity (moreover, in Catalonia they competed for the same votes as the Esquerra Catalana), in conservative areas (Old Castile), or in those in which the Unión Republicana had a major influence. Actually, the Unión Republicana and the Izquierda Republicana showed a geography of complementary provincial roots, which led one to think of a possible simplification of the party system on the basis of the contraction of these two parties into a single party. The Unión Republicana had its principal support in the southern half of the peninsula, especially in Andalusia.

The Communist party had a rather extensive (candidates in nineteen circumscriptions) but little concentrated influence (only two candidates in Córdoba). Its main support lay in industrial zones (the Basque provinces, Asturias) or in latifundist provinces of the south. The Socialist party was absent from only five circumscriptions, of which four were Catalan (and the Unió Socialista de Catalunya existed there and represented the same ideology at a regional level as the PSOE). Its greatest influence was found in the latifundist provinces of the south and in industrial centers, but it was also important in conservative provinces as an alternative to the right (Salamanca). On the other hand, the number of its candidates decreased, as is logical, in areas of anarchosyndicalist influence (the Mediterranean coast and the lower Guadalquivir River), where the bourgeois left played a principal role among the Popular Front candidates.

3. The Election campaign.

If the errors of the right were serious at the moment of drawing up the slates of candidates (although they were probably also inevitable), this was also true with respect to the election campaign. While the Popular Front elaborated a program of governmental action and hurled it at public opinion, the right was incapable of doing so. Even though its street propaganda of leaflets and pamphlets was abundant, this was often counterproductive because of its content.

The forces of the united left coincided on two basic objectives (amnesty for captured revolutionaries and the necessity of reviving the political experience of the first two years of the Republic), which formed a sufficient base for reaching complete agreement. However, the fulfillment of that agreement was not easy: When the program of the Popular Front was announced on January 16, Sánchez Román, leader of the small Partido Nacional Republicano (National Republican party), abandoned the alliance fundamentally because he did not want to be allied with the Communist party and other revolutionary proletarian groups. Concerning the content of the program, it is true, as Gil Robles pointed out, that it was "a record of disagreements." The allies demonstrated their concurrence on amnesty, replacement of civil servants, and the readmission of dismissed workers, but the Republican parties rejected "a class Republic," opposing nationalization of land and banking, worker control, or even subsidized work stoppage. It is very possible that this enumeration of differences had an electoral significance in the sense that it attracted the votes of the center, who were little disposed to any revolutionary adventure.

For its part, the government made public on January 28 an electoral manifesto in which it announced its principal purpose of carrying out a program of "pacification and national reconstruction." This affirmation was accompanied, however, by absolute imprecision at the moment of fulfilling it, probably because of a desire to remain on a vague level that would offend no one. It is curious, however, that in a certain way Portela's program (it was elaborated by Portela himself and even some of his collaborators were ignorant of its content until its publication) was more conservative than had been the positions of some of the CEDA members such as Giménez Fernández (Portela's ideal in economic matters was simply "to return to private initiative that free play which would give such a good result").

As we have said, the right was incapable of elaborating an electoral manifesto. In 1933 they had only managed to unite around some points of an essentially negative character (amnesty, protection of economic interests, and constitutional reform), but now their differences were so great that they could not even manage this. In a certain sense, their failure to reach an agreement was positive, because it demonstrated that in spite of appearances the CEDA, the principal force of the right, continued to be a moderate political group. In effect, immediately following the dissolution of the Cortes, the Monarchists proposed to the CEDA a program of a completely subversive tone, which included the declaration of the new Cortes as a constitutional assembly, the dismissal of Alcalá Zamora and his replacement by a general. The CEDA ended up by rejecting this program, in part because of the attitude of an important sector of its leaders (among them Gil Robles, Giménez Fernández, and Lucia) and in part because, as is logical, the acceptance of these principles supposed the pure and simple impossiblity of reaching an electoral agreement with the right Republicans.

With the rejection of this program, the extreme right issued manifestos that augmented it: For example, they asked for a declaration of the illegality of the Socialist party and the separatists and "the organization of a new state on a corporate and authoritarian base." Calvo Sotelo put it more strongly: He even admitted that in his words there had been "a direct call for force," for "military force in the service of the state," since the army was the backbone of the nation.

On the other hand, Gil Robles, obliged by circumstances to make no programmatic manifestation at all, was obliged to remain at a level of imprecision which was quite similar to that adopted on many occasions by the party in power. On January 23 he gave a speech in Toledo which is a good example of his ambiguity, logical considering the attitude of a goodly number of the masses which followed him (and which, on this occasion, received General Franco with acclaim). After stating that the alliance of the right was purely electoral, he rejected the necessity of enunciating a program because "whoever comes before us knows that for us the first thing is God and then Spain because there is nothing else."

A voter is not moved only by programs but also, and especially, by the oratory of the leaders and by simplifications consisting of brief phrases or mottoes which condense the antagonism among the participants in the contest. In the case of the Popular Front the propaganda of this type insisted that its victory would be simply the recuperation of the Republic of April 14 for the realization of a program which would differ little from that carried out during the Republic's first two years. It was a question, according to Azaña, of executing "a Republican policy developed by a Republican government with the support of the Spanish proletariat." There was, however, a sector of the Socialist party, represented by Largo Caballero, that did not forget its revolutionary pretensions, but at the moment of the electoral campaign he neglected them somewhat so as not to frighten the conservative voter. In short, a good example of Popular Front propaganda is provided by this selection taken from a leftist daily in Granada:

For the Republic of April 14th
Against the kidnappers of public liberties
Against those who evict the laborers from their lands
Against those who hate the Republic because it is a
  regime of freedom and of justice
Against administrative immoralities.

Naturally, as a result of statements such as the one quoted, the majority tone of Popular Front propaganda was moderate, very much in agreement with the image they wanted to present to the electorate. The situation was very different with the right. Toward the end of the summer of 1935 Giménez Fernández had pointed out the necessity of avoiding during the electoral contest the "mistaken dilemmas" such as Socialism and Catholicism, republic and monarchy, revolution and counterrevolution. Nevertheless, the reality was that when the elections were held, the CEDA fell into precisely those errors that the former minister of agriculture had pointed out. *El Debate* tried to identify the CEDA with the center, but the propaganda mottoes of this organization, the largest on the right, were the antithesis of what they should have been if they wanted the CEDA's image to be one of moderation. "Against the revolution and its accomplices," an oft-repeated slogan, ran the danger that in a more or less direct way it referred to the President of the Republic and to other center politicians; "All power for the leader" supposed in practice little less than a call for a dictatorship; "Vote for the three hundred [deputies]" was absurd since the CEDA was not running so many candidates; "For God and for Spain" supposed an exasperated clericalism which would have painful consequences in the future. The impact of mottoes such as those quoted must have been, in all probability, pointedly negative for the independent voter at the moment of casting his ballot, but it expressed very well the exasperation of the CEDA members at the failure of the second two years of the Republic.

In spite of all this (the failures of the right in the elaboration of the election slates and the program) there is not the slightest doubt that the electoral forecasts were clearly in its favor. The rightist press as well as the left assumed that the new Cortes, even with a certain recuperation by the left, would be obliged to elect cabinets of the same persuasion as those that had existed during the previous two years, thanks to the replacement of the Radicals by Portela's party and the maintenance of the CEDA as the most numerous group.

That this was not the result is explained, at least partially, by anarchist intervention in the elections. The anarchists had always placed maximum importance on their comrades jailed as a consequence of the repression of a revolutionary movement and now this factor seems to have played a primary role. Throughout January 1936 the anarchist press posed the question of what to do during the coming elections. From the theoretical point of view the question presented no problems, because the anarchists never intended to intervene directly in politics, but, on the other hand, they could either mount an active abstentionist propaganda as in 1933 or omit it, which, of course, would have quite considerable importance at the moment of counting the votes. In conclusion, at the beginning of February the attitude of the CNT consisted of recommending abstention and propagandizing in its favor, although it indicated in this respect that a great difference would exist between the 1933 campaign and the current one. However, although the anarchist press recommended abstention it did so with such coolness that it could not compensate for the attitude of any well-known anarchist leader such as Durruti, who declared to the press that "I cannot recommend to anyone that he not vote." As a consequence, the anarchists participated much more in this election than in 1933, although not all did and the situation varied considerably in the provinces.

4. The electoral results.

Given the passion with which the campaign developed and the evolution of events once the Popular Front won at the ballot box, it is not at all strange that the results of the Spanish election of February 1936 have been much discussed. In almost all the works concerning the Spanish Civil War, recent or not, a different evaluation is given, depending often on the political view of the author. However, the truth is that the results are not so difficult to obtain. Those which are found here derive mainly from provincial sources: either the *Boletines Oficiales (Official Bulletins)* where, according to the electoral law, the results were to be published, or the daily press, which provided the data certified as valid by the Junta Provincial del Censo Electoral (as we shall see, this data was later modified in some cases by the Cortes, which had jurisdiction over the final validity of the results).

The task of analyzing the results is difficult because of the peculiarities of the electoral law and the complication of the alliances produced during the campaign. Maintaining the affiliations of the candidacies as they were presented to the voter, the following table has been drawn up from which one may deduce a first conclusion upon which many authors have insisted: The electoral results signify an almost absolute tie. The difference between the right and center-right candidates and those of the Popular Front is less than 1 percent of the electorate. The Popular Front victory is undeniable, but this does not mean that the absolute majority of Spaniards, nor even the absolute majority of the voters, voted for the Popular Front; because if the center votes are added to those of the right and the center and right alliances the result would have favored the latter. Doing this, however, would be abusive, because in many aspects the followers of Portela Valladares and the Basque Nationalists were closer to the Popular Front than to, for example, the Monarchists, as was later shown during the Civil War.

This first impression should be complemented by a deeper and more detailed examination. In the first place, it is necessary to refer to abstentionism. All contemporary witnesses indicated that the passion of the contest was translated in a considerable increase in voter participation, which the statistics confirm: The percentage of voters rose from 67.4 percent to 72 percent; this last figure is not very high if it is compared with other European countries at that time, but it is probably the highest ever in any Spanish election. The provincial distribution of abstentionism shows us in general a greater homogeneity than in 1933: On this occasion the difference between the circumscription with the greatest abstentionism and the one with the least is about 60 percent, while in 1936 it was approximately half. In this instance abstentionism was less in the urban environment than in the rural (in all urban circumscriptions the percentage of voters exceeded 66 percent). As is logical, a map of the distribution of abstentionism would show us that it was especially great on the periphery and, above all, in the anarchist triangle of Cádiz-Sevilla-Málaga where the voting percentage reached only 55 percent to 60 percent. On the other hand, in five provinces of the northern plateau the percentage of voters surpassed 76 percent. Nevertheless, in spite of having maintained to good measure the traditional abstentionism in the areas of anarchist influence, an important percentage of the electorate addicted to these doctrines participated in this election, while they did not in 1933. This fact is especially visible in Málaga and Sevilla (capitals) where the percentage of voters rose from 50-55 percent to more than 90 percent (in their respective provinces the increase is less).

The vote obtained by the Popular Front was localized, first of all, in the urban environment. Not only did the Popular Front always win in the eight urban circumscriptions (obtaining at least 35 percent of the vote), but, moreover, it also triumphed in many other provincial capitals whose rural areas, on the other hand, gave a complete victory to the right: So it happened, for example, in León, in the middle of Old Castile, where the left obtained some 7,000 votes as opposed to only some 4,000 for the right.

On the other hand, the periphery showed a much more definite support for the left than the center of the country (with the single exception of the province

TABLE 4-2

Final results of the February 1936 election

Electors	13,553,710	
Voters	9,864,783	72.0%
Popular Front	4,555,401	
Popular Front and		
Center (Lugo)	98,715	34.3%
Basque Nationalists	125,714	
Center	400,901	5.4%
Right	1,866,981	
Right and Center	2,636,524	33.2%

TABLE 4-3

Final results of the 1933 election

	According to El Debate (2-2-1936)		According to Largo Caballero [1]
Voters		67.4%	
Right	4,806,094		3,345,504
Center	512,371		1,351,174
Left	3,191,100		3,375,432
Right and Center	5,318,465		4,726,606

[1] "Discursos a los trabajadores," p. 161.

The differences between the two calculations are due to the different manner of considering the votes of certain coalitions. The computation from El Debate was based upon the alignment of the parties in 1936.

of Madrid). The entire Mediterranean coast gave a victory to the Popular Front: sociological factors were important here (for example, Andalusian latifundism), as well as cultural factors (the Mediterranean region had been the principal support of the Spanish left since the First Republic). The left was also victorious in Extremadura, in three Galician provinces (although here the main reason was found in the existence of triple candidacies), and in Asturias. As for the right, their major support was located in Castile, especially Old Castile, coinciding with the provinces of the greatest index of religious practice and the smallest of illiteracy. In two provinces in Old Castile as well as in two from New Castile, the center and right candidates gained all the popular representation and the same thing occurred in Navarre and Vizcaya (province). This link between religious practice and voting for the right was also apparent in the urban environment: Bilbao was the provincial capital where the right and the center obtained the largest percentage of votes.

When we interpret the electoral results of 1936 a fundamental question which arises is to what degree the electoral behavior in 1936 varied radically with respect to that of 1933. The fact is that, if we take into account only the final results, a certain stability is perceptible: As in 1936, in 1933 the total votes obtained by the center and the right was superior to that of the left. However, this stability in the electorate's decision was most clearly appreciated at the provincial level: For example, the case of the Balearic Islands, whose results from both elections are found in the following table. In this instance as in that of Málaga (capital) the electorate's decision seems to have been very similar. The only change was that the vote obtained by the Radicals (who presented themselves in 1933 as the personification of the Republic) was switched to the Popular Front (and more concretely to Azaña, the great benefactor from these elections). This (together with the fact that the Centrist party could not even remotely make itself into the successor of the Radicals) is a prime factor in understanding the Popular Front victory.

Another factor of no less importance is the participation of a sector of the electorate which was absent from the 1933 elections and which now voted for the left: anarchism. The case of Cádiz showed that in 1933 the right probably obtained the maximum possible votes, while the left saw their vote almost triple thanks to the participation of the anarchist electorate (even if the percentage of voters had increased, the most probable occurrence is that the great beneficiary would have been the left).

On the other hand, it is clear that given the peculiarities of the electoral law the vote would tend to be concentrated in that slate with the greatest possibilities of winning: Therefore, although it may not properly be said, as we shall see, that the center was the great loser in this election, in several circumscriptions (as, for example, in Bilbao) the political groups of the center were seriously hurt.

A final factor, which explains the results and proves that the disconformity in electoral behavior from 1933 to 1936 is not as great as is sometimes stated, is the scattered vote of the right and the center. We have already said that the majority of Spaniards who voted in February 1936 did not vote for the Popular Front. Therefore, if the center and the right had been perfectly united (an unreal possibility), they would have been the winners. This fact is especially evident in Galicia, the Canary Islands, and the Levant.

Thus, this contradicts the relatively frequent affirmation according to which

TABLE 4-4

Stability of electoral behavior, 1933-1936

1. The case of the Balearic Islands.

	1933		1936
Right	102,327		
Radicals	19,661	Right	118,076
Independents	3,427		
Left	30,239		
Communists	1,059	Popular Front	54,413

2. The collapse of the Radicals.

Votes in Málaga (capital)

	1933	1936
Right	11,808	14,452
Radicals	10,328	1,510
Left	27,488	55,295

3. The impact on the results of new voters.

Results from Cádiz

	1933	1936
Voters	98,654	163,004
Left	30,967	98,437
Right	65,425	64,325

4. The difficulties of the center parties when they did not ally themselves with the right.

Results from Bilbao

	1933		1936
Basque Nationalists	57,239		43,529
Right	20,049		30,274
Left and PSOE	50,467		
Communists	9,139	Popular Front	69,684
Radical-Socialists	1,093		

the 1936 elections would have supposed a revolution. Another quite common affirmation is that the 1936 elections were an antecedent of the Civil War in the sense that they supposed the triumph of the extremes. This does not seem to be the case however. It is disproven, in the first place, by the very fact of the composition of the slates of candidates and the propaganda of the two large groups which contested the election, but it is also disproven by the election results themselves. In each slate in each province the most moderate groups won the most votes. This is due to the fact that one sector of the electorate crossed out those names that their ideology rejected and is a good proof that a current of moderation existed within each party, often unperceived if the total results were analyzed (for example, it would be wrong to judge that only 5 percent of the electorate were from the center because moderate personages such as Martínez Barrios or Giménez Fernández were in fact found, under electoral law, in the left and right respectively). There is no indication that the Communist party had increased their vote and, as for the independent slates of the Falange, they obtained a minimum vote: at the most some 40,000 votes out of an electorate of more than 13 million. It seems clear that at this time the country did not desire a civil war: This was only the thought of some very radicalized minorities, though a few months later this possibility began to become real.

In short, the interpretation which, after a careful examination of the electoral data, we reach here does not differ essentially from that proposed by historians such as Madariaga or Pabón. It agrees with the former that in February 1936 "everyone was in agreement as to the bases of the regime and in particular the parliamentary regime." The latter affirmed, as without doubt seemed certain, that the CEDA had maintained its electoral strength in spite of the fact that radicalism had disappeared and centrism had not yet arrived.

If, however, the contrary has been affirmed (that is to say, that the electorate did not generally maintain a moderate and relatively stable posture with respect to 1933), that derives, at least in good measure, from the fact that the results in the number of deputies differed greatly from that almost exact tie that we have been able to perceive by comparing the number of voters. The reason is based, of course, on the electoral law which in 1933 had favored the right (probably more than it did the left in 1936) and which now favored the left. The best proof of this is found in the following table: In agreement with the results of the first round, 10 percent more deputies would have corresponded to the Popular Front than to the center and right together (in the event that they had been united) though in votes the latter would have obtained a majority of approximately 4 percent of the electorate. Each Popular Front deputy represented in reality some 6,000 votes less than those of the right and center. It is true that the electoral law was not proportional, but it would be unjust to state that to this alone was due the defeat of the opponents of the Popular Front, for the simple reason that the right had had in the two previous years the possibility of reforming it and did not do so, committing the further error of going to the polls disunited.

At any rate we must bear in mind when we examine the following table that the data found in it are incomplete not only because of the changes soon introduced by the Cortes but also because they do not take into account the second electoral round. This second round of 1936 (as distinct from what had occurred in 1933) affected few provinces (only the Basque provinces, Soria, and Castellón). Nevertheless, the result of the first round had been so surprising for the right that we may suppose that they were sufficiently discouraged so as not to give their full support to the second round.

5. Electoral fraud.

The results of the 1936 election, like those of 1931 which supposed a change of regime, have been much discussed. During the Civl War a "Commission formed in order to express an opinion on the illegitimacy of the acting powers of July 18, 1936" judged that the results had been modified "in perfect execution of a plan mapped out in advance." The first thing which must be said concerning this opinion is that, although explicable in the period in which it was issued, it does not coincide with that which the political groupings of the right declared in the days immediately following the voting. In the greater part of the peninsula the results which appeared in the press were accepted as valid: The principal organization of the right (the CEDA) recognized that it had been defeated, and it may even be said that the groups of the extreme right were much busier demonstrating that the CEDA tactics had failed and that parliamentarianism was not viable than in proclaiming the invalidity of the results. Of course, at the provincial level this general impression that the Popular Front had won and had won honestly varied somewhat, especially in certain regions, but the dominant feeling was still that the left had been triumphant at the national level.

The attitude with which the left and right attended the Cortes was very different and already began to foretell the intolerance which was going to take possession of Spanish opinion. The right, probably through fear more than anything else, amended their electoral demagogy, showed themselves disposed to collaborate with the government, and, consequently, urged that the criteria employed in the proceedings of the Cortes be strictly legal. In the Popular Front, although it was probably not the majority opinion, there were those who did not hesitate to urge a partisan attitude (perhaps the position of the rightist deputies in 1933 had not been neutral either). *El Socialista* stated, for example, that "having rigorously examined the question, not even one rightist deputy can affirm that he obtained his election certificate honestly."

The reading of the records of the Cortes sessions corresponding to the discussion of the electoral proceedings permits the conclusion that, in the first

TABLE 4—5.

Provincial distribution of votes

	Voters	Popular Front	Center	Center-Right	Right	Falange
Álava	(74.1)	16.4	14.9		27.6	
Albacete	(75.7)	31.9		41.5		
Alicante	(73.0)	39.1		33.9		
Almería	63.9	34.7		29.4		
Ávila	(80.2)	34.1		38.1		
Badajoz	75.3	40.9		34.8		
Baleares	72.1	22.6		49.5		
Barcelona (C)	68.8	43.7		25.6		
Barcelona (P)	75.2	38.7		28.6		
Burgos	71.5	20.6		50.8		
Cáceres	(76.4)	38.8		37.6		?
Cádiz	(59.5)	35.9		23.5		2.7
Castellón	71.7	27.0	15.1		27.1	
Ciudad Real	72.3	30.4		39.4		
Ceuta	57.9	41.3		16.7		
Córdoba	73.4	43.5		30.3		0.4
Cuenca	75.0	19.7			55.2	
Gerona	71.3	41.0		30.1		
Granada	74.7	30.0		44.6		
Guadalajara	74.0	22.9			51.0	
Guipúzcoa	(75.9)	23.7	26.0		26.0	
Huelva	70.7	37.6		36.2		
Huesca	65.8	35.6			31.3	
Jaén	(74.9)	38.6		34.9		?
La Coruña	(70.6)	37.2	14.4		27.8	4.1
Las Palmas	59.6	25.2	24.2		14.2	
León	(71.5)	30.0			37.3	
Lérida	(69.5)	38.0		31.5		
Logroño	74.5	32.5			39.9	
Lugo	62.8	34.6		30.6		
Madrid (C)	77.2	41.7		34.7		0.9
Madrid (P)	(77.6)	44.5			33.0	
Málaga (C)	93.4	71.1			14.9	

TABLE 4—5 (continued)

	Voters	Popular Front	Center	Center-Right	Right	Falange
Málaga (P)	(55.0)	33.7		21.1		
Melilla	(62.7)	45.5		17.2		
Murcia (C)	(85.0)	51.4		33.6		
Murcia (P)	(67.5)	35.2		32.4		
Navarra	80.0	17.9			61.9	
Orense	(83.9)	18.5	30.3		34.5	
Oviedo	(74.1)	39.3		34.8		0.1
Palencia	80.1	21.6			58.5	
Pontevedra	58.6	30.7	20.9	21.1		
Salamanca	76.6	27.1			49.4	
S.C. de Tenerife	56.9	24.8	12.4		25.4	
Santander	75.2	31.4			39.6	1.4
Segovia	(72.8)	27.0			40.4	
Sevilla (C)	97.4	61.5			35.8	0.7
Sevilla (P)	59.2	32.7		26.5		?
Soria	(76.1)	23.7	26.8		27.7	
Tarragona	(73.1)	41.9		31.2		
Teruel	67.7	25.4			42.2	
Toledo	(80.0)	29.7			47.7	0.5
Valencia (C)	86.8	43.6	8.2		35.3	
Valencia (P)	70.5	31.1	12.1		31.0	
Valladolid	77.9	28.8		40.9		3.2
Vizcaya (C)	77.8	37.7	23.5		16.3	
Vizcaya (P)	74.6	10.9	29.7		25.9	
Zamora	71.2	21.7		42.0		0.7
Zaragoza (C)	85.7	45.1			39.4	0.6
Zaragoza (P)	69.3	32.1			34.9	

Estimated results in parenthesis.

TABLE 4—6.

Deputies elected in February 1936 (in accord with the first round results)

Right

CEDA	101
Traditionalists	15

TABLE 4—6 (continued)

Right		
Renovación Española	13	
Monarchists	2	
Others	2	Right Total: 133
Center-Right		
Centrists	21	
Liberal Democrats	1	
Agrarios	11	
Progresistas	6	
Radicals	9	
Independents	10	
Lliga	12	
Basque Nationalists	5	
Conservatives	2	Center-Right Total: 77
Bourgeois Left		
Izquierda Republicana	79	
Unión Republicana	34	
Esquerra	22	
Acció Catalana	5	
Galleguistas	3	
Others	8	Bourgeois Left Total: 151
Proletarian Left		
PSOE	88	
Communists	14	
Others	10	Proletarian Left Total: 112

	Deputies		*Votes*	*Votes per deputy*
Popular Front	263	55.5%	4,654,116	17,696
Right and Center	210	45.5%	5,029,823	23,951

place, impartiality was not always maintained and, in the second place, that since it was not, of course, a determinate factor in the final result of the elections, a degree of electoral corruption existed even if its limits are difficult to define.

The best proof that the Popular Front did not act impartially at the moment of conferring the certificates of election is, without doubt, that Indalecio Prieto himself, president of the commission in charge of judging them, ended up by resigning his post because he was not in agreement with the standards of the rest of his committee. On the other hand, a good indication that there was a certain degree of corruption is found in the debate over the election certificates from Granada. This was the only Andalusian and Mediterranean province where the right had won. The left attributed this victory to coercion and the fact that the province had a long tradition of electoral corruption, that there were several villages where the total census was shaped in favor of the right, as well as the fact that there were abundant weapons in the area; the very tepidity of the rightists in defense of these certificates seems to prove that their nullification was correct. In Cuenca where the certificates were also nullified, it is more difficult to determine if the nullification followed criteria of strict justice or not. Of course, it was a matter of a province that also had a long cacique tradition, but at the same time its geographic location placed it in a conservative environment that may make one think that the original results (which gave a victory to the right) were correct.

It clearly began to be evident that the Popular Front deputies were not acting impartially in the debate over the certificates from Pontevedra, which gave the appearance of multiple irregularities, but which were approved because according to the results the former president of the Council of Ministers, Portela Valladares, was elected. It appears that on this occasion he counted on the support of the Popular Front deputies. During the debates on the certificates from Ciudad Real, Albacete, Salamanca, and, especially, Orense, not only was that limited impartiality evident but, concerning this subject as well as others, the union among the leftist groups was at times precarious. In these four provinces the socialists and communists demanded the nullification of certificates for which evidence was nonexistent and, therefore, the moderate left could not accept it. For example, without explanation the extreme left voted against the admission of the deputy elected from Ciudad Real, Pérez Madrigal. The decision on the certificates from Salamanca and Orense was even more relevant from the political point of view, since they returned to the Cortes two rightist leaders as important as Gil Robles and Calvo Sotelo. With regard to the certificates from Salamanca, the extreme left admitted explicitly that they lacked proof of coercion (Dolores Ibarurri stated as the ultimate argument that of "could one imagine Gil Robles representing the country people of Salamanca"). The case of Orense was even more strange: In the middle of the Cortes session the Commission on Certificates changed its own opinion according to which Calvo Sotelo had not been admitted and substituted an opinion by which he was. This change was probably brought about by the direct influence of the government on the deputies from the moderate left who were on the commission, to the great indignation of the socialists and the communists. Therefore, it seems clear from the examination of the five cases mentioned that the left omitted impartiality at the time of judging the election certificates. Although the right had probably acted in a similar manner, that such a thing happened was a serious attack against the democratic system. As Giménez Fernández would say in his final speech in the Cortes, such an action provided an argument for those who said that a legal battle was not possible and, moreover, it accomplished nothing since the Popular Front already had a majority with which to govern. Rather than simply examining the results of the election, when we approach our study of the origins of the Civil War it is more important to verify how the election certificates were judged.

At any rate, the behavior of the Popular Front in the debate over certificates is only one part of the entire question. It remains for us to inquire to what point electoral corruption still existed in Spain in 1936. The answer to this question is difficult if one tries to be absolutely precise because there are no data on which to base it (and there probably never will be). Nevertheless, it is possible to state, in the first place, that even if there was corruption (and it appears that there was) in no case may it be said to have had the magnitude which it reached during the reign of Alfonso XIII when the entire system existed by means of political corruption. In the 1931 municipal elections as well as in the legislative elections in 1933 and 1936 the winner was a political group which was not in power; thus, we must judge that the party in power was not in a good position to impose its will. In this respect one may say that Spain was a country sufficiently undeveloped for political corruption to have completely disappeared but sufficiently advanced for it not to have a determinate character. In fact, if one observes which are the provinces in which the accusations of alteration of the results are most frequent it is found that they are the same as under the constitutional monarchy of Alfonso XIII. There is a coincidence worthy of noting between the structure of agrarian property and accusations of corruption: In the latifundist areas as well as in the minifundist regions the protests arising from this are especially acute. One may even add something more: The procedures were also similar to those of earlier periods (violence in the south and the theft of election certificates in Galicia).

The fact that corruption exists in some elections is, above all, demonstrative of the degree of civic culture of the country where they occur. Therefore, to think that only those of one faction used dishonest methods is probably false. In the case of the 1936 Spanish elections there are sufficiently convincing indications to believe that the right as well as the left used dishonest methods. If the left could accuse their opponents because of the distribution of weapons in

Granada, the accusation could be reversed in other provinces such as Cáceres where it seems certain that the leftist masses assaulted the electors. When the Popular Front deputies pointed out that in many areas of small villages the entire population had voted for the rightist candidate, which seemed extremely suspicious, the right could reply that the same thing had occurred in locations where the results had been exactly reversed. At most it is possible to judge that since the center-right of Portela Valladares was in power it was the main beneficiary of the corruption. In more than one province Portela's followers seem to have arranged the complete census of certain towns that were especially docile for the object of, for example, in case of defeat, assuring themselves the first position on the minority list.

In short, the judgment which should be made concerning the 1936 Spanish elections is that which Jackson suggests for all the elections held during the Spanish Second Republic. "Compared with the elections in Western Europe, Scandinavia, England, or the United States," this author assures, "even the most honest of the Republican elections are characterized by election day violence and corruption during the tabulation. However, the results were not known beforehand and therefore they better represented the popular will than the results of the Mexican elections. They admit favorable comparison with the freer elections in countries such as Argentina, Chile, and Uruguay and, of course, they were infinitely more democratic than those in the peoples' democracies of Eastern Europe."

6. Final evaluation.

In a more strictly historical view it may be useful in conclusion to compare the 1936 Spanish elections and those held the same year in France, the latter characterized, as were the Spanish, by the presence of a large alliance among the left with an identical title of Popular Front. In good measure this comparison may help explain the different path which both Popular Fronts followed in future years.

As in Spain, the program of the French Popular Front also had above all a defensive character: Fear of the right produced it and its goals were rooted in the maintenance of Republican legality. However, the differences were greater than the similarities. In the first place, the role of leftist extremism in the French Popular Front was quite inferior to that of the Spanish Popular Front. In Spain the moderate left, in spite of having more candidates than the socialists and the communists, probably had less strength. The Spanish extreme left not only had more strength but was also much more radical: It is sufficient to compare Léon Blum with Largo Caballero in order to demonstrate this (in the Spanish Socialist party De los Ríos would correspond rather well to the figure of Blum). The Communist party was more numerous in France, but on this occasion it obtained an important electoral advance thanks to an exceptional moderation in its programmatic aspirations: It is very probable that Thorez understood the instructions of the Third International much better than José Díaz or Dolores Ibarurri. In the electoral propaganda itself the difference seems clear since in France the question of political regime was not presented, because its existence was accepted by the majority; in Spain the matter appears to be more or less hidden. The same results show an important divergence between the French case and the Spanish. In France the general acceptance of the democratic system and its praxis is shown in a much higher percentage of voter participation than the Spanish (12 percent more). The absence of anarchism is, of course, the reason which explains it. The percentages of voters obtained by each political group showed a stability superior to the Spanish among other things because in France there was not, as there was in Spain, the disappearance of the political group which was judged to be the backbone of the Third Republic (the Radical party).

The stability of electoral behavior and its moderation was found in a greater degree in France than in Spain (in spite of the fact that to a lesser degree it was also found there and the Civil War was not, therefore, inevitable). This is what explains the different path followed by the two Popular Fronts. A time arrived in Spain when the government could not control the situation, not only because it was faced with a more quarrelsome right but also because it could not maintain order among its own extreme left. Although the elections supposed, in terms already indicated, a last attempt to revive the Republican system, this final opportunity was soon seen to be a failure. In France the relevance of the Popular Front period is great, but when all is said and done it was only a parenthesis, closed exactly when the Spanish war imposed a regrouping of the center which definitively had the situation in hand. In short, the differences between one country and the other are rooted in the fact that France was a stable democracy which suffered a serious crisis and Spain was a nation attempting democracy for the first time, probably under conditions that could not have been worse.

5

The Ominous Spring of 1936

Stanley G. Payne (Stalinist)

The political atmosphere in Spain during the months that followed the Popular Front elections of 1936 was vastly different from the halcyon period of the Republic in 1931. By the spring of 1936 forces on both the left and right had become much more radical and intransigent. In some cases they were also severely divided within themselves, most notably in the case of the Socialists, the most important group on the left. The Socialists soon showed themselves to be bitterly split between the moderate reformist elements led by Indalecio Prieto and the "Bolshevized" revolutionaries whose main chief was Francisco Largo Caballero, and proved incapable either of supporting parliamentary reformism or of following an effective revolutionary policy. In an atmosphere of growing hate and violence, the new left Republican government found little opportunity to pursue the ideals of 1931, exhausting itself in a futile effort to pacify the revolutionary left and restrain the authoritarian right.

The following selection appeared as a chapter in the author's The Spanish Revolution *(New York, 1970). It de-*

*scribes the breakdown of the Spanish polity during the
spring and early summer of 1936, a breakdown without
precedent or parallel in twentieth-century Europe. It is reprinted by permission of the author, who is professor of
history at the University of Wisconsin.*

After resuming office, Azaña announced that he would carry out the Popular
Front program as rapidly as possible. The Cortes was not scheduled to con-
vene for nearly a month, but pressure was so great from the revolutionary parties for an immediate amnesty of the 15,000 imprisoned insurrectionists that
Azaña felt he could not wait for full congressional approval of his first measures. Though the constitution stipulated that political amnesties could only be
voted by a regular parliamentary majority, such niceties were no longer observed. On February 21 the Permanent Commission of the Cortes, representing all major parties, granted approval of a complete amnesty for the insurrectionists, some of whom had already been freed in mass jailbreaks. Several
days later similar approval was given for the restoration of Catalan autonomy
under the 1932 statute. A government decree reestablished labor tribunals
with the same prolabor majority they had under the previous Azaña administration. Another order restored local officials and functionaries dismissed because of complicity in the insurrection and established commissions to rule on
claims by workers who had been fired for allegedly political reasons. Those
whose claims were upheld were to be rehired by their old employers and com-
pensated for wages lost in the interim, though this might constitute a crushing
burden to small businessmen.

The Communist party had achieved noticeable political influence for the first
time and immediately established itself as the most active member of the Popular Front, constantly pressing for further goals. The party's over-all strategy
was summarized in *Mundo Obrero* on February 18, two days after the election:

> We shall follow the path of completing the bourgeois democratic revolution until it
> brings us to a situation in which the proletariat and the peasantry themselves assume
> the responsibility of making the people of Spain as happy and free as are the Soviet
> people, through the victorious achievement of socialism, through the dictatorship of
> the proletariat.

The left Republican government was to be encouraged to a swift completion of
the Popular Front program, then to further measures outlined by the Communists during the electoral campaign; these included expropriation of land on a
large scale without compensation and the outlawing of the rightist parties. After the conservatives had been eliminated and the revolutionary left had ex-

panded, the Republican left, according to a *Mundo Obrero* editorial of February 24, would have to give way to a "Worker-Peasant government." The latter concept in Communist planning represented the transitional phase from parliamentary democracy to socialist dictatorship. Communist leaders emphasized that the change could only be carried out by stages, and chided the revolutionary Socialists about premature talk of the "dictatorship of the proletariat." [1]

The Spanish Communist party emerged from the elections with 21 deputies (16 representing the party itself and 5 from the pro-Stalinist Catalan Marxist parties) and possibly 30,000 regular members. It is still asserted in historical studies that the Spanish Communist party was too small in the winter and spring of 1936 to be taken seriously. If Spain had in 1936 been a modern western country under normal political conditions, a Communist party of that size would have held comparatively little importance. Proportionate to the total population, however, the Communist party of Spain was larger at the beginning of 1936 than was the Bolshevik group in Russia at the start of 1917. Spain was entering a phase of political disintegration, with political opinion increasingly polarized and the established moderate and conservative parties nearly impotent. There were two mass revolutionary movements in the country, but neither knew exactly what it wanted and how to get it. Only the Communist party had the nerve and discipline of an effective revolutionary group. In such a climate it flourished and began to expand even more rapidly than before. Within five months its membership increased threefold. To achieve a position of predominance, however, the indispensable preconditions were continued deterioration of political and social conditions, complete Bolshevization of the Socialist party, and its fusion with the smaller Communist organization.

As soon as the elections were over, Largo Caballero's supporters demanded that the Socialist national committee hold new elections to choose more representative leaders. Prieto suggested that a congress be convened in Asturias, where the Socialist miners were disgusted with Largo Caballero and the Madrid maximalists for having failed to support them effectively in the insurrection. On March 8 new elections were held for the executive commission of the Madrid section of the party. After Largo and his followers won by a margin of three to one, Largo insisted that any party congress must be held in the national capital, where he was assured of strong support.

On March 12 *Claridad* published the text of a long letter from the central committee of the Communist party to the executive commission of the Socialist party, dated March 4. It proposed the creation of joint Socialist-Communist Worker-Peasant Alliance groups on all levels from the local to the national. The proposed twelve-point program was almost identical to the thirteen-point program announced in the party's 1935 manifesto, save that the earlier point ten, urging financial support of small property owners, was dropped, and a new concluding goal was added. This announced the ultimate aim as formation of a "Worker-Peasant Government" based on the Worker-Peasant Alliance, with the Alliance committees playing the same role in Spain as the soviets in Russia.

The letter proposed that the Worker-Peasant Alliance prepare for the establishment of a united party on the following conditions:

> Complete independence vis-a-vis the bourgeoisie and a complete break of the social democratic bloc with the bourgeoisie; prior achievement of unity of action; recognition of the need for the revolutionary overthrow of the domination of the bourgeoisie and the installation of the dictatorship of the proletariat in the form of Soviets; renunciation of support for the national bourgeoisie in the event of an imperialist war; construction of the unified party on the basis of democratic centralism, assuring unity of will and of action, tempered by the experience of the Russian Bolshevists.

The Socialist executive commission made no immediate reply, but on the following day (March 5) the *caballerista* executive commission of the UGT proposed to the executives of the Socialist party and Socialist Youth that a joint committee be formed of two representatives of each of the working-class parties of the Popular Front to unite energies for the execution of the Popular Front program. Two weeks later, the *caballerista* leadership of the Madrid section of the Socialist party announced that it would ask the next party congress to grant priority to achieving a united party with the Communists.

That same month the Socialist moderate Gabriel Mario de Coca finished writing a brief book criticizing the "Bolshevization of the party." He concluded with these words:

> I close my work with an impression of Bolshevist victory in every sector of the party. The Socialist parliamentary minority in the Cortes will be impregnated with a strong Leninist tone. Prieto will have few deputies on his side while Besteiro will be completely isolated as a Marxist dissenter . . . .
>
> The outlook that all this leaves for the future of the working class and of the nation could not be more pessimistic. The Bolshevist centipede dominates the proletariat's horizon and Marxist analysis indicates that it is on its way to another of its resounding victories. So that if in October 1934 it only achieved a short-lived Gil Robles government accompanied by the suspension of the constitution and the most horrible, sterile shedding of working class blood, it can now be expected to complete its definitive work in the future [cataclysm]. [2]

This prophecy, ~~absolutely~~ completely accurate, was repeated many times by men of varying background; it had little effect.

The Communists and revolutionary Socialists built strong pressure against the government to follow up its amnesty of the insurrectionists by punishing those who had repressed the insurrection. Dolores Ibarruri (La Pasionaria), the most influential member of the Spanish Communist central committee, exhorted in a speech of March 1:

> We live in a revolutionary situation and cannot be delayed by legal obstacles, of which we have had too many since April 14 [1931]. The people impose their own legality and on February 16 asked for the execution of their murderers. The Republic must satisfy the needs of the people. If it does not, the people will throw it out and impose their will. [3]

The government made a symbolic concession on March 11 when it ordered the arrest of General López de Ochoa, the commander of the army forces that had pacified Asturias. It took another step five days later, ordering the arrest of the national leaders of the small (20,000-man) fascist party, Falange Española, and the closure of its main headquarters. Henceforth the Falange became in effect an illegal party as more and more headquarters were shut down and an increasing number of party members were arrested throughout the spring. The government's explanation was that the Falangists had been guilty of terrorist acts. That was entirely true, but if such deeds merited the closing of the party, the Socialist party, Communist party, POUM, and CNT ought also to have been closed down. In addition to engaging in intermittent terrorism, they had attempted armed rebellion against the constitutional Republic, something that the Falange had not yet done. But the Azaña administration was making little effort to carry on impartial government. Its only policy seems to have been more and more concessions to the left to win the revolutionaries' support so it could stay in office as long as possible. After proscription of the Falange, violence and disorders continued to increase. The official line of the government and the leftist parties was that nearly all the violence was either due to the Falangists or was a response to "provocations" by them.

The government was rapidly outflanked by the revolutionaries in the acceleration of agrarian reform. Responding to heavy pressure, the newly reenergized Institute of Agrarian Reform decreed on March 20 that the principle of "social utility" (under terms of which a law passed by the moderates in 1935 had provided that in special circumstances land might be expropriated without compensation) would be extended to all categories of land, and particularly to land in townships where "property is heavily concentrated" or "a high proportion of the population consists of poor peasants." The Socialist FNTT did not wait for this measure to be put into effect. It had reorganized its following in the southwest, and on the night of March 25 carried out a well-planned occupation of large properties by peasants in Badajoz province. *The New York Times* correspondent reported that 60,000 peasants in 263 villages participated. Though this mass action was technically illegal, the government quickly decided it was better to legitimize the take-over ex post facto, even though not all the property involved belonged to large holders. According to the study by Edward Malefakis, the following amount of land was redistributed during the next months:

March	249,616 hectares	
April	150,000 hectares	(approximate)
May	46,391 hectares	(statistical averages for May and June)
June	46,391 hectares	
July 1 – 17	40,000 hectares	
July 18	23,000 hectares	announced

By April the government had largely gained control of the land transfers, whose volume declined during May as the spring plowing neared completion. On June 2 the Cortes passed new legislation reversing the eviction of tenant farmers that had taken place during 1935, and on June 11 the original Agrarian Reform bill of 1932 was restored, including the 1935 "social utility" clause, but dropping the 1932 provision that had been prejudicial to medium-sized properties.

Nevertheless, the degree of effervescence in the southern countryside only increased as the spring advanced. From May 1 to July 18 there were at least 196 peasant strikes and one of them, organized by the CNT in Málaga province early in June, claimed to have the support of 100,000 peasants. As the summer advanced, nearing the start of a new agricultural season, it seemed that the pressure for occupation would be greater than ever.

In the southwest the larger landowners had in many cases deserted their properties after the elections. The medium and small owners had little alternative, however, but to stay on, so that it was the rural middle classes, not the latifundists, who bore the brunt of the harassment, violence, and property destruction which wracked much of southern and central Spain during the spring and early summer. In Extremadura the Socialist Youth set up "civic guard" militia groups that were given official police authorization in towns with Socialist mayors. These activists made many arbitrary arrests and sometimes beat up landowners and conservatives. Though there were comparatively few political murders in the rural areas of southern and central Spain, the wave of anarchy, regularized only to the extent that the revolutionaries were actually beginning to take over local authority in some areas, had the rural middle classes in a state of absolute panic.

And yet much of the Socialist- and anarchist-dominated peasantry had little notion of a thoroughgoing social revolution. All that most of them wanted was either higher wages or a reasonable amount of land of their own to work on easy terms. As Julián Besteiro warned in the Cortes and as an agrarian expert warned in the pages of El Sol (July 15 and 17), the real effect of all the strikes and rural harassment in southwest Spain was not to effect a positive revolution in terms of ownership and production but to divert as much as possible of the short-run profits to the poorer peasants and laborers. Mechanization was thwarted and small and medium holders were being ruined without any real attempt to lay the basis for a more efficient and equitable rural economy. The economic consequences of the agrarian prerevolution in the south were primarily destructive.

After the acceleration of the agrarian reform, the next major move of the left was the deposition of the moderate president of the Republic, Alcalá-Zamora. Both left and right were disgusted with him, the left because he had refused to support the Azaña government in 1933, the right because he had blocked the formation of further moderate conservative coalition ministries at the end of 1935. Alcalá-Zamora conceived the function of the presidency in a Republic with a unicameral legislature as that of a moderating authority that must exercise direct initiative to keep the government from diverging too sharply toward either extreme. His continuation in office, restricted though his prerogatives were, was the last remaining guarantee of moderation within the Republican system. For that reason the left was determined to be rid of him. The excuse used was Article 81 of the constitution, which stipulated that the action of a president who dissolved the Cortes twice during his term of office would be reviewed by the new Cortes chosen in the second election to determine whether or not he had properly fulfilled his functions in accordance with the popular will. There could be no question from the Popular Front point of view of the need to dissolve the previous Cortes; without new elections the left would never have had the majority with which to depose the president. Throughout 1935 spokesmen of all the leftist groups reiterated that their major request of the president was dissolution of the Cortes. As Azaña had said in a speech of October 20, 1935:

Calling new elections is the immediate goal of the Republican Left. Our abstention from any kind of government coalition that might be formed before calling new elections is total and irrevocable . . . . The Left has only one recommendation: new elections.

After their constant petition had been granted, they then argued that Alcalá-Zamora was still culpable for not having dissolved the preceding Cortes earlier. Despite the dubious applicability of Article 81, it was the only tactic that could be invoked, for the section on impeachment—Article 82—required a two-thirds majority of parliament, and the left was not sure it could muster that. On April 7, with the right abstaining, the left voted the deposition of the president of the Republic.

When special elections for presidential electors (compromisarios) were held on April 26, there was massive middle-class abstention. The choice of the leftist candidate, Azaña, seemed inevitable, for the center and right were demoralized and even more disunited than before. Only a little more than one-third of the registered electorate voted, and the Permanent Commission lowered quorum requirements below the customary 40 percent in order to register a valid contest.

All the while activity of the Communists and revolutionary Socialists increased. By April the Communist party claimed 50,000 members and by May 60,000, a figure nominally equal to that of the Socialists (which officially stood at 60,000 at the end of June, though the actual Socialist membership was probably larger than the moderate-controlled executive commission was willing to admit, most of the new Socialist members being caballeristas). During the spring of 1936 Spain was inundated with Communist propaganda, and its self-assured demagogy about constituting the "wave of the future" attracted not merely working-class militants but other thousands of self-selected middle-class elitists who wanted to be part of the vanguard of tomorrow.

According to the central committeeman Hernández, the chief Comintern adviser in Spain, Artur Stepanov, outlined Communist plans in the following terms: "There is no doubt that Spain is undergoing the same historical process begun in Russia in February 1917. The party must learn to apply the tactic of the Bolsheviks: a brief transitory phase and then the soviets!"[4] This rise in Comintern expectations paralleled exactly the excited interpretations of the Socialist intellectuals, the most articulate of whom was Araquistain. [5]

Delegations were sent to Moscow by both the Communist and Socialist

Youth groups to arrange their fusion under the blessing of the Comintern. Organization of the United Socialist Youth (JSU) [6] was announced on April 1. The JSU's 41,200 members [7] made it the largest political youth movement in the country. Though some of the local groups of the Socialist Youth did not recognize the fusion, the non-Communist leadership of the Madrid section was deposed. In Catalonia the liaison committee of the small pro-Stalinist Marxist parties of that region continued to function. Plans were made for a Communist-dominated United Socialist party of Catalonia, which could bypass the POUM and challenge the CNT for leadership of the revolutionary left in Catalonia.

The Popular Front Cortes reconvened for its second session on April 15. This was the most disorderly assembly in the history of Spanish parliamentarianism. As the Socialist historian Ramos Oliveira observed,

> Each session was in continuous tumult, and since nearly all the representatives of the nation went about armed, a catastrophe could have been feared at any meeting. In view of the frequency with which firearms were displayed or made reference to, the insulting precaution of frisking the legislators on their entry had to be adopted. [8]

An attempt was made to shout down the more prominent conservative spokesmen whenever they took the floor. Socialist and Communist deputies vied with each other in hurling threats at Gil Robles and at Calvo Sotelo, the monarchist leader. The president of the assembly made feeble attempts to restore decorum.

At the beginning of the new session Gil Robles and Calvo Sotelo warned that the explosion of violent strikes, street brawls, *atentados,* barn burnings, and church burnings that the government did little or nothing to restrain was bringing the country near a state of de facto civil war. Gil Robles declared that the government should not think that the middle classes would bend their necks meekly before the axes of the revolutionaries.

On May 10 Azaña was formally elected president of the Republic. There was speculation that he might be succeeded as prime minister by Indalecio Prieto, who would form a stable moderate Socialist-left Republican cabinet. Meanwhile, negotiations were also carried on by one of the most liberal of the CEDA leaders, Giménez Fernández, with Prieto and other comparatively moderate elements about the possibility of forming a broad national coalition government extending from moderate conservatives to the moderate Socialists, in which the CEDA would not actually participate but which it would support with its votes. Some such realignment was the only constructive, legal means of holding the revolutionaries in check, but all efforts came to naught. Hopes for a moderate coalition cabinet led by Prieto were dashed by a caucus of most of the Socialist Cortes deputies on May 12. It voted 49 to 19 against participating in any sort of government coalition, even with the middle-class left.

Prieto later claimed that Azaña showed no real interest in the formation of such a ministry. Whether or not that was really the case, the new president ended by appointing a "domestic cabinet," led by one of his most trusted and aggressive supporters, Casares Quiroga. It is clear that by this time Azaña was profoundly depressed—indeed almost benumbed—by the hopeless political situation into which he had maneuvered himself. His reaction was one of personal withdrawal, leaving the administration of affairs in the hands of his new prime minister. Casares Quiroga had the reputation of being the "hardest" of Azaña's lieutenants, but he suffered from tuberculosis and was not a truly energetic leader. His reputation for toughness was based mainly on his speeches, which were usually aggressive and provocative. Casares Quiroga would admit of no danger to the left, but instead blamed all difficulties on the right. Under his leadership the government of the Republican left followed a consistent policy of appeasing the revolutionary left and antagonizing the right, thus consummating the political polarization of Spain.

On May 5, approximately one week before becoming prime minister, Casares Quiroga responded serenely to complaints about the collapse of public order:

Calm, señor Calvo Sotelo! What worries me at present is the right, for . . . the social revolution does not worry me at all. In a difficult moment the other day I did not find these men [the revolutionary leaders] and the masses whom they represent wielding a knife to stab me in the back; I found on certain occasions some excesses, but loyalty nonetheless, and in difficult moments I found the support of leaders, of public opinion and of a working class that enabled us to conjure the peril. But yourselves—not yourselves: rather those on your flank, who, separating themselves from you, rush toward violence, which you claim to condemn but which at times you seem to encourage—these are the people who are making every effort to subvert the Spanish state, or rebel against it, or create an atmosphere of perpetual disquiet, which is much worse than an armed rebellion. [9]

To the Popular Front denunciations of a "fascist" danger forming on the right, Calvo Sotelo replied accurately:

Fascism, here and elsewhere, is not an original postulate, but an antithesis, not an action, but a reaction. In England, where there is no Communism, there is scarcely any fascism. In Spain, where Communism is a reality—and even when you utter words of almost Panglossian optimism to show your lack of concern for the social danger, I am fully convinced that secretly you think otherwise—since in Spain Communism advances, whether you desire it or not, within the government and expands by force, fascism—not as a specific organized force, which is least significant—but as an uncoerced, indefinable sentiment of national defense, which man do not know how to define or organize, will continue to grow until the social danger disappears. [10]

Indalecio Prieto himself warned in a speech at Cuenca on May 2:

A country can survive a revolution, which is ended one way or another. What a country cannot survive is the constant attrition of public disorder without any immediate revolutionary goal; what a nation cannot survive is the waste of public power and economic strength in a constant state of uneasiness, of anxiety and worry. Naive souls may say that this uneasiness, this anxiety, this worry, is only suffered by the upper classes. In my judgment that is incorrect. The working class itself will soon suffer from the pernicious effects of this uneasiness, this anxiety, this worry, because of the disarray and possible collapse of the economy, because though we aspire to transform the economic structure, we cannot escape the consequences of that structure so long as it does exist. . . .

Let it not be said, to the discredit of democracy, that sterile disorder is only possible when there is a democratic government in power, because then such disorder would mean that only democracy permits excesses and that only the lash of dictatorship is capable of restraining them. . . . If disorder and excess are turned into a permanent system, one does not achieve socialism, nor does one consolidate a democratic republic—which I think is to our advantage—nor does one achieve communism. You achieve a completely desperate anarchy that is not even advocated by anarchist ideology. You achieve economic disorder that can ruin the country. [11]

The program of the ~~revolutionaries~~ Stalinists for achieving public order was simple: to arm the left and outlaw the right. On April 2 *Claridad* headlined: THE PEOPLE'S MILITIA. THEY MUST BE ORGANIZED IN EVERY VILLAGE OF SPAIN. One week later the Communist press demanded that the government officially shut down all the rightist parties and newspapers as "fascist" and "counter-revolutionary."

On April 18 a public meeting of the Madrid section of the Socialist party was held. The *caballerista* majority demanded the calling of a new party congress to ratify the dominance of the revolutionaries, and the exertion of greater pressure on the Azaña government to complete the Popular Front program so that they could move on to a Socialist Republic under the dictatorship of the proletariat. The elderly Besteiro rose once more to challenge the "Bolshevizing" trend, and asked if they were proposing the dictatorship of the Spanish proletariat or the dictatorship of the Spanish Socialist party. He asserted that the revolutionaries were transforming the formerly democratic Spanish Socialist party into a Russian-style Communist party; to face the issue squarely, a vote on that question should be taken among all party members. As so often in the past, Besteiro told the militants unpleasant truths which they refused to hear. He suggested that the forces opposed to the Popular Front were stronger than the revolutionaries cared to admit, and that the analogies drawn with Russia were as false as ever. There the established system had been totally exhausted by an enormous world war, permitting the Bolshevists to build through the use of force and terror an artificial majority. By no stretch of the imagination, he went on, could it be claimed that the Spanish Marxist parties in 1936 had a majority of the population behind them. Nor did Spanish socialism have the kind of leaders who could impose a terrorist dictatorship even if they wanted to.

> In Russia there were revolutionary redeemers because there existed revolutionaries trained in the hard, cruel struggle of persecution and emigration. Those men had the fiber and determination of violent revolutionaries. But regarding yourselves, comrades—do you think that you are equal to that?[12]

These harsh realities were greeted by the crowd with loud protests, jeers, and threats.

The only political position more advanced than that of the Communists and revolutionary Socialists was the stand taken by the Leninist POUM, which held that the electoral victory opened a phase of permanent revolution in which the revolutionary forces should proceed as quickly as possible. For the POUM, the Azaña administration existed only to be superseded immediately. Its organ, *La Batalla,* on April 10 denounced the parliamentary support being given Azaña by the rest of the left: "This fundamentally false position of the working-class parties in supporting the bourgeois government, when the moment is extremely propitious for revolutionary action, will be of disastrous consequences." In a speech at Gijón, the POUM chief Maurín said on April 19 that a union of all the proletarian forces could rally 4 million workers and conquer power directly. He urged a united revolutionary front so "that Spain could become the second country to brandish the lighted red torch of a soviet regime."[13]

This proposal was too precipitous even for the Communists, who continued to urge support of the Popular Front at least until its legislative program had been completed. Moreover, the Communists were determined to isolate the POUM, whose leaders remained staunchly anti-Stalinist and opposed to Comintern control. On April 24, *Mundo Obrero* denounced "The renegade Maurín, enemy of the Popular Front."

Meanwhile, the Communists continued to work for the same policy—a union of all the revolutionary forces—but excluding the POUM. From the middle of April they stepped up requests for syndical unity between the UGT and the CNT. The latter, relatively quiescent in 1934–35, had entered a new phase of expansion since the beginning of 1936. The fact that many local CNT leaders had urged their followers to vote for the Popular Front in the recent election also encouraged the hope that the anarchosyndicalists might finally be enticed out of their apoliticism.

The national congress of the CNT met in Zaragoza, headquarters of the FAI as well as of the syndicalist Confederation, on May 10. The delegates represented 988 Sindicatos Unicos totaling 560,000 workers. Of these the largest concentration was still Catalonia, followed by Andalusia-Extremadura with approximately 120,000, and the Levant with more than 50,000. As the spokesmen at the congress related, it was very hard to determine the exact membership of the Confederation due to its "revolutionary, combative character." The total following of the CNT must have been at least 50 percent greater than the total represented, amounting to some 800,000 to 900,000, and was in a period of rapid growth. [14] Moreover, the syndicalist movement was partially reunited at the congress with the return of most of the separate Libertarian Syndicalist Federation, which was disbanded.

In response to Largo Caballero's gesture toward revolutionary syndical unity, 884 syndicates voted in favor of a "Revolutionary Alliance" with the UGT, while only 12 were opposed, but this was based on the proviso that the UGT follow Largo's line renouncing any collaboration with the middle-class left or the existing Republican system and move directly toward the total destruction of the existing politicoeconomic order. If such a program were to be adopted at the next UGT congress, it was agreed that a liaison committee be named to negotiate an alliance between the syndical movements which would then be submitted to a binding referendum by both groups. The classic revolutionary program of Spanish anarchosyndicalism was explicitly reaffirmed, stressing the collectivization of industry, expropriation without indemnity of all landed property larger than 50 hectares, and the restructuring of the country on the basis of a confederation of autonomous communes. The official report also denounced Azaña as "the leader of socializing radicalism, the most cynical and coldly cruel politician known to Spain," and the Catalan Companys as "a cheap politician who once lived off his flattery of anarchism and subsequently persecuted it passionately."

Concurrent with this "transcendent event," as Largo termed the Zaragoza congress, important sectors of the Catalanist left were moving toward the revolutionaries. On May 14−15, an assembly in Barcelona representing 50,000 members of the Unió de Rabassaires approved a five-point program calling for: (a) expropriation without indemnity of "private property"; (b) collective ownership of land, with profits therefrom to be received by those who worked it; (c) formation of compact family cultivation units; (d) establishment of cooperatives where needed; (e) syndical organization of all farmers and farm workers. This program, affirming both family farms and collectivization, was contradictory. The general tone of the meetings left little doubt that rank-and-file Rabassaires adhered strongly to the institution of private family farms, but the leaders were strongly influenced by allies among the small Marxist parties in Catalonia and, amid the hysteria of those weeks, pushed through a much more radical, if vague and contradictory, line. The Rabassaires then voted to separate from the governing Esquerra federation in order to carry out their program in association with the Catalan Socialist groups. At exactly the same time the small, formerly reformist Unió Socialista de Catalunya rejected future collaboration with the Generalist and announced plans to join the Comintern. The new leaders of Estat Català had already repudiated the "rightist" line of Dencàs, who was drummed out of the party that same month in order to facilitate closer approximation to the Catalan revolutionary left.

While the revolutionaries went on from strength to strength, nonpolitical and Catholic syndicates languished. At the end of 1935, the Free Syndicates, the National Confederation of Catholic Syndicates, and a Spanish Federation of Workers, recently organized by the Jesuit priest Jesús Ballesta, came together in a United National Labor Front, claiming 276,389 members—no more than 15 to 20 percent of organized labor in Spain. The UNLF found its organizational efforts stymied in 1936; in June the Madrid headquarters were closed by the government on the ground of alleged "provocations."

On May 19 the new prime minister, Casares Quiroga, declared the government to be in a state of war against the Falange and all supporters of "fascism." Conservative spokesmen protested the incorrectness of a constitutional government declaring war on fascist extremists while maintaining a political alliance with violent leftist revolutionary associations.

In view of the attitude of Casares Quiroga and further deterioration in the political situation during the days that followed, Sánchez Román and his National Republican associates urged that a change in policy be adopted before it was too late. The National Republican party approved the following motion on May 25:

At the present time, the PNR, its authority increased by having foreseen the difficulties that the Popular Front would face and enjoying the freedom of movement provided by its absence from the government, has the responsibility of uniting other Republicans in an understanding of the seriousness of the political situation, recognizing the failure of the so-called Popular Front in its present form and the need to take measures to save the country and the Republic.

Political agreement should be based on the following measures:

Immediate execution of the program of defense of the Republican state [perhaps referring to the stringent security law passed by the first Azaña government], vigorously reestablishing the principle of authority together with a program of social reform and economic development agreed upon by the Republican Left, Republican Union and National Republican Parties.

Fulfillment of the reforms benefiting the working class that were included in the Popular Front electoral program.

Necessary measures must be taken to prevent those social and political forces that are actually most interested in the execution of this program from being the greatest obstacle to its accomplishment.

The following steps should be taken:

a) Severe repression of incitement to revolutionary violence.

b) General disarmament [of political militias].

c) Dissolution of all political, professional, economic or religious organizations whose activity gravely threatens the independence, constitutional unity, democratic-republican form or security of the Spanish Republic.

d) Prohibition of uniformed or paramilitary societies.

e) A law establishing the legal responsibility of leaders of political organizations for the crimes provoked by the latter's propaganda.

f) Prosecution of local government authorities for the infractions of law which they may commit in exercising their functions. Where circumstance requires, mayors may be relieved of supervision of public order and this function transferred to other authorities.

g) The rules of parliament will be reformed to improve the structure and functioning of parliamentary committees, so that with the assistance of technical agencies new legislation can be completed more quickly.

Señor Sánchez Román will present our request to the leaders of the Republican Union and Republican Left Parties. Once an agreement has been reached, the Socialist Party will be publicly invited to participate in a new government in order to carry out this program.

Should the Socialists refuse to collaborate, the [left] Republicans will urge the President to form a government of representatives of all the Republican forces [presumably referring to the center parties] willing to support the program approved by the left Republican parties. A team of Republican ministers recognized for their authority, competence and prestige will be appointed. They will govern above the level of party politics, rejecting any kind of demagogic appeal.

If the government does not receive parliamentary support, Cortes sessions will be suspended in conformity with constitutional statutes.

Alternatively, parliament might be presented with a bill authorizing the government to legislate by decree, under the powers granted by Article 61 of the constitution, regarding concrete matters that demand urgent attention. [15]

The formation of a government endowed with decree powers to restore order was suggested by various moderate and conservative spokesmen. The most widely publicized proposal came in a series of six articles by Miguel Maura in *El Sol* between June 18 and 27. Maura declared that the Republican left had been performing a national service in channeling the onslaught of the revolutionaries, but that in recent months its leadership had completely collapsed. He said that his fear was not so much that Spain might fall under a Communist-type dictatorship—for which Spanish conditions were hardly suited—as that the country would soon disintegrate in unprecedented anarchy.

> Peaceful citizens, whatever their political sympathies, now believe that the laws are a dead letter and that public insults, assaults, arson, property destruction, homicide, and attacks on the armed forces have ceased to count in the penal code when committed by those in red and blue shirts [the JSU] or under the starred emblem of the hammer and sickle. The clenched fist [the Communist salute] has become safe conduct for the worst excesses.
>
> A reaction against this was inevitable and gives cause for concern in taking a form that is called "fascism," . . . though of authentic Italian fascism it has only the name and a few doctrinal postulates of which the majority of its affiliates are ignorant.
>
> Today the Republic is no more—though I would like to believe unconsciously—than the tool of the violent, revolutionary sector of the working classes, which, shielded by the liberal democratic system and the blindness of certain leaders of the Republican parties, is preparing in minute detail an assault on the government and the extermination of capitalist and middle-class society. . . . They tell us this themselves in their newspapers and public meetings.
>
> . . . We Republicans who made the greatest personal sacrifice to collaborate with the regime are called "fascists."
>
> . . . If the Republic is to be this, it is inexorably condemned to swift extinction at the hands of those who claim to be its defenders, or what is more probable, at the hands of a reaction from the opposite direction.

Maura called for a multiparty coalition "national Republican dictatorship" to save the country, but added, "I do not harbor the slightest hope that my reasoning could convince those who currently bear responsibility for government."

There is no indication that these appeals from former associates, men of proven liberal principles, had any effect on the president. In 1933 Azaña had said he did not fear seeing the Republic "fail" so much as seeing it "corrupted." To avoid corruption through compromise, Azaña presided over the progressive disintegration of the regime. He was willing to risk the destruction of his country rather than infringe his principles.

The scope of Communist activity steadily increased. Great attention was given to paramilitary work. By June the militia organization (MAOC) had 2,000 organized members in the Madrid district, and was given the goal of expanding into "a mass organization of semimilitary character" as "the organizational basis for the future worker-peasant Red Army." [16] Parallel to the MAOC was the "Antimilitarist section" of the party, led by the Russian-trained Galician Communist Enrique Líster, who had undergone a year or more of preparation at the Frunze Academy. Simply put, the task of Líster's bureau was the subversion of the Spanish Army. It set up Communist cells in as many military detachments as possible and was particularly successful among noncommis-sioned officers in the Madrid garrison. Another semisecret military organization manipulated by the party was the Republican Antifascist Military Union (UMRA), first organized by leftist army officers in 1934 to combat the union of conservative nationalists within the Army (UME). The UMRA's chief organizer was a Communist officer on the General Staff, Capt. Eleuterio Díaz Tendero. Such groups were further complemented by Communist infiltration into the security forces in Madrid and certain other cities where conditions were propitious. Unofficial contacts were established between the security forces and the Communist and Socialist militia in some areas, and police offi-cers played a role in training the latter.

After the Comintern agent Vittorio Vidali (Carlos Contreras) arrived in Spain in May to assume supervision of paramilitary activities, Communist terrorist squads were separated from the regular MAOC groups in order not to com-promise the latter. Terrorist deeds were directed primarily against Falangists under terms of the urban guerrilla civil war that was under way, and an effort was made to avoid killing policemen in order not to antagonize the middle-class left.

The Socialist militia was much less well organized; in fact, in most areas regular Socialist paramilitary forces did not exist save on paper. A major ex-ception was the Socialist-Communist stronghold, Madrid, where the main So-cialist militia unit, La Motorizada, had its own transportation facilities and sev-eral thousand organized volunteers. In addition, the Socialists had expanded their *grupos de choque* in Madrid and other key centers. These, in turn, were becoming honeycombed with Communists so that it became increasingly diffi-cult to distinguish Socialist members from the MAOC.

The strike wave initiated by Spanish labor had international repercussions by May, when a big maritime strike tied up Spanish shipping in a number of foreign ports. By early June the dockers and crewmen had won a total victory with a large wage increase, a reduction in hours, and massive fringe benefits. Terms of the new contract required such an increase in manpower to get the work done that there were neither enough new crewmen nor enough space in the crewmen's quarters of Spanish merchant ships to hold them, leaving many ships idle in port and Spanish commerce facing catastrophic loss. Indalecio Prieto had earlier warned in a major speech that though Spain could survive a revolution, what the country could not survive was prolongation of merely neg-ative anarchy and disorder, which destroyed national institutions and ruined the economy. On May 25 he warned that because of their economic absurdity the terms of the impending seamen's settlement would provoke "a crisis in-

Impossible demands serve a useful purpose - if you cannot come up with the goods we'll take over!

finitely greater" than the preceding exploitation of dockers and crewmen. [17]

Prieto was, as usual, denounced as a "social fascist" and the strike wave spread. The total number of strikes reported in the liberal newspaper *El Sol* increased to 139 during the month of June and to 145 during the first seventeen days of July. These figures are far from complete, since most strikes did not draw mention, but they serve to indicate the trend. On June 9 the newspaper calculated that 1 million workmen were out on strike.

The CNT's *Solidaridad Obrera* tried to mitigate the rash of local strikes by urging workers not to waste their energy on walkouts with merely economic goals so as to save their strength for the final revolutionary general strike. But regional CNT groups could not resist the temptation to go the Socialists one better in syndical extremism, outflanking the UGT by making impossible demands that employers could not match. Adopting a position even more extreme than the Socialists, the CNT seized the initiative and began to expand membership more rapidly than its rivals. This revolutionary competition, however, soon degenerated into gunfights between the unions with dead and wounded on both sides.

In Barcelona, the terms demanded by hotel workers would have wrecked the hotel industry. When owners offered to cede part of their property to workers as shares in return for a more cooperative settlement, the CNT refused. In similar revolutionary local strikes, the Valencia streetcar company and the Andalusian Railway Company were forced into dissolution, their services taken over by the government. Less spectacularly, hundreds of small businessmen were being ruined. After the contractor's association gave in to exorbitant demands of striking CNT construction workers in Seville, the secretary of the CNT national committee, Horacio Prieto, urged his comrades to moderate demands before desperate employers, who were now willing to concede anything that was reasonable, were pushed into the arms of a protofascist reaction. His warnings, like those of Indalecio Prieto among the Socialists, were ignored.

Unemployment continued to increase (insofar as unemployed workers could be distinguished from strikers), production began to decline once more, tax receipts dropped, and more capital left the country. It became increasingly difficult to fund the debt and float government bonds. The balance of payments was running so strongly against Spain in June as to threaten the value of the peseta. Spanish business leaders pleaded with the government to try to do something to stabilize the economy and reach some sort of agreement with the revolutionary trade unions. On June 7 *La Veu de Catalunya* published a "Manifesto" signed by 126 employers' associations. It expressed willingness to accept most of the Popular Front's economic program, but urged the government to take immediate measures to control economic anarchy, suggesting a temporary end to wage increases, reform of the labor tribunals to achieve fair arbitration, and a national "Labor Conference" to try to straighten things out. Resolutions of the extraordinary assembly of the national Chambers of Commerce and Industry in Madrid, as reported in *El Sol* on June 26 and July 5, expressed the same attitude. These urgent pleas were, as usual, ignored by the Azaña regime.

On June 16 Gil Robles rose again to protest in the Cortes, emphasizing that the present government had met no parliamentary opposition whatever to any of its measures, had been able to have everything its own way, fully dominated the legislature, yet was completely unable or unwilling to maintain order in the country. The state of alarm had been prolonged since February 17, but to no avail. The government imposed censorship on moderate and conservative newspapers to prevent them from reporting the full dimensions of the problem, while doing nothing to curb incendiary outbursts of the revolutionary press.

The only available police figures on political violence in Spain between February 17 and July 17, 1936, show the following: [18]

	Killed	Injured
February 17 – 29	13	58
March	53	210
April	52	109
May	43	124
June	29	11
July 1 – 17	25	25
	215	537

Insofar as these figures have any validity, they indicate that there may have been a decline in violence during June, though the rate shot up again during the first half of July. The statistics for injured mean little, for the majority of those slightly injured in street affrays were probably never reported in official figures.

Política, the organ of Azaña's party, admitted that there had been a significant increase in politically motivated strikes, but excused them as the inevitable response to fascist provocation. Even the Communist *Mundo Obrero* began to warn that the strike wave was getting out of hand and condemned indiscriminate CNT agitation. Within a few more days, however, the joint UGT-CNT strike of construction workers in Madrid pulled 85,000 off the job; when the UGT reached a settlement, the CNT kept the strike going and attacked UGT members returning to work.

Violence spread almost blindly. Street warfare between gunmen of the extreme left and extreme right was paralleled by a series of lethal shootings between the CNT and the Marxist groups. Strife between the two factions of the Socialist party also flared into the open. During a Socialist meeting at Ecija in the south on May 31, shots were fired by revolutionaries at Indalecio Prieto and other moderate leaders.

Prieto and his associates clung desperately to their control of the party executive in the hope that they could ride out the storm, and the next party congress was postponed until October to provide a cooling-off period. Communist fellow travelers urged the revolutionaries to split the party and fuse with the Communists, but Largo still had too much sense of Socialist loyalty and legality to do such a thing. Since the date of the congress had been postponed, the executive commission conceded the holding of new elections on June 28 to elect a regular president and vice-president in place of the current interim leadership. This solved nothing, for the same disagreements immediately reappeared. The moderates on the national committee refused to recognize the membership rolls of all the *caballerista*-dominated local sections. Moreover, *Claridad* demanded that an entire new executive commission be elected. According to the moderates' count, 10,993 valid votes were cast for González Peña and only 2,976 valid votes were admitted for Largo Caballero. [19]

The revolutionary Socialists cried gross fraud. In view of the heavy majorities they were drawing in most local sections, they seemed to have reason to doubt the accuracy of the executive commission's report. *Claridad* claimed that the latter was undermining the party's strength and making it look ridiculous by having it appear that there were only 23,000 Socialists in Spain sufficiently concerned about Socialist affairs to cast their votes. Moreover, charged *Claridad,* the executive commission manipulated membership lists at will and arbitrarily struck out many names, including whole sections of the party that had been unable to pay their dues during the repression of 1934 – 35. On July 2 *Claridad* insisted that nearly 22,000 votes had been cast for Largo, and published a long list of totals from the local sections in different parts of the country. Moreover, it protested accounts in the moderate press of the recent provincial Socialist congress in Jaén, where, according to *Claridad,* the moderate line had once more been rejected and the revolutionary platform, including the building of a broad Worker-Peasant Alliance and a unified Socialist-Communist party, had carried by 1,438 votes to 523.

The executive commission's report gave the membership of the party as less than 60,000, which if correct would have indicated a decline of at least 20 percent since 1932. The Communist party was claiming nearly 100,000 members. Largo declared that if the executive commission was so confident of its statistics it should call a general congress immediately to resolve the major is-sues. *Claridad* suggested that a special investigative commission, selected half by the executive commission and half by the *caballerista*-dominated Ma-drid section of the party, be chosen to scrutinize the electoral results. The ex-ecutive commission decided to have none of that.

During the second week of July, Largo Caballero was in London to represent the UGT at the international trade union congress. There, once more, he struck down the line assiduously cultivated by Socialist moderates and left Re-publicans which tried to present the 1934 insurrection as merely an effort to "save the Republican constitution." Largo stressed that the insurrection had been strictly a "class movement." [20] On July 10 another Andalusian provincial Socialist congress, this time at Cádiz, supported the radical position by a vote of 88 to 2. [21]

Meanwhile, on July 1 the Communist delegation in the Cortes submitted to other Popular Front factions a legislative proposal to require the arrest of ev-eryone in any position of responsibility at the time of the Asturian repression from Lerroux on down, subjecting them to plenary prosecution and con-fiscation of property. [22] This measure was unconstitutional and was not sup-ported by most of the middle-class left. It was an attempt to implement the an-nounced Communist tactic of using the Popular Front majority to eliminate the conservatives, after which the collapse of the Republican middle-class left could be easily accomplished. On July 9 the Communists won a pledge from the other Popular Front groups to delay the normal summer closure of the Cor-tes until the question of "responsibilities" for the Asturian repression had been settled. [23]

After a special caucus of the Popular Front deputies and visits by the Social-ist executive commission to the prime minister on July 9 and 10, there was re-newed speculation about a change in government. Though no precise informa-tion was available, rumors suggested that despite Communist encouragement the revolutionaries had lost control of the Socialist Cortes delegation, which might be willing to support a more moderate and broadly based ministry. In an interview with an Argentine reporter on July 11, Calvo Sotelo, who had become the strongest spokesman for the parliamentary opposition, opined that despite the increase in strikes he believed there was less danger of another leftist in-surrection than there had been in February.

The rumors and conversations of July 10 and 11 proved a brief lull before the final storm. Calvo Sotelo and key leaders of the CEDA had already been in-formed that a military revolt against the Azaña regime was imminent and had pledged support. Conversely, the Communists and revolutionary Socialists would do all they could to oppose formation of a moderate coalition ministry.

The last word was spoken by the terrorists. With one exception early in March, both sides had restricted their targets to the opposition's rank-and-file or low-echelon leaders. The murder of Calvo Sotelo in the early hours of July 13 by a heterogeneous squad of off-duty police officers and leftist terrorists broke this unwritten rule. It was an assassination without precedent, for never before in the history of a western European parliamentary government had a co-leader of the parliamentary opposition been murdered by a group composed mainly of members of the official state security forces.

Since the elections, a number of ultra-left-wing police officers who had participated in the 1934 insurrection had been restored to their commands, even though previously convicted by the courts. Alcalá-Zamora had refused to permit right-wing army officers purged for their complicity in the 1932 revolt to be reinstated, but the Popular Front regime felt no such scruples concerning revolutionary leftists in the police, some of whom were leaders of the UMRA. The Undersecretary of the Interior, Bibiano Ossorio Tafall, a member of Casares Quiroga's Galicianist left, was assiduously courted by the Communists and emerged as a leading crypto-Communist during the Civil War. He apparently gave active support to left-wing extremists in the police and may have encouraged their association with the Marxist paramilitary units. [24] One UMRA militant, the retired Engineers officer Carlos Faraudo, who helped train Socialist militia, had been murdered by Falangist gunmen on a Madrid street corner on May 9. Another, an Assault Guard lieutenant, José del Castillo, was killed near his home on July 12 when on his way to night duty. There is some evidence that leftist police officers conferred that evening with the Minister of the Interior, a bland, middle-aged incompetent of the Catalanist left, Juan Moles, to demand measures against the conservative leaders. [25] At any rate, within a few hours of Castillo's death, a special detachment set out from Assault Guard barracks, led not by an Assault Guard officer but by a Communist Civil Guard captain, Fernando Condés, who had earlier been condemned to life imprisonment for his part in the 1934 insurrection. Calvo Sotelo was hauled out of his apartment in the middle of the night, carried off in an Assault Guard troop truck, shot in the back of the head, and dumped in a suburban cemetery. The triggerman in the murder was a leftist gunman, Victoriano Cuenca (onetime bodyguard of the Cuban dictator Machado), who had been provided with an Assault Guard identification card by leftist officers. [26]

Within forty-eight hours both Calvo Sotelo and Castillo were buried in Madrid. Prieto drew the following image of the funeral processions in an article entitled "Today's Spain Reflected in the Cemetery":

After burying José del Castillo, the workers walk downhill toward Madrid with their jackets over their arms. When they pass in front of the arcade of the General Cemetery, they brush against a barrier of Civil Guards on horseback, who look like an extension of the wall that ends there. Behind the mounted guards file groups of fascists escorting the corpse of Calvo Sotelo. There is an exchange of wrathful stares. This perfectly symbolizes the Spain of today. [27]

On the afternoon of July 13, the Communist party presented the other Popular Front parties with a draft of proposed legislation that it planned to submit to the Cortes on the following day. It read:

Article 1. All organizations of fascist or reactionary character, such as Falange Española, Renovación Española, CEDA, Derecha Regional Valenciana, and those whose characteristics are related to these, will be dissolved, and all properties of these organizations and their leaders will be confiscated. . . .

Article 2. All persons known for their fascist, reactionary and anti-Republican activities will be jailed and prosecuted.

Article 3. The government will confiscate the newspapers *El Debate, Ya, Informaciones, ABC* and all the reactionary press of the provinces. [28]

There was no opportunity to present this proposal, for reopening of the Cortes was postponed for eight days to avoid parliamentary debate of the murder. Several members of the assassination squad were placed under arrest, but little attempt was made to detain Condés, Cuenca, or several other leftist officers implicated. [29] The government did shut down the headquarters of the two monarchist parties in Madrid and suspended two leading conservative newspapers. [30] On the day after the murder, Azaña's *Política* made a verbal appeal for "discipline" in support of the all-out struggle being waged between "so-called fascism" and a government determined to "extirpate the last residues of feudalism." This lame terminology, ill-suited to Spanish political realities in mid-1936, reflected the inability of the middle-class left to come to grips with the breakdown of constitutional government. It has sometimes been observed that fewer Spanish governments are overthrown than commit suicide.

NOTES

1. In a joint Communist-Socialist meeting shortly before the elections, José Díaz had stressed that a "Worker-Peasant government does not mean either the dictatorship of the proletariat or the construction of socialism," according to *El Socialista,* February 12, 1936, in Pozharskaya, p. 128.

2. *Anti-Caballero: Crítica marxista de la bolchevización del Partido Socialista* (Madrid, 1936), pp. 207, 211.

3. *Mundo Obrero,* March 2, 1936.

4. Jesús Hernández, *La Grande trahison* (Paris, 1953), pp. 12−13.

5. The most coherent statement of the Spanish Socialists' fascination with a comparison between their situation and that of Russia was made in a lecture by Luis Araquistain on February 8 entitled "Historical Parallel Between the Russian and Spanish Revolutions." He denied the validity of Besteiro's explanation that it was the wartime disintegration of established institutions that had permitted Bolshevism to triumph in Russia. Furthermore, he denied the validity of Besteiro's emphasis, similar to that of the Mensheviks, that Spain would not be ready for socialism until it had completed the full series of phases of social and economic development prescribed by Marx. According to Araquistain, "history, like biology, is full of leaps." In Russia and Spain, the relative backwardness of society made it all the more susceptible to revolution. Conditions in prerevolutionary Russia and contemporary Spain were said to be analogous. The working-class movement was strong, the resistance of middle-class and conservative groups was weak. The Republican upsurge of 1930−31 was "Spain's 1905." The Spanish Republic had built "a weak state," whose institutions could not resist revolutionaries. "These objective, undeniable facts lead me to think that Spain may very well be the second country where the proletarian revolution triumphs and becomes consolidated. Nor am I particularly worried about the danger of counterrevolutionary intervention from abroad. Neighboring great powers are fully occupied with their own problems. . . . And finally, the U.S.S.R. would not permit other European states to intervene directly in the internal affairs of a Socialist Spain." He concluded that "the historical dilemma is fascism or socialism, and only violence will decide the issue," but since what passed for "fascism" in Spain was weak, socialism would win. *Claridad,* February 13, 1936.

6. Socialist moderates dubbed the Juventud Socialista Unificada the "Juventud Socialista URSSificada," making a pun on the Spanish letters for U.S.S.R.

7. According to a JSU memo of July 1937. (Bolloten Collection, Hoover Institution.) Cf. Santiago Carrillo, *En marcha hacia la victoria* (Valencia, 1937).

8. *Historia de España* (Mexico City, 1952), III, p. 244. According to an official announcement 270,000 new gun licenses were taken out in Spain within a period of less than thirty-six months between mid-1933 and mid-1937.

9. "Diario de las Sesiones de las Cortes," in José Pla, *Historia de la segunda República española* (Barcelona, 1940), IV, p. 428.

10. *Ibid.,* pp. 429−430.

11. *Ibid.,* pp. 437−438.

12. *Claridad,* April 20, 1936.

13. ABC, April 21, 1936.

14. It might be noted that the revolutionary old guard of the CNT had a low opinion of the tone and commitment of the new influx into the organization. A spokesman for the

Barcelona Textile Syndicate lamented that revolution would actually be harder in the spring of 1936 than in the spring of 1931, when political institutions lay in shambles. A delegate from the Sagunto dock workers complained:

> Since 1934 the organization has changed radically. The anarchist blood that used to flow through its veins has diminished greatly. Unless a salutary reaction occurs, the CNT of today is not the same as in 1932 and 1933, in essence or in revolutionary vitality. The virus of politics has wrought great damage. It suffers from the obsession of gaining more and more members without stopping to consider the harm this causes its internal structure. It has completely forgotten the ideological formation of its members and only seeks to incorporate them numerically. . . .
> Let us carry out a thorough, conscientious campaign of libertarian education.

El Congreso confederal de Zaragoza (Mayo, 1936) (Toulouse, 1955), pp. 145 – 146.

15. Garcia Venero, *Internacionales*, III, pp. 106 – 108. Garcia Venero says that he has seen the original document and has "no doubt of its authenticity."

16. *Material de discusión para el Congreso Provincial del Partido Communista que se celebrará en Madrid, durante los dias 20, 21 y 22 de junio de 1936.*

17. *El Sol,* May 26, 1936. This data was first brought out in a seminar paper at UCLA by Mr. C. Sheldon Thorne.

18. Comín Colomer, *Partido Comunista,* III, pp. 681 – 749.

19. *El Socialista,* July 1, 1936. The commission also reported that even if all invalid votes were counted, the total would rise to 12,088 for González Peña and 10,318 for Largo Caballero.

20. *Claridad,* July 10, 1936.

21. *Ibid.,* July 13, 1936.

22. *Claridad,* July 3, 1936.

23. *Mundo Obrero,* July 10, 1936. It should be noted that at no time between February and July 1936 did the government or the leftist parties present concrete evidence substantiating the vociferous charges of extreme ruthlessness in the police repression in Asturias during 1934 and 1935, of which so much propaganda capital was made.

24. Ossorio Tafall's role was first pointed out to me by one of the principal leaders of the Galicianist left.

25. The Communist Manuel Benavides wrote in *La Publicitat* (Barcelona) on December 1, 1937, that Moles had "authorized house searches" of leading conservatives. This is not, however, corroborated by other evidence.

26. These details were brought out by the subsequent judicial investigation by the Nationalist regime.

27. *El Liberal,* July 15, 1936.

28. *Mundo Obrero,* July 13, 1936.

29. Cf. Indalecio Prieto, *Cartas a un escultor* (Buenos Aires, 1961), pp. 39 – 41.

30. The Madrid headquarters of the CNT, which had been provoking severe labor disturbance and was also strongly opposed to the Marxist parties, was also closed.

6

Internal Political Problems and Loyalties: The Republican Side in the Spanish Civil War

Edward E. Malefakis

The Spanish Civil War of 1936 – 1939 became the most notorious and controversial event of the 1930's prior to the beginning of World War II. However, the intense passion that it aroused throughout the Western world was not primarily due to the issues at stake in Spain itself but rather to the transformation of the Spanish conflict in the attitudes of foreign observers, who primarily interpreted it in terms of international and non-Spanish issues. Thus what was fundamentally a life-and-death struggle between the revolutionary left and counterrevolutionary right in one Southwest European country was inflated to symbolic and mythical proportions of a conflict between "fascism" and "democracy," though the left was not primarily democratic and the right not primarily fascist.

The following selection is focused on the internal problems and conflicts of the Spanish left during the Civil War. Though many factors contributed to the latter's defeat, none was more important than internal division. The author is professor of history at Columbia University and has also written Agrarian Reform and Peasant Revolution in Spain *(Yale, 1970). This selection was originally published in*

Civil Wars in the Twentieth Century, *ed., Robin Higham
(Kentucky, 1972), and is reprinted by permission of the
author and the University of Kentucky Press.*

SOCIAL

The Spanish Civil War has often been described as "the last great cause," the
last instance in our increasingly complex world when moral issues were
sharply drawn and men of goodwill could unreservedly support the cause of
freedom against the encroachments of totalitarian fascism. This was the feeling of many of those who lived during the conflict. Because of the peculiar inability of World War II (in truth a much more profound and clear-cut moral cru-
sade) to arouse similar emotional involvement among intellectuals, the feeling
persists.

However one chooses to explain this great outpouring of emotions which the
Western world channeled into the Spanish Civil War, the fact remains that it
was not a struggle between united, homogeneous blocs. Rather, probably
more than any other civil war of this century, the Spanish conflict was characterized by internal divisions, particularly on the Republican side. it resembled
less a medieval morality play, with its emphasis on the struggle between undi-
vided good and evil, than Greek tragedy or modern drama, with their por-
trayal of the protagonist as his own chief enemy, unable to triumph because he
is unable to gain ascendancy over himself.

That this was so should not be surprising, given the history of Spain in the
years immediately preceding the Civil War. The nonviolent overthrow of the
monarchy in 1931 by a coalition of middle-class progressives and Socialists
did not bring a solid national consensus in favor of the Republic that followed.
From the start, what was then the largest working-class group in Spain, the
Anarchosyndicalist Confederación Nacional del Trabajo (CNT), sought to
overthrow the new regime by means of a second social revolution which, going
far beyond the reforms advocated by the Republicans, would completely destroy capitalism, traditional forms of government, and all other manifestations
of what it considered to be the eternal oppression of man by man.

The intense opposition of the CNT might have been contained had the left
Republican-Socialist alliance which gave birth to the Republic been maintained. This did not occur, however. The middle-class left Republican parties
proved unwilling to accept the implications of the social policies they had so
bravely proclaimed in 1931. The underdeveloped Spanish economy was unable to solve the perennial problem of unemployment, now aggravated by
world depression. Above all, the Socialists abandoned their acceptance of par-

liamentary democracy, partly because of its slowness in bringing about reforms, partly because of the fear engendered by the fascist victories in Germany and Austria in 1933 – 34, and partly because the first electoral test of the Republic after the initial enthusiasm for it had waned went against them.

In the autumn of 1933 the Socialists abandoned their left Republican allies as weak, incompetent, or treasonous. Instead, they unsuccessfully attempted to create a working-class bloc with the CNT and, in October 1934, launched a hopelessly badly organized revolution against the Center-Right government that had taken power. Defeat in the October Revolution split the Socialist movement. One wing, headed by Indalecio Prieto, worked to reestablish the former Socialist commitment to reformist tactics, with its corollary of close cooperation with the left Republicans. The other wing, headed by Francisco Largo Caballero, sought its remedy in renewal and intensification of the revolutionary spirit.

Had the Center-Right been more flexible and far-sighted, the divisions within the Left might have kept it from recapturing power almost indefinitely. As it was, reactionaries gained control of the Center-Right bloc in 1935 and by their purely negative policies forced the Left to reunite temporarily into a Popular Front coalition during the elections of February 1936. Those elections won, the old divisions within the Left immediately reasserted themselves. The Popular Front cabinet, composed exclusively of left Republicans, could rely on full support only from middle-class progressives and the Prieto Socialists. The Caballero Socialists, the CNT, and the Communists (who now began to assume importance for the first time) vacillated between advocacy of the immediate overthrow of what they considered to be still another "bourgeois" regime and toleration of that regime until conditions were ripe for full-scale social revolution. This ambiguity was never resolved during the six months between the elections and the Civil War, in great part because the working-class Left was once again unable to unite within itself. The CNT demanded as the price of union a complete break with all parliamentary forms and an exclusive reliance on insurrectionary tactics. Neither the Caballeristas nor the Communists were willing to accept these terms, partly because their grounding in Marxist philosophy left a greater residue of caution among them than the millenarian CNT possessed.

To summarize, on the eve of the Civil War the Spanish Left was doubly divided. Its working-class components were separated from its middle-class components by their desire for social revolution. The working-class groups in turn were themselves divided by the intensity with which they pressed this revolutionary goal and the tactics by which they sought to achieve it.

As though these divisions were not enough, the middle-class Left was also divided because of the regional question, uniquely important in Spain. The failure of the country to modernize itself during the nineteenth century had given rise to separatist tendencies in its two most industrialized regions, Catalonia and the Basque country. Both joined the Loyalists so as to preserve or secure their regional autonomy against the Nationalist determination to restore a unitary Spain. Yet the bond that tied them to the Republic simultaneously separated them from it, since their fear that the regional principle would also be violated by their allies frequently led them to excessive insistence on their rights of autonomous government.

The divisions within the Spanish Right need not concern us in as much detail for several reasons. First, although they existed, they had never become so profound during the peacetime Republic, partly because the Right had usually been on the defensive rather than in power. Second, the army, an organization without specific ideological commitments and not previously involved in daily political life, immediately established its ascendancy over the Right when it rebelled against the Republic on July 18, 1936. In so doing, it reduced to secondary importance the hatreds between monarchists and conservative Republicans, as well as those between these more traditional groups and the small fascist party, the Falange. The main danger of internal conflict for the Nationalists stemmed from rivalry among the leading generals. This danger was avoided by the astuteness of Franco, the early deaths of his two main competitors, Sanjurjo and Mola, and the continuous success of Nationalist arms on the battlefield. The unwillingness of Hitler and Mussolini to risk alienating Franco by supporting their ideological counterpart, the Falange, during the coup by which Franco won control of that movement in April 1937 removed the only other threat of serious internal discord. Consequently, the Right was able to maintain far greater unity during the Civil War than it had previously. Rivalries there were aplenty, but none achieved major political significance.

The outbreak of war had quite different effects on the Left. In one sense it diminished factional strife: for the first time since 1931, a common enemy had appeared against whom all Republican factions could join. This was more than counterbalanced, however, by the fact that the insurrection momentarily destroyed the central state appartus and left power in the hands of Anarchist and Socialist groups. This power was used to launch a profound social revolution which, because it was conducted more or less independently in each locality and lacked a single ideological impulse, transformed Republican Spain into a veritable mosaic of separate and often competing authorities. Within days after the military insurrection there were several different levels of government in the Loyalist zone: the central government in Madrid; the autonomous Catalan and Basque governments in Barcelona and Bilbao, respectively; an almost fully autonomous CNT-sponsored Regional Council in eastern Aragon; somewhat less independent Socialist or Communist regional councils in Asturias, Santander, and Valencia; and finally, hundreds of local village and town antifascist committees that often claimed the right to independent action. The same pattern characterized the Loyalist military forces: rather than a single army under unified command, there was an unstable mixture of increasingly outnumbered regular army and police units, which had remained loyal to the Republic, and steadily expanding, self-assertive miltias spontaneously created under Anarchist, Socialist, Communist, left Communist, and sometimes even left Republican auspices.

The history of the Civil War on the Loyalist side was in large measure one of trying to come to terms with this extraordinary fragmentation of political and military power in the latter part of July 1936. Two predominant points of view emerged very quickly. One maintained essentially that victory could be achieved only if the war was fought primarily through conventional means, defined in three ways. First, the power of the central government must be restored. Second, a new army must be created through conscription and must operate on hierarchial principles under unified command. Finally, the social revolution that had occurred must be checked and even partially reversed so as to enlist the support of the urban middle classes and small peasant proprietors within Spain as well as that of the bourgeois governments of England and France, the most logical suppliers of arms to the Republic.

As one would expect, this viewpoint was strongly advocated by the middle-class left Republicans and the Prieto Socialists, the two moderate groups of the Popular Front coalition. Its most energetic and effective champions, however, were the Communists, whose seemingly uncharacteristic stance stemmed from a complex mixture of foreign, domestic, and ideological considerations. The chief goal of the Soviet Union during the mid-1930's was to escape, through rapprochement with the Western democracies, the threat to its existence posed by Hitler. Consequently, Stalin sought to transform the previous Communist reputation for universal, unrelenting class antagonism into one of working-class reasonableness. Domestically, the Spanish Communist party, because of its relatively small size and lack of a fully developed union apparatus in 1936, found that the principal gains in the social revolution of late July had been made by the Anarchists and Socialists, not by itself. Moreover, new left Communist groups, particularly the POUM, had gained strength in certain localities, from which they launched Trotsky-like attacks against the Stalinists. As to ideology, spontaneous, undirected popular revolution had been deprecated in the teachings of Lenin from a very early date; moreover, the Russian Revolution seemed to reaffirm the necessity of a vanguard party exercising strong control over the people.

This curious coalition of middle-class Republicans, moderate Socialists, and Stalinist Communists was opposed by an even more complex de facto alliance of the Anarchists, the POUM, and many left Socialists. For these groups victory could be won only if the war was fought entirely by revolutionary means— that is, by abandoning conventional political, economic, and military organization and relying instead on the new types that had appeared. It would be futile to try to win over the Spanish middle classes or England and France by checking the social revolution, they asserted; rather, the revolution must be carried further so as to inspire the Spanish masses to still greater efforts.

For all three groups, this position was a continuation of their policies of the preceding few years, when they had worked to overthrow the peacetime Republic through a second revolution, as well as an expression of their determination to hold on to the great gains they had made in late July. For the Anarchosyndicalists, an ideological motive was added. The very essence of Bakunin's teachings, and the point ultimately at issue between him and Marx, was the romantic conception that man had survived whole and good despite the sufferings to which the feudal and capitalistic systems had subjected him. Therefore, not only did Bakunin believe in the efficacy of spontaneous revolution, he also thought that as soon as it had triumphed traditional forms of government could be dispensed with so that men would be free to establish looser, more humane forms. The Spanish Anarchists, having gained this freedom in several regions where they were principally responsible for frustrating the military insurrection, were unwilling to return to centralized control, whoever might exercise it. They made their stance most strongly in eastern Aragon, whose Regional Council was led by CNT extremists, and where rural collectives sprang up by the hundreds after July.

As had been the case in the immediate prewar period, the twofold division in the Spanish Left did not erupt into open conflict, even though the rival factions now possessed their own militas and, to some extent, their own territorial bases. The internal struggle as newly defined continued to be waged mainly through propaganda and political maneuvering. The revolutionary side held the initial advantage because its mass following and enthusiasm enabled it to fill most rapidly the power vacuum created by the military insurrection. But the tide gradually began to shift in the late summer and early autumn of 1936 for two fundamental reasons: steady military defeat, and the Communist switch to the anti-revolutionary side, at least in the context of Spain.

Defeat on the battlefield during this period was in large part the price paid for the fact that many of those who collectively came to be known (more outside than inside Spain) as the Loyalists were more loyal to their particular ideology or revolutionary achievement than to a commonly defined Republic. The recent attempt of Noam Chomsky to revive the Anarchist interpretation of the war may have validity for later periods and in the exceedingly important sense that without the social revolution the Republic might well have collapsed without a fight instead of resisting the military insurrection. However, for the critical period from July to October 1936, when the basic military positions for the rest of the war were being decided, a major reason for the Republic's failure to take advantage of the opportunities open to it was the inability of the newly dominant Anarchist and left Socialist groups to wage an effective struggle of their own, and their simultaneous refusal to accept the revival of alternative forms of organization that might have proven militarily more efficacious.

The army insurrection in itself, without reference to the social revolution it set off, disorganized the Republic but did not render it completely helpless. Of the seven major Spanish cities, five remained in Republican hands. The two most industrialized regions were also Republican. The gold reserves and most other financial assets were Republican. The air force and navy remained primarily Republican, as did the large, semi-militarized police forces. Finally, the army itself was by no means united behind the insurrection of some of its generals; more than half of the units stationed on the peninsula seem to have remained on the Republican side.

Against this array, the Nationalists had two material assets of similar magnitude at the very start: command of the units stationed in Spanish Morocco, by far the best in the army, and support of most of the rural population of northern and north central Spain. Yet since the army in Morocco was rendered ineffective for more than two weeks by its inability to cross the Straits of Gibraltar and the northern rural population was far smaller than that of the Republican zone, the true advantage of the Nationalists during this period was probably psychological: their single, desperately held sense of purpose as opposed to the divided allegiances and multiple purposes of their opponents.

The Republic's inability to implement its potentially greater power was partly inherent in the situation and could not have been entirely overcome under any circumstances. The insurrection inevitably sowed suspicion as to the loyalty of all officers; defections and a handful of treasonous acts deepened the distrust. Yet the army and police strength left in the Republican zone might have been used more effectively, and a larger number of initially neutral officers might have been won over had not the ideological presuppositions of the Anarchist and Socialist militias led to their being branded "fascist" almost automatically. Similarly, in many areas, particularly Barcelona, social revolution was inherent in the very act of resisting the insurrection and could not have been avoided. But once successful in these places, revolutionaries diverted precious military resources in ridding themselves of "class enemies" and in imposing the new order upon populations to whom it did not come so naturally. Some scarcity of weapons was also unavoidable, but thousands of rifles that might have been used on the fronts were instead stowed away in CNT headquarters or strutted around the streets by militiamen celebrating their momentary triumph. All this was not without effect on Republican foreign relations. Given the overriding English and French desire to avoid conflict during the 1930's and the aggressive assertiveness of Germany and Italy, an international alignment unfavorable to the Republic would probably have developed in any event. Yet the revolutionary chaos among the Loyalists and their attendant lack of military success enabled each country to overcome, sooner than it otherwise might have, its initial doubts as to what course to follow.

In short, had the Spanish Left not been so disunited before the July insurrection and by the social revolution that immediately followed, it is conceivable (though admittedly not very likely) that the outcome of the French army rebellions in Algeria in 1960 – 61 might have been anticipated: the relatively weak opposition in the metropolitan country might have been suppressed and the strong force in the trans-Mediterranean colony therefore rendered permanently ineffective. [1] As it was, by August 5 sufficient troops had been transported from Morocco with German and Italian aid to alter completely the military situation on the peninsula. Instead of the weak Nationalist forces of the north, which had been able to do little more than maintain their positions during the preceding two and a half weeks, the Republicans were suddenly confronted by small but effective units that immediately launched an offensive. Against this force the true extent of their lack of preparation revealed itself. Within a month much of Andalusia and nearly all of Estremadura, two vast regions of southern Spain where the Anarchist and Socialist peasant following was most numerous, had fallen to the Nationalists. In another month they had taken San Sebastian in the north and penetrated deep into south central Spain. As the Nationalists approached Madrid in October, resistance stiffened. Only when they actually reached the outskirts of the capital in early November and were stopped short by its defenders, however, did it become clear that they were faced with a true war rather than a military promenade. In the three months between August 6, the start of the Moroccan army's offensive from Seville, and November 7, its first setback in Madrid, the Nationalists conquered approximately 25,000 square miles of territory. In the next three months, to the start of the Málaga offensive on February 3, 1937, they conquered not much more than 250.

So profound a setback could not but alter internal political relationships in the Republican zone. The extreme revolutionary position eroded, and the position of those who called for sacrifice of ideology and particular revolutionary achievements in favor of greater unity grew stronger. All factions were affected to some extent. The Largo Caballero Socialists drew back from their revolutionary intransigence, accepted leadership of the Madrid government in September, and thereupon lent their support to the drive to create a new, hierarchically organized Republican army. Despite cries of treason from many of their followers, several CNT leaders abandoned their ideological principles and accepted posts in the Catalan government in September and in the Madrid government in November. The Communists gained enormously in strength, both because their units, having shunned revolutionary delirium, had proven most effective in the fighting, and because the Soviet Union had emerged in early October as the Republic's chief supplier of arms. With the Communist increase in power and the growing left Socialist acceptance of centralization, the regional councils in Santander and Asturias, which these two forces dominated, became more closely linked to the central government. The same effect was achieved in Valencia when that government, fleeing before the Nationalist onslaught, transferred itself from Madrid to the Mediterranean coastal city.

Yet if these changes, together with continuous Soviet aid after October and the appearance on the battlefield of the International Brigades in November, converted the Republicans into a much more formidable military force than before, the Loyalist side continued to be handicapped by its internal divisions. Republican strength approximated its potential only in the central zone around Madrid, where Anarchist influence was weakest and regionalist sentiment did not exist. Elsewhere, the situation was far different. In the northern war zone, the autonomous Basque government continued to operate more or less independently of other Republican forces, whether those immediately adjacent to it in Santander and Asturias or those in the central zone, from which it was cut off by Nationalist territory. Only once did this populous, highly industrialized region launch an offensive, which lasted for six days; otherwise it vainly guarded its strength and was preoccupied by its own internal conflicts. Catalonia participated more actively in the war effort, but the gap between its actual and its potential performance was of even greater importance since the area was even more populous and industrialized than the Basque region.

In Catalonia, because it had not been so directly affected as Madrid by the great Nationalist advance of August-October, and because of its different internal political composition, the inner transformation that had taken place in the central zone did not occur to the same degree. The Communists and Socialists achieved a closer union there than elsewhere and greatly increased their prewar following, but the superiority of the CNT had been so great that they were not yet able to impose their policy of centralization, particularly since the POUM supported the CNT revolutionary line, and the middle-class Catalan regionalists, seeing their autonomy threatened by both groups, played a vacillating role. In consequence, the Catalan sector of the front (which lay in Aragon, some miles west of Catalonia proper) continued to display the military ineffectiveness characteristic of the Republic as a whole in the months immediately after the July insurrection. Internal conflict was rampant; offensives were infrequent and poorly executed; and the CNT and POUM generally refused integration into the new Republican army and insisted upon retaining their special prerogatives and separate structure. Under these circumstances, the manpower and extensive material resources of Catalonia were rendered meaningless, even though directed against Nationalist forces that were much smaller and more poorly equipped than those ranged against Madrid. After an entire year of intermittent combat, the lines on the Aragon front remained essentially what they had been in July 1936.

There are two possible explanations for the next major political transformation in the Republican zone, the events of May 1937 in which the rivalries between the Republican forces burst into several days of street fighting in Barcelona and left the Communists the dominant force. The more popular explanation emphasizes the ruthlessness and duplicity of the Communists, characteristics certainly not foreign to them. Having gained a strong position by their discipline and influence over the arms supply from the U.S.S.R., it is said, the Communists, though unable to assume open command because they feared to alienate England and France, decided to take over de facto control of the Republic. This they achieved in three ways: by honeycombing the Republican army with their political commissars, by reducing the power of the CNT and destroying completely the POUM (more because it was "Trotskyite," the argument runs, than because of its specific actions within Spain), and by substituting a more pliable leader, the moderate Socialist Juan Negrín, in the central government when Largo Caballero sought to resist them.

The other, less ideological explanation is that the ambiguous situation that arose after the Nationalists had been stopped at Madrid in November 1936 could have continued only so long as the war remained stalemated. Once the Nationalists began to move again, with their rapid conquest of Málaga in February 1937 and the opening of their offensive on the northern front in April, the same kind of transformation that had been experienced in the central zone earlier would have to be imposed upon Catalonia. The May events, in essence, were a desperate attempt to prevent further defeat by forcing Catalonia to shoulder more of the war effort. They may have been hastened by Communist fears that the CNT and POUM would stage a coup of their own, perhaps with the support of the Caballero Socialists, who were increasingly resentful of the growth in Communist power. But primarily the Communists sought to create a more effective war machine rather than secure personal dominance as such.

Insofar as these two motives can be separated (for they are by no means mutually exclusive), the second seems the more plausible, though the savageness of the suppression of the POUM leaves room for doubt. The Communists could not have won the Barcelona street fighting in early May or ousted Largo Caballero from the premiership in the latter part of that month had they not enjoyed the support of the Prieto Socialists and the reluctant acquiescence of many CNT leaders (who, while refusing to join the new Negrin government, did not try to turn their massive following actively against it). The same was true of the changes that occurred in the summer of 1937 as an aftermath to these two decisive events. The Communists alone could not have disbanded the semi-independent Regional Council of Aragon, undone the nearly universal collectivization that had existed under the CNT in that region since the 1936 social revolution, nor reduced Catalan autonomy to a shadow of its former self.

Yet having been achieved by force rather than consent, the victory of the Communists had its price. Their chief allies of the prewar period, the Caballero Socialists, now began to tread rapidly down the road that by 1939 would lead them to regard the Communists as a greater evil than the Nationalists. The Anarchosyndicalists, who had been psychologically buffeted since the autumn of 1936 by the failure of reality to correspond to their theories, now became almost completely dispirited. The Catalan regionalists were in a similar condition for similar reasons. The dominance achieved by the Communists subtly affected even those groups not directly injured by the May events by raising doubts as to their tactics and suspicions as to their ultimate motives.

The Communists were successful in their purpose of integrating Catalonia more closely with the war effort, but they could have enabled the Republic to transcend the new divisions that had appeared only if this integration had led to victory on the battlefield. Such was not to be the case. The Nationalists, because of their conquest of industrial Bilbao in June 1937 and of the rest of the northern Republican zone by October, and because of the steady flow of arms and men they had been receiving from Germany and Italy since the autumn of the previous year, now held material as well as psychological superiority.

Thus while the Republicans were able (as they had not been earlier in the war) to convert Aragon, not Madrid, into the principal scene of battle, the greater military effectiveness that this shift symbolized was no longer enough. The Aragon offensives of August and September 1937, by which the Republicans sought to divert the Nationalist army from completing its conquest of northern Spain, failed in their purpose. The massive Teruel offensive of December-January won its initial objectives but so exhausted Republican forces that it enabled the Nationalists to stage a breakthrough unmatched since their drive of August-October 1936. In four months, from early March to early July 1938, the Republicans lost some 15,000 square miles of territory on the Aragon front and saw the Nationalists reach the Mediterranean Sea, splitting the Loyalist zone in two. The valor of the Republican army was proven in late July when, managing to take the overextended Nationalists by surprise, it pushed their forces back some ten to fifteen miles in exceedingly difficult terrain along the Ebro River. But this momentary victory had little effect except to lead to several months of a battle of attrition, which the diminishing Republican forces could ill afford.

Communist dominance after May 1937 had led—at a tremendous cost in lives—only to a greater ability to resist, not to a turn in the tide of battle. Thus the Communists, militarily the most formidable of the Republican groups, were no more able than their rivals to create a consensus of loyalties behind their version of the Republic. War weariness inevitably spread among large sectors of the population as defeat followed defeat, the hope that England and France might change their policies became more untenable, and even the Soviet Union first reduced and then entirely stopped its flow of arms. Aside from the battles mentioned, there were three major milestones in the Republican descent into hopelessness. Prieto's dismissal from the Ministry of War under Communist pressure in April 1938, after the Teruel disaster, narrowed the base of Negrín's coalition government still further. Franco's rejection of Negrín's thirteen-point peace proposal in May raised demands for an alternative government that would negotiate surrender. Moreoever, the British and French collapse before Hitler at the Munich Conference in September destroyed the illusion of a dramatic shift in international alignments that had sustained the Republicans during the Czech crisis of the late summer.

Because of the destruction of the POUM and the disintegration of the Anarchists and Caballero Socialists, the opposition to Negrín and the Communists came from more individual middle-class and moderate Socialist leaders than from working-class groups, as it had in the past. The Republican masses might still occasionally express their valor in battle, as on the Ebro, but no longer acted in the streets under the inspiration of some ideological vision. For the urban masses, food shortages and destruction of the revolutionary factory workers' councils in favor of government control ended the enthusiasm of 1936 and early 1937. For the peasantry, which retained control of most of the land it had seized in July 1936, social gains were rendered meaningless by ever greater government crop requisitions and the growing horror of war. In short, a general consensus had finally arisen within the Republic, but it was the consensus of defeatism.

Under these circumstances, the success of the Nationalist offensive against Catalonia in January 1939 should not be surprising. There was no repetition of the saga of Madrid, no stubborn stand as the armies approached the Catalan capital, only steady retreat. Within two months the Nationalists conquered the most populous and industrialized region of Spain, captured vast quantities of military supplies, and forced a major portion of the Republican army to intern itself in France. Because of the sudden change that occurred in the European political scene soon after, the Republican cause might not have been entirely hopeless even after this amputation of its resources. Given the slowness with which the cautious Franco planned each major move, it is conceivable that the struggle might have dragged on until the outbreak of World War II in September, and that the Western democracies then might possibly have come to the Republic's aid (though this was unlikely because of England's generally good relations with Franco and its tendency to regard the Spanish war as a separate conflict).[2] But the will to fight was gone from everyone except the Communists and Negrín.

The final act of the Republican drama was the one which had long been threatening: open warfare among the Republic's component elements. The conflict took the form of an anti-Communist coup in Madrid, headed by a non-political military man, Colonel Casado, and supported by most Socialists and Anarchists as well as by what was left of the middle-class Republican groups. Some 2,000 lives were lost in a week-long battle in early March. Had Franco been more generous, this new tragedy might have been expiated by his agreement to the general amnesty which the Casado forces sought as the basis for peace. Instead, Spain was finally delivered from the horror of war on April 1, 1939, only to be plunged into a new horror of prison camps and political executions by the tens of thousands.

The principal lesson of the Spanish Civil War, insofar as internal political loyalties are concerned, is that a common cause can be maintained only if it has been generally accepted prior to the opening of hostilities. If it has not and either of the combatants is riven, as was Republican Spain, by a multiplicity of social, ideological, and regional conflicts, two consequences are probable. Moments of apparent triumph are unlikely to be converted into full victory because each of the rival factions will try to anticipate the final settlement and secure as strong a position as possible for itself by imposing its particular political vision within the territory under its control. This is what occurred in Spain from July to October 1936. Times of defeat, on the other hand, may enable or compel the faction that can draw upon the widest assortment of politically effective partial allegiances to impose a forced unity upon the others, thus weakening still further their attachment to the general cause and creating new divisions that may eventually erupt into internecine conflict if the forced union is not militarily victorious. This is what occurred in Spain under the Communists after May 1937. The tragedy of Republican Spain, in short, was that a civil war of its own always lurked within its ranks as it fought the greater Civil War against the Nationalists.

NOTES

1. The major differences between the two situations were that the rebellious French generals had won no territorial base in France as well as in Algeria, held insecure control over their own forces and the native population, and confronted a powerful leader in De Gaulle. Nevertheless, the analogy helps illuminate some of the reasons for Republican failure in the Civil War.

2. This kind of miraculous, last-minute salvation of the Republic was also improbable because Hitler might not have chosen to risk general war over Poland in September had the Spanish conflict still continued.

7

An Authoritarian Regime: Spain

Juan J. Linz

The Franco regime that came to power in the Spanish Civil War has been one of the most anomalous of twentieth-century European political systems. Linked to some extent with Nazi Germany and Fascist Italy, it was treated with hostility by most other Western governments yet survived both World War II (in which Spain remained neutral) and a brief period of international ostracism that followed. After 1945 it slowly but steadily evolved in a more moderate direction, divesting itself of certain fascistic trappings that it featured in earlier years. In the process it emerged as a leading exemplar of a different kind of political system— the rightist authoritarian but not totalitarian system, distinct at one and the same time from fascism, communism, and parliamentary democracy.

The following selection has come to be recognized as the classic definition of the Franco regime and more generally of the broader category of the right authoritarian state. The author is professor of sociology and political science at Yale University and has published numerous monographs on modern Spanish society and politics. This selection first appeared in Cleavages, Ideologies and Party Systems, *ed., E. Allardt and Y. Littunen (Helsinki, 1964), and is reprinted by permission of the author and the Westermarck Society.*

I

TYPES OF POLITICAL SYSTEMS

This paper attempts to conceptualize some differences between political systems, taking the present Spanish regime as example and point of departure. In the decades since World War II, the distinction elaborated by political scientists between democratic governments and totalitarian societies has proven useful scientifically and even more polemically. The terms democratic and totalitarian have come to be used as dichotomous or at least as a continuum. An effort is made to fit various regimes into one or the other type, often basing the decision on nonscientific criteria. While the classification has been useful, it is increasingly necessary to go beyond it. From the beginning social scientists have felt uneasy about placing countries like Spain, and even Fascist Italy or pre-1945 Japan, into the totalitarian category. The uneasiness has grown as they came to deal with the "progressive" one-party regimes of the underdeveloped areas and the "modernizing" military dictatorships. So, for example, A. Inkeles remarks on

. . . a mode of analysis which can encompass totalitarian systems as divergent in their concrete institutional structure as the Communist and Nazi systems, which most closely approximate the ideal type; Fascist Italy, which only imperfectly approximated it; and Franco Spain which only imperfectly fits the model in a few crucial respects.[1]

Even a correspondent like Herbert Matthews, far from friendly to the Spanish regime, writes:

The power [of Franco] is almost unlimited. This does not make Spain a totalitarian country in either the Communist or the Fascist sense. It is an authoritarian country. The authority is exercised by keeping all parts of the regime weak or in conflict with each other. Order is kept essentially because the Spanish people want it, and through the Army and police. This makes Franco's power supreme when he wants to exercise it. Since, like all modern dictators, he does not allow any single man or group to become strong and threaten his power, there is no alternative to Francisco Franco, at least no visible alternative. As long as his position is not attacked and the nation's affairs function smoothly, he keeps hands off.[2]

Raymond Aron faced the same problem after characterizing the constitutional pluralist regimes and the regimes *de parti monopoliste,* when he wrote about a "third class of regime where there is no single party nor multiple parties, not based on electoral legitimacy nor on revolutionary legitimacy," [3] giving as examples Portugal, Spain, and the first phase of Vichy.

Gabriel Almond, in his important article on comparative political systems, has formulated most clearly some main characteristics of this type of regime which we shall call authoritarian; the term is used by many in this connection, even by spokesmen of such regimes. Almond writes:

> [The totalitarian political structure] is anti-pluralistic in intent and method if not in accomplishment. . . . Recent developments in the Soviet Union seem to be directed toward providing some explicit structural bases for policy discussion and conflict. . . . But what has so far been attained . . . is far from the structural pluralism which is so typical for authoritarian regimes. If one takes such a system as that of Spain, it is evident that religious bodies, organized interests, status groups, bureaucratic agencies, as well as the Falange party are "acknowledged" elements in a pluralistic political structure. Interest confict is built into the system, and is not merely latent and spasmodic as in the totalitarian pattern.
>
> The structures of the two systems differ in a second significant respect. The totalitarian system tends to be highly mobilized, tense and expansive internally and externally. The authoritarian tends to be more stable, more relaxed, although these are differences in degree. [4]

It could be argued that there is no need for a new type—the authoritarian—since regimes so described are really imperfect forms of either totalitarian or democratic polities, tending ultimately in one or the other direction and close, at least in their ideals, to one or the other pole. Failure to reach the totalitarian stage might be due to administrative inefficiency, economic underdevelopment, or external influences and pressures. In regimes approving in principle a Western "progressive" conception of democracy—like the Mexican or Turkish leadership after their national revolutions—failure might be attributed to economic backwardness and religious traditionalism. To formulate it as sociologists, we might say that when certain functional prerequisites for a stable democracy are absent, some form of authoritarianism is established, in order—presumably—to prepare the country for it; or in other cases a premature transition to democracy leads to a setback in the form of an authoritarian regime. From another angle, we might say that certain characteristics of the social structure make it impossible for those in power to move toward true totalitarianism without endangering their own position. This hypothesis assumes that those in power are deliberately pursuing a totalitarian social order, which strictly speaking may not be the case even for some stages in a transition which actually results in a totalitarian society.

We prefer for purposes of analysis to reject the idea of a continuum from

democracy to totalitarianism and to stress the distinctive nature of authoritarian regimes. Unless we examine the features unique to them, the conditions under which they emerge, the conceptions of power held by those who
shape them, regimes which are not clearly either democratic or totalitarian will
be treated merely as deviations from these ideal types and will not be studied
systematically and comparatively.

Like any ideal type, the notion of the authoritarian regime is an abstraction
which underlines certain characteristics and ignores, at least for the time
being, the fluidity of reality, differences in degree, and contradictory tendencies present in the real world. In any of the European regimes of the interwar
years that we would call authoritarian, Fascist elements played a role and significant minorities were striving for a totalitarian state; the Hungary of Horthy,
the colonels' regime in Poland, the Rumanian and Yugoslav royal dictatorships, the Portuguese Estado Novo, the Austrian corporative Dollfuss regime,
Vichy, are examples. Today the model of the Soviet Union operates similarly in
many underdeveloped areas. Such regimes exist under many formal garments
and their lack of an elaborate and consistent ideology makes them particularly
susceptible to mimicry. [5]

The external forms of the thirties and forties, the uniforms and ceremonies
and terminology, and the appeals of today to democratic or socialist values are
more easily assimilated than the institutional realities they represent. We may
be seriously misled if we study such regimes through constitutions, laws,
speeches, the writing of unknown and unrewarded "ideologists," without in-
quiring how these are actually translated into social reality. The laws may say,
for example, that everyone has to be a member of certain organizations, but
later almost nobody is; the law gives the corporative system a monopoly of interest representation, but a study of businessmen shows that they belong to lit-
erally hundreds of autonomous interest groups which existed before the regime came to power; a political indoctrination course is provided for in the
universities but it turns out to be a course in labor and welfare institutions, and
everyone is allowed to pass.

The utility of treating authoritarian regimes as a distinct type will lie in help-
ing us understand the distinctive ways in which they resolve problems common to all political systems: maintaining control and gaining legitimacy, recruiting elites, articulating interests and aggregating them, making decisions
and relating to various institutional spheres like the armed forces, religious
bodies, the intelligentsia, the economy, etc. If we can find that they handle
such problems differently from both democratic and totalitarian regimes, and
furthermore if quite different regimes, classified as authoritarian, handle them

in ways that turn out to be similar, the distinction will have been justified. Later we will explore in some detail a few examples along these lines.

Before defining an authoritarian regime, let us refer briefly to the conceptions of democracy and totalitarianism from which we start in our comparative analysis. This is particularly important since many authoritarian systems claim to be "organic," "basic," "selective" or "guided" democracies, or at least to govern for the people, if not in fact to be "people's" democracies. We consider a government democratic if it supplies regular constitutional opportunities for peaceful competition for political power (and not just a share of it) to different groups without excluding any significant sector of the population by force. This definition is based on those of Schumpeter, Aron and Lipset, [6] with the addition of the last qualification to include censitary regimes of the nineteenth century, democracies in which the vote has been denied to some groups, but with real competition for support from a limited electorate. As long as new claimants to suffrage were not suppressed forcibly for more than a limited time, we can consider such regimes democratic.

As Schumpeter has stressed, the element of competition for votes makes the whole gamut of civil liberties necessary, since without them there could be no true free competition; this is the link between classical liberalism and democracy. It could be argued that authoritarian regimes, even preconstitutional monarchies, have or had certain civil liberties, but we would not call them democracies for this reason. To give an example in recent years, legalization of a right to strike—perhaps not under that name—has been discussed in Spain, particularly since de facto strikes are tolerated and government officials participate in the negotiations between workers and employers despite their illegality. Similarly, the courts have assumed quite extensive control over administrative acts through the Law of Administrative Procedure, following the model of continental European administrative law and jurisprudence. Many elements of the Rechtsstaat are not incompatible with an authoritarian state and perhaps not even with a "secularized" totalitarian state. However, full civil liberties, including an unlimited right of association and assembly, for example, inevitably create pressures toward political democracy. In this sense, against a strong tradition in continental political theory, we can say that liberalism and democracy are inseparable.

In defining totalitarianism we also want to limit the term somewhat and reserve it for the unique new forms autocratic government has taken since World War I, without denying that similar tendencies existed in the past. Perhaps Kornhauser's characterization is as good as any other, even if it overstresses somewhat the arbitrary aspects, when he writes:

Totalitarian dictatorship involves total domination, limited neither by received laws or codes (as in traditional authoritarianism) nor even the boundaries of governmental functions (as in classical tyranny), since they obliterate the distinction between State and society. Totalitarianism is limited only by the need to keep large numbers of people in a state of constant activity controlled by the elite. [7]

C. J. Friedrich's well-known definition [8] includes the following five clusters of characteristics: an official ideology, often with chiliastic elements; a single mass party unquestioningly dedicated to the ideology, near complete control of mass media, complete political control of the armed forces, and a system of terroristic police control not directed against demonstrable enemies only. In another version central control and direction of the economy is added. This more descriptive definition provides a clearer yardstick, although in view of recent developments I would not give as much emphasis to the role of the police and terror. [9]

Definition of an Authoritarian Regime

Authoritarian regimes are political systems with limited, not responsible, political pluralism: without elaborate and guiding ideology (but with distinctive mentalities); without intensive nor extensive political mobilization (except some points in their development); and in which a leader (or occasionally a small group) exercises power within formally ill-defined limits but actually quite predictable ones.

To avoid any confusion we want to make it clear that personal leadership is a frequent characteristic but not a necessary one, since a junta arrangement can exist and the leader's personality might not be the decisive factor. Furthermore, the leader does not need to have charismatic qualities, at least not for large segments of the population nor at all stages of development of the system. In fact he may combine elements of charismatic, legal, and traditional authority in varying degrees, often at different points in time—though the charismatic element often tends to be more important than the legal authority, at least for some sectors of the population.

Pluralism

We speak of regime, rather than government, to indicate the relatively low specificity of the political institutions: they often penetrate the life of the society, preventing, even forcibly, the political expression of certain group interests (as religion in Turkey and Mexico, labor in Spain) or shaping them by interventionist economic policies. But in contrast to some of the analysts of totalitarianism, such as Inkeles, we speak of regimes rather than societies be-

cause the distinction between state and society is not obliterated. The pluralistic element is the most distinctive feature of these regimes, but let us empha-
size that in contrast to democracies with their almost unlimited pluralism, we
deal here with limited pluralism. The limitation may be legal or de facto, serious or less so, confined to strictly political groups or extended to interest
groups, as long as there remain groups not created by nor dependent on the
state which influence the political process one way or another. Some regimes
even institutionalize the political participation of a limited number of independently existing groups or institutions, and actually encourage their emergence.
To take an example, when Primo de Rivera created his National Assembly he
provided for the representation of the church, cultural institutions, the nobility,
the army, and the business community, as well as the newly created party; at
the same time he encouraged the creation of economic interest groups that
have been the pressure groups of Spanish business ever since.[10] [11] Another
example is the institutionalization of a complex pluralism in the officially dominant Partido Revolucionario Institucional of Mexico that prompts V. Padgett to
write: "An 'official' party need not necessarily be an instrument of imposition.
It may be a device for bridging the gap between authoritarianism and representative democracy." [12] With such a limited but relatively autonomous pluralism, there is likely to be some competition for power, more or less informal,
despite open declarations of monopoly. It is quite characteristic in this respect
that the Falange, after entering the Franco coalition, dropped Point 27, which
read:

> We shall work to triumph in the struggle with only the forces subject to our discipline.
> We shall make very few pacts. Only in the final push for conquest of the state will the
> command arrange for the necessary collaborations, always provided that our pre-
> dominance be assured. [13]

This pluralism contrasts with the strong domination, if not the monopoly, imposed by the totalitarian party after conquering power; its penetration, through
the process the Nazis called *Gleichschaltung* (synchronization), of all kinds of
groups and organizations; the creation of functional organizations serving as
transmission belts and auxiliaries for the party; politicizing even areas remote
from politics, like sports and leisure. [14]

Serrano Suñer, the once powerful brother-in-law of Franco, head of the
Junta Politica, minister of interior and foreign affairs and master engineer of
the decree founding the unified party, writes quite accurately and with awareness of the alternatives, as follows:

In truth, be it an advantage or disadvantage, it is time to say that in Spain there has never been anything that would really look like a totalitarian state, since for this it seems to be a necessary condition that the single party should exist in strength and be really the sole basis of support for the regime—the only instrument and in a sense the only holder of power. . . . The complex of forces participating in the Uprising—the army, traditional elements, parties, etc.—has never disappeared, thanks to a policy of equilibrium and through the persistence of the unified elements without ever fusing and without deciding in favor of a total pre-eminence of the official party.

To give each his due: this regime has not been totalitarian as it has not been democratic or liberal. What it would have been without the world war only God knows. What it will finally be is still to be seen. [15]

The difference between authoritarian and democratic pluralism is that the latter is in principle almost unlimited; it is not only tolerated but legitimate; and its open participation in the competition for power, through political parties, is institutionalized. In a democracy political forces not only reflect social forces, but represent them and to some extent commit them to the support of government policies once these are arrived at; political forces are dependent on the support of constituencies. The "iron law of oligarchy" may make this relative, but the formal principle is upheld.

In authoritarian regimes the men who come to power reflecting the views of various groups and institutions do not derive their positions from the support of these groups alone, but from the trust placed in them by the leader, monarch, or "junta," who certainly takes into account their prestige and influence. They have a kind of constituency, we might call it a potential constituency, but this is not solely or even principally the source of their power.

The co-optation of leaders is a constant process by which different sectors or institutions become participants in the system. In the consolidated totalitarian system this process takes place between bureaucracies or organizations that are part of the political structure created by the system, generally dependent on the party or an outgrowth of it; in the authoritarian regime pre-existent or newly emergent elements of the society can be represented by this means. The authoritarian regime may go very far toward suppressing existing groups or institutions inimical to the social order; this process of control may affect others, and the threat of control is always present; but due to a number of circumstances the control process is arrested. The strength of ideological commitments; the size, integration, quality of the group wishing a monopoly of power; the strength and legitimacy of existing institutions, and their international ties; the degree of economic autarchy possible; all are factors which may limit maximum suppression of dissidence. Ultimately, the conception of power held by the authoritarian leader may make the decisive difference.

Mentality Versus Ideology

Styles of leadership, and different ways of conceiving the relation between state power and society, must be examined if we are to analyze the authoritarian regime in its various forms.

We will purposely use the term mentality rather than "ideology." The German sociologist Theodor Geiger [16] has formulated a useful distinction between ideologies, which are systems of thought more or less intellectually elaborated and organized, often in written form, by intellectuals, pseudo-intellectuals, or with their assistance; and mentalities, which are ways of thinking and feeling, more emotional than rational, that provide non-codified ways of reacting to situations. Ideologies have a strong utopian element; mentalities are closer to the present or the past. Totalitarian systems have ideologies, a point emphasized by all students of such systems, while authoritarian regimes are based more on distinctive mentalities which are difficult to define. The more traditional an authoritarian regime is, the greater the role of the military and civil servants, the more important "mentalities" become in understanding the system, and the more a focus on ideologies, even those loudly proclaimed by the regime, may be misleading. [17]

It is interesting to note that Naguib, a participant in the creation of such a regime, was aware of a distinction along the same lines when he wrote:

> I shall not enumerate my specific differences with the Council here. It is enough, I think, for me to say that most of them revolved around what Abd Nasser has called the "philosophy" of the revolution. Perhaps, since neither of us are philosophers, it would be better to call it the "psychology" of the revolution. [18] [Emphasis supplied.]

The result of Nasser's "philosophy" has been described by Nadav Safran in these terms:

> The young authors of the revolution who have presided over Egypt's destinies for the last eight years came to power with no guiding political philosophy beyond a few generalities, and little in the way of a positive program beyond good intentions. They proceeded to work out philosophy and program in a pragmatic experimental fashion, fighting at the same time against the forces of reaction and counter-revolution and struggling among themselves for predominance in their own councils. The result was many false starts, mistaken courses, abrupt reversals, and a high degree of uncertainty. [19]

The new authoritarian leader's lack of clear ideology is evident when we read excerpts like these from Franco's lengthy manifesto of July 18, 1936:

The situation of Spain is more critical every day; anarchy reigns in the majority of its farms and villages; authorities appointed by the government preside over, if not encourage, the revolts. Differences between factions of citizens are fought out by guns and machine guns. . . . We offer you Justice and equality before the law. Peace and love among the Spaniards. Liberty and fraternity free from license and tyranny. Work for everybody. Social justice without bitterness; an equitable and progressive distribution of wealth without destroying or endangering the Spanish economy. . . . The purity of our intentions does not allow us to throttle those conquests which represent a step forward in the socio-political improvement . . . and of the inevitable ship-wreck of some legislative attempts, we will know how to save whatever is compatible with the inner peace of Spain and its desired grandeur, making real in our Fatherland for the first time, and in this order, the trilogy Fraternity, Liberty, Equality. Spaniards: Viva España! Viva the honest Spanish people! [20]

The same lack of novelty in themes and symbols can be seen when Vargas said on October 4, 1930, after a similar but less vehement description of the regime's crisis,

Sheltered by the support of public opinion, with the prestige given us by the adherence of the Brazilians . . . counting on the sympathy of the armed forces and the collaboration of its best part, strengthened by justice and by arms, we hope that the Nation will reassume possession of its sovereignty, without major opposition by the reactionaries, to avoid useless loss of lives and goods, hasten the return to normality of the country and the restoration of a regime of peace, harmony and tranquility, under the sign of the law. [21]

Given the reliance of many authoritarian regimes—those of Salazar, Dollfuss, Franco, even Pétain—on conservative interpretations of Catholic social doctrine, we might ask whether this system of thought is an ideology. Inkeles, writing about the ideological aims of totalitarianism, raises the issue as follows:

Invariably this higher goal involves some mystique, some principle above man, some force that responds to laws of its own and that merely requires the state as an instrument through which it may work out its inner imperatives. The mystique may be the dialectical laws of history and social development for the Marxist, the destiny of the nation and race for the Hitlerian, or the ideal of the true Christian society for Franco. [22]

In some cases this ideology competes and coexists with other ideological currents, but even where it is dominant we would argue that it cannot provide the basis for a totalitarian system because of its heteronomous nature. How can a regime base total power on an ideology whose only legitimate interpreters are ultimately outside its control? Given the distinctiveness of Church and State, the internationalism of the Church and the powers of the Pope, the use of a conservative Catholic ideology in itself limits monolithic tendencies toward totalitarianism. The Franco regime's difficulties in the face of a growing labor movement, church inspired or supported, are due largely to this ideological heteronomy. Shifting and divergent interpretations of the Catholic social doctrine in themselves introduce a strong element of pluralism, where the ultimate doctrinal decision is outside the political realm. [23]

Apathy Versus Mobilization

Stabilized authoritarian regimes are characterized by lack of extensive and intensive political mobilization of the population. Membership participation is low in political and para-political organizations and participation in the single party or similar bodies, whether coerced, manipulated or voluntary, is infrequent and limited. The common citizen expresses little enthusiastic support for the regime in elections, referenda, and rallies. Rather than enthusiasm or support, the regime often expects—even from office holders and civil servants—passive acceptance, or at least they refrain from public anti-government activity. Let us stress this depolitization is characteristic of stabilized authoritarian regimes, but would not be necessarily true for their formative stages, particularly since their emergence in a crisis would involve considerable and often very intensive popular participation. We would like to argue that this participation is not likely to be maintained over a long period of time, unless the regime moves into a totalitarian or a more formally democratic direction. However, the degrees of mobilization might be the most useful criteria on which to distinguish subtypes of authoritarian regimes. [24]

On the one side we have those that Raymond Aron [25] has characterized as "regimes without parties" which "require a kind of depolitization of the governed" and others we could call "populistic" in which there is a more continuous effort of mobilization, without reaching the pervasiveness and intensity of the totalitarian model. Recognizing the importance of such a distinction, [26] we would like to suggest that often the difference might be more that of stages in the development of nondemocratic regimes than a substantive difference. It would be to misunderstand contemporary Spain to ignore the high level of participation in party activities, youth groups, political oriented welfare activities—not to mention rallies, parades, etc.—during the years of the Civil War in Nationalistic Spain; and the intensity of involvement, ideological and emotional, of people in all sectors of the population must be stressed. [27] No one can deny that this disappeared during the years after the victory. This was not only because, first, the leadership lacked interest in maintaining it, but also because the social structure of a semideveloped country, and the social, institutional, and ideological pluralism made such levels of participation untenable without either channeling them through organized parties or substituting that pluralism with a hierarchical, disciplined, and ideologically committed single party. In the contest of the early forties, the first possibility was excluded and the will to impose a truly totalitarian system, destructive of the coalition character of the forces Franco led to victory, was absent from an army (including its leaders) which had no single well-defined ideology. I would like to leave the question open if in the future some of the more "populistic" one-party regimes in Africa and the Moslem countries will not undergo a similar process, transforming the parties and connected organizations into adjuncts of the state apparatus (the bureaucracy) or/and patronage organizations, [28] with little genuine participation, even of a manipulative type.

However, even admitting that the degree of mobilization may depend on the phase in which the system finds itself, we should not ignore that the leaders of such regimes may opt between regarding political mobilization as desirable or preferring to rule without it. The option may reflect ideological predispositions and influences toward social change or arresting such change, but we should not consider this the only or decisive factor. In fact, we could argue that the choice will depend more on the opportunities offered by the social structure, the political context, and the international situation for a mobilization in support of those in power than on the outlook of the rulers. On the other side, the "outcomes," the capacity to do things, and the power for social change may in part depend on the capacity for sustained mobilization.

Thus on the one side we have regimes coming to power after periods of considerable organized political strife, lack of consensus under democratic governments, and aborted revolutions: all these will tend to use apathy to consolidate their power, at least the apathy of those not likely to be won over to their policies. The depolitization in these cases would be one way to reduce the tension in the society and achieve a minimum of re-integration, which otherwise could probably be reached only by totalitarian suppression of the dissidents. Privatization under authoritarian regimes has a certain parallel in the "internal migration" of totalitarianism, but differs in that this privatization is consciously or unconsciously encouraged by those in power. Such apoliticism would bar people from positions of power and influence in a totalitarian system; in some authoritarian regimes it is even valued as an asset, or so it is publicly claimed by persons appointed to high office who state they have never been actively involved in "politics." Referring to this depolitization some cynics have called the three F's—Fatima, football, and *fados* (folk songs)—the *arcana imperii* of Portugal.

On the other side we have regimes trying to gain control of societies in which the masses have never been mobilized by any political force, particularly if the preceding regime had been one of colonial rule, or a traditional monarchy, or even an oligarchic democracy. These situations are likely to coincide with underdeveloped rather than semideveloped societies, where the underprivileged masses have not given their loyalty to any organized movement, and consequently their manipulation is easy, at least initially. The populistic dictators of Latin America could create a certain mass base among workers that the supporters of Franco, even with socially progressive policies and demagogic appeals, would never have succeeded in creating given the previous history of Spain. The content of the policies might not depend as much on the desires of the rulers as on the opportunities for mobilization, shaped by previous history, economic and social development, and even the degree of pluralism and complexity of the society. Last but not least, the international situation of the country, the possibility to use or not to use a xenophobic appeal, rallying people of all classes and degrees of identification with the system, to a national cause might be decisive. Foreign pressure can maintain participation in an authoritarian system as nothing else can. After all, in Spain the last successful manifestations of mass participation were achieved when the United Nations exercised their pressure or under the cry of Spanish Gibraltar.

It would take too long to analyze here all the causes of low mobilization or our doubts about the capacity of such regimes to sustain a significant degree of mobilization for any length of time (without considerable changes in other respects—limitation of pluralism and emphasis on an ideology—in a totalitarian direction), but we may list at least some factors. In the absence of a modern revolutionary ideology, reformism, particularly bureaucratic and technocratic reformism, does not provide a chiliastic vision for action, and the structure of underdeveloped countries does not motivate sustained, regular day-to-day activity. Existent or emergent status differences are another obstacle; for example, the equalitarian Falangist *"tu,"* as distinct from the respectful *"usted"* as a form of address, was incompatible with differences in education and style of life, and slowly lost appeal. Pluralistic elements of authoritarian regimes resist mobilization as a threat to their distinct constituencies; so, for example, in Spain the church-controlled secondary education system prevented the creation of an effective, large-scale, youth organization across class lines; the women's organizations of the party had to compete with Catholic Action and the traditional welfare organizations like the Red Cross, and so on. Family loyalties, friendship, and other particularistic ties divert time and energy from politically inspired secondary groups. With social and economic change come the growth of private interests and the struggle to improve one's living standard. Only in a society where the government is the principal employer, or controls the economy as through cooperatives, can it offer financial rewards to the citizens who participate, but this does not insure that participation will be political; it may come to resemble participation in interest groups like those characterizing democratic society. Economic development and industrialization seem to be a precondition for a lively associational life under any system. [29] Limited literacy and low incomes are such obstacles that only the diversion of considerable resources can assure participation for any length of time.

Undoubtedly such social and structural factors may be overcome if the leadership is really committed to the idea of a mobilized society, as the Communist and, even to a minor extent, the Italian Fascist experiences show. The very different attitude of one typical authoritarian leader is well described in these comments of Macartney in writing about a Hungarian political leader in the twenties:

> He did not mean opposition ever to be in a position to seriously challenge his own will. But he did not think it any part of the duty of government to pry into and regiment each detail of the subject's conduct, much less his thoughts. For this he was too large-minded, or too cynical, too little a perfectionist. . . .[30]

This contrasts markedly with the activism of totalitarian systems, their many forms of participation: the 99 per cent referenda, and more importantly, the myriad of politically closed activities associated with women's organizations, Komsomol, Kraft durch Freude, factory committees, and so on. This widespread participation grows out of democratic ideology, whether of a rationalistic classless society or a classless Volksgemeinschaft. Some of these activities end in resembling those in democratic societies more than the totalitarian rulers wish, with the participants becoming hostile or indifferent to their political aspects, and therefore we may say that both democratic and totalitarian regimes encourage a participative rather than a parochial, or subject, political culture, to use the terms of Almond and Verba. [31] In totalitarian systems membership is either obligatory or necessary for success, in democracies there is generally a free choice among multiple groups.

In authoritarian regimes, intermediate systems are frequent: membership may be obligatory but involves nothing more than paying dues, or strictly voluntary without creating any advantages. Presumably political goals take primacy in totalitarian organizations while specific interests predominate in democratic organizations. In Spain, many voluntary associations linked with the party have been consciously depoliticized, as when the official youth organization discontinued its fascist accoutrements and substituted leadership training guides based on Kurt Lewin's experiments in democratic group climates and sociometry. (Changes in terminology were avoided, however, to avoid hurting old-timers' feelings.) In other cases like the SEU—the official student organization—free elections up to the faculty level have allowed even dissidents from the regime to occupy influential positions, something that certainly was not intended.

The depoliticization of officially created associations has certainly not been unique to Spain; with the "end of ideology," the politicization of interest and leisure groups characteristic of European democratic parties from the turn of the century to World War II has also receded. In fact it could be argued that authoritariansim provided a welcome relief from overpoliticization in democratic societies which had not developed apolitical voluntary associations in proportion to the number of fiercely conflicting political groups. An Italian metal worker in his fifties expressed this when he said of his working-class neighborhood in Genoa:

> I was born here. Then everyone used to know each other, we used to get together, loved each other. After the war came politics. Now we all hate each other. You are a Communist, I am a Socialist, he is a Demo-Christian. And so we avoid each other as much as possible. [32]

In fact, in countries like Spain we find a rapid and accelerated growth [33] of voluntary associations, necessarily not openly political and generally apolitical, in recent years, particularly in areas where their numbers had been smallest. In this sense some of Lavau's observations would also be applicable to the apoliticism of the masses in Spain. [34]

I would suggest that the closer an authoritarian regime is to pursuing either the totalitarian or democratic model, the greater will its efforts be toward some kind of mobilization. So the Spanish regime made greater efforts to organize mass meetings, parades, public ceremonies, in the Fascist-inspired period than today; while it has become more pluralistic, it has become less participative. Since both pluralism and participation characterize democratic polities, we can say that certain political systems are more or less "democratic," depending on which element we focus on; using participation as a criterion, Nazi Germany was relatively democratic; using pluralism, a regime like Horthy's, which was certainly not participative, could be termed relatively democratic.

The content of the policies being pursued, socially progressive or conservative, may have something to do with the degree of mobilization a regime encourages, but the social context in which such programs are enacted may have as much importance. I would not be surprised to find quite different degrees of mobilization even where economic development policies, expansion of education or mass media, and welfare state measures are quite similar. Still, I would agree that without such mobilization the introduction of such measures becomes more difficult and their socially integrative function may not be achieved.

The Authoritarian Party

According to the legal texts of many authoritarian regimes, their single parties occupy a similarly dominant position: to the totalitarian party monopolizing power, recruiting the elite, transmitting both the aspirations of the people and the directives of the leadership. [35] In fact, however, some regimes that in reality approach the totalitarian model legally have multi-party systems, while in others which are legally single party monopolies, the party plays a comparatively limited role. Therefore it is imperative to examine the authoritarian party in its sociological reality.

First and foremost, the authoritarian party is not a well-organized ideological organization which monopolizes all access to power. As we will see later, a considerable part of the elite has no connection with the party and does not identify with it. Party membership creates few visible advantages and imposes few, if any, duties. Ideological indoctrination is often minimal, the conformity and loyalty required may be slight, and expulsions and purges are not frequent and do not represent an important mechanism of social control. The party is often ideologically and socially heterogeneous. Far from branching out into many functional organizations, in an effort to control the state apparatus and penetrate other spheres of life as the Nazi party did, it is a skeleton organization of second-rate bureaucrats. The party becomes only one more element in the power pluralism; one more group pressing for particular interests; one more channel through which divergent interests try to find access to power; one more recruiting ground for elite members. [36] Since tight discipline lacks widespread ideological legitimacy, various functional groups that might have been transmission belts for the leadership's directives become apolitical interest groups or autonomous nuclei where a few activists, even those emerging from the grass roots, may follow independent policies.

The importance of the party has many indicators: the number of high officials that were active in the party before entering the elite; the membership figures; the degree of activity indicated by the party budget; agit-prop activity; the prestige or power accorded to party officials; the presence of party cells or representatives in other institutions; the importance of training centers; the attention paid to party organs and publications; the vigor of ideological polemics within the party factions. By all these criteria the Spanish party has never been too strong and today is obviously weak. A look at the party's provincial headquarters, in contrast to other government offices or the Sindicatos (a functional organization theoretically dependent on the party), should convince anyone of the party's second-rate role in Spain.

The different roles of the authoritarian and totalitarian parties may be explained by differences in their origin. Most single parties in authoritarian countries have been created after accession to power rather than before. [37] They have been created by fusing a variety of groups with different ideological traditions and varying social bases, not by completely subordinating some elements to one dominant force. Where politicians of other groupings, including the minor Fascist parties, have been co-opted, no disciplined, integrated organization emerged. In other cases, when the military dictator has tried to create a patriotic national unity organization, the effort was carried out by officers and bureaucrats, who typically do not have the demagogic skills needed to create a lively organization. They are further hampered because they continue devoting most of their attention to government or army offices, where real power, and not merely the promise of it, lies. The old politicians, rallying to organizations like the Imperial Rule Assistance Association [38] or the ex-CEDA (conservative-demochristian deputies in the Republic) leaders in the Falange, are not able to adopt the new style that a totalitarian party requires. Since the party is not tested in a struggle for power, it attracts more than its share of office seekers and opportunists, few idealists, true believers, real revolutionaries. Since its ideology is not defined, indoctrination of the numerous newcomers, entering en masse, is likely to be scanty, and the facts of life soon disillusion the more utopian. Since the primary staff need is to staff the state apparatus, the premium will be on recruiting professionals and bureaucrats, and not the armed intellectuals or bohemians, the marginal men that give the totalitarian movement its peculiar style.

The prominence of the army or civil service in the regime before the party was created, and the solidarity of these groups against newcomers when it comes to making key appointments, make the rewards of party activity less appealing than membership in the NSDAP or, later, the SS. In underdeveloped countries the army is particularly important, since it does not like the rise of rivals and will seek to prevent the creation of anything like party militias or workers' guards. Any attempt to build up the party beyond a certain point, particularly after the German experience, is likely to encounter the open opposition of the army, as Perón soon discovered. In Spain the relation between party and army during the forties was not without tension and the overlap in leadership was used to bridge the gap, but from the beginning a law giving all army officers party membership gave them the opportunity (never exercised) to control the party directly. [39] A comment by Serrano Suñer, former chairman of the Junta Politica of the party, describes the relation between army and political groups in many such regimes:

> In the last analysis the center of gravity, the true support of the regime (despite all the appearances which we foolishly try to exaggerate) was and would continue to be the army; the nationalist army—an army that was not politically defined. [40]

In some regimes the fact that the leader, an army officer or politician·with army support like Salazar, was not the leader of a party before assuming power makes for an ambivalent and uneasy relation between the pre-existing parties now subordinated to his leadership. Their identification with the program and ideology is weak; the leader lacks charismatic appeal for the members; his personal ties with the subgroup leaders are likely to be uneven, even when he succeeds in creating them as Franco has done to a large extent. General Antonescu's relation with the Iron Guard, Pétain's with various nationalistic and fascist political groups, are examples of this. Nasser's difficulties with the Baathists in Syria are another.

Forms of Social Control

Similarities between authoritarian regimes and the totalitarians can perhaps go furthest in the control of mass media, particularly in countries in the process of modernization where the technological and capital requirements for setting up the media make such control very easy. Media may vary greatly in autonomy, even under the same regime, but limited pluralism readily creates some islands of exemption; in Spain, for example, church publications are free from government censorship.

The small size of the elite and the persistence within the regime of ties created prior to it, allow for considerable free communication, unless the regime is willing to use a good deal of coercion. The same may be said of contacts with other countries, particularly by the elite. While the monopoly of mass media may be as great as that in totalitarian societies, the impact of this monopoly is less because it is not enhanced by intensive personal propagandizing through agitators and other informal leaders. Even when the freedom of the press is curtailed, truly totalitarian control is not present if there is freedom of travel and, at least, freedom of conversation. (As long as one does not make more than five copies of one's opinions, one cannot be prosecuted for illegal propaganda in Spain.) It may well be that the excesses of control to which a Stalin or Hitler went are really unnecessary.

Terror and police control figure prominently among the characteristics of totalitarianism listed by Friedrich, Brzezinski, Arendt, and others, as they should in view of the recent Hitlerian and Stalinist experiments. However, recent tendencies toward "socialist legality" may reduce this; and the need for political justice or terror in democracies during crisis situations, while not comparable in volume, suggests that this may not be a good distinction between various types of political systems. Undoubtedly there are differences in the ways in which coercion is used. Whatever repressive practices a democracy may resort to, they are more a reflection of public opinion than of government policy, and the importance of civil rights for the functioning of the system put serious limits to their extension beyond a crisis situation. In authoritarian regimes the existing legal barriers may be weak (though not to be discounted), but the equilibrium of forces on which limited pluralism is based may be a serious restraint. While repression of the system's open enemies may go far, dissenters within the coalition, or potential members of it, must be handled with more care. While in totalitarian systems members of the elite have often been punished with great harshness, and the setting of examples in show trials has been frequent, in authoritarian regimes exile, kicking upstairs, retirement to private life are more frequent.

While Arendt [41] could perceive no decrease in terror, in fact an increase, after the totalitarian consolidation of power, we may argue that after the birth pangs of an authoritarian regime are over it may relax. The absence of full ideological self-righteousness is an important restraint. Another is the presence in the elite of men who have held power under states of law and are themselves lawyers; or, if military, they share at least the military conception of law: legalism may not inhibit repression of the State's enemies, but it does lead to certain procedural rules, to an emphasis on actions rather than intentions. The importance of the armed forces limits the political autonomy and development of the police apparatus; its concern is with actual rather than merely potential opponents. The less dynamic character of such regimes also tends to make the use of force less necessary. The distinction between society and politics, private and public life; limited party membership means information about citizens is also limited, and consequently so is control. Without a "Blockwart"—the Nazi party representative in each dwelling area—gossip available for control purposes is reduced.

The Position of the Military

All political systems face the problem of subordinating the military to political authority, and once military dictators start devoting their energies to political problems, they face the same issue. Methods of controlling the military differ in democracies, totalitarian systems, and authoritarian regimes; the equilibrium established between political and military authority will differ as well. In most authoritarian regimes the limited popular consensus, which made such forms of rule necessary or possible in the first place, means there is more need for potential force; this gives the army a privileged position. Normally military affairs are left to military men and not to civilians. The absence of a mass party, and in some countries of a trustworthy and specialized bureaucracy, often leads to the use of military men in political appointments, patronage positions, and the administration. The technical branches provide experts for public service or nationalized industries. Nationalism as a simple ideology, easily shared by all classes, makes for an emphasis on the army as a bearer of national prestige. If the break with the past was made by a military coup, the position of the army is likely to be even more enhanced.

> The army is the shield of Egypt. . . . It carries the responsibility of a heavy and difficult duty . . . the task represented in its defense of the nation against external foes . . . the defense of the nation against internal exploitation and domination. [42]

On the other hand we find the army presented as essentially apolitical, above parties and classes, hoping to transfer its powers to the "people" once order is re-established and the corruption of the previous regime cleaned out. In the manifestos and speeches of the first period of the regime's rise to power, we find expressions like the following:

> Everybody knows that I did not initiate the movement with any political objective. I have never been interested in politics nor did I ever think of representing the supreme power of the nation. If at the head of my comrades I raised the national flag I did it only as a patriot and soldier. One cannot judge that way, because there is no army that struggles alone. Our revolution would have failed from the first moment due to lack of interest on the part of the civilian population, if it had only been a military uprising. (Franco, 1938). [43]

> I imagined that the whole nation was on tiptoes and prepared for action. . . . After July 23rd I was shocked by the reality. The vanguard performed its task; it stormed the wall of the fort of tyranny . . . and stood by expecting the mass formations to arrive. . . . It waited and waited. Endless crowds showed up, but how different is the reality from the vision. . . . We needed action but found nothing but surrender and idleness. (Nasser). [44]

In such regimes emerging from a military action, the army may enjoy a privileged position and hold on to key positions, but it soon co-opts politicians, civil servants, and technicians who increasingly make most decisions. [45] The more a regime becomes consolidated, the fewer purely military men staff the government, except when there are no alternative sources of elites. In this sense it may be misleading to speak of a military dictatorship, even when the head of state is an army man. In fact he is likely to carry out a careful policy of depoliticization and professionalization of the army, while he maintains close ties with the officer corps to hold its loyalty. [46]

The military background of key men in authoritarian regimes, and their usual lack of ideological sophistication, make it particularly important to understand the military mentality in relation to internal politics, to styles of political life, conceptions of authority, ideas about cost versus results, legitimate forms of expressing grievances, and so on. [47] The few studies on the role of the military in politics have only raised the issue; real data are still to be assembled.

Authoritarian Regimes and Weber's Types of Legitimacy

Due to the prominent role of the leader in authoritarian regimes, there is some temptation to identify them with charismatic rule. However, we would like to argue that Max Weber's categories can and should be used independently of the distinction between democracy, authoritarianism, and totalitarianism. Within each of these systems the legitimacy of the ruler, for the population or his staff, can be based on one or another of these types of belief.

Undoubtedly charisma has played an important role for masses and staff under Hitler [48] and Lenin; totalitarian regimes have also made demands on their civil service, based on legal authority; and democratic prime ministers have enjoyed charisma. Authoritarian regimes may also have a charismatic element, since they often come into being during serious crisis situations, and control of the mass media facilitates the creation of an "image" of the unique leader. Genuine belief in charisma is likely to be limited, however, since the man assuming leadership was often unknown before, and to his fellow officers is often a *primus inter pares,* who owes his position often simply to rank. With notable exceptions—Perón or Nasser—the modern army as a rational institution does not breed the irrational leadership type, full of passion, demagogic, convinced of his mission. He is not likely to have, at least for his fellow officers and collaborators, the same appeal that a Lenin or a Hitler could have for those who initiated with him, as marginal men, the long hard struggle for power.

At the same time limited pluralism and the lack of ideological self-right-

eousness allow more room for the development of general rules institutional-
izing the exercise of power, and there is thus a trend toward the secularization
of whatever charisma was acquired during crisis. This transition to legal authority has been emphasized in the case of the Spanish regime by one of its
leading political theorists and is even reflected in legal texts. [49] Staffing the
system with officers and civil servants, rather than the "old shirts" of street
fighting days, contributes to the growth of legalism.

Authoritarian regimes may come to power as de facto authorities with little
legitimacy and develop some charismatic appeal; but they end in a mixture of
legal, charismatic, and traditional authority. The low level of mobilization may
often mean that large parts of the population remain in the position of subjects,
recognizing agents of power without questioning their legitimacy; for them
habit and self-interest may be more important, and belief unnecessary for effective control.

Traditional and Authoritarian Regimes

One question some of our readers raise is: Aren't many such regimes really
only a form of autocratic and conservative rule like we find in preconstitutional
and traditional monarchies? It would be foolish to deny that the distinctions are
fluid, that a number of authoritarian regimes have emerged out of such political forms, and that the formal constitutional framework may still be a monarchical one. However, we want to stress that we would not want to include in
our concept any political system which would strictly fit under the concept of
traditional authority in Weber's sense and where rule is based on historical
continuity, impersonal familial or institutionalized charisma or various mixtures
of patrimonial or feudal rule—using these terms in a somewhat technical
sense. [50] To make it clear, neither Abyssinia, nor Yemen before the recent
revolution, nor Tibet, Afghanistan, nor some of the other political entities along
the Himalayan border, fit our concept, to mention contemporary systems. Nor
would the prerevolutionary European absolute monarchies of the past. Authoritarian regimes are a likely outcome of the breakdown of such traditional forms
of legitimacy. This results from a partial social and political mobilization and a
questioning of the traditional principles of legitimacy (largely due to their secularization) by significant segments of the society. Authoritarian systems—
even those we might call reactionary—are modernizing in the sense that
they represent a discontinuity with tradition, introducing criteria of efficiency
and rationality, personal achievement and populistic appeals. It should not
be forgotten that the regimes we call royal dictatorships in Southeastern
Europe were created by kings with very limited traditional legitimacy and that

those kings who supported dictators, as did Alphonso XIII in Spain, Victor Emmanuel III in Italy, and several mideastern monarchs, lost their thrones, giving way to democratic republics or authoritarian regimes without a king. The enormous ambivalences surrounding the legitimacy of the Iranian monarchy [51] that was restored by an authoritarian military leader, Reza Pahlevi, are obvious and certainly would not allow this monarchy to be regarded as a purely traditional regime. The attempts of the present Spanish regime to find its constitutional and legitimacy form as a traditional monarchy certainly suggest the difficulties encountered when moving from an authoritarian regime to a traditional one. There can be no doubt that many of those who are willing to recognize the claims to legitimate rule of Franco would not transfer their allegiance to a traditional monarchy. In our times authoritarian rule almost inevitably leads to questioning traditional authority, if for no reason than by making the people aware of the importance of the effective head of the government and its secular character. Authoritarian rule might be an intermediate stage in or after the breakdown of traditional authority, but not the route toward its restoration. To specify further the differences would take us at this time too far from the Spanish case.

This might be the place to stress a very important characteristic of many, if not most, authoritarian regimes: the coexistence in them of different legitimizing formulae. [52] The actual pluralism of such regimes, and the lack of effective legitimate institutionalization of that pluralism within a single legitimate political formula allowing competition of the pluralistic elements for power, almost inevitably lead to the coexistence of competing legitimacy formulae. So in the case of Spain the traditionalist monarchy desired by the Carlists, a restoration of the pre-1931 monarchy, some form of Catholic corporativism like the present regime under monarchical (or even republican) form, a more dynamic totalitarian vision along fascist lines, even a transition to a democratic republic under Christian democratic leadership, are all different formulas open to the supporters of the regime. These supporters give their support in the hope that the regime will satisfy their aspirations, and they withdraw their support in so far as they realize that the regime is not doing so, or is unable to do so. If we had more space we could develop some of the parallels with Binder's description of the Iranian situation.

Fortunately for many such systems, the great mass of the population in semi- or under-developed societies is not concerned with the legitimizing formulae. Instead the population obeys out of a mixture of habit and self-interest, [53] either characterizing the political culture of passive subjects or the parochial (to use the terminology of Almond and Verba). [54] The confusion concerning the sources of legitimacy inherent in many such regimes contributes much of the confusion and pessimism of those most likely to be politically involved. Because of this often the more privileged and those close to the centers of power may appear more alienated from the regime than they really are (at least for all practical purposes). This can help to explain the relative stability of many such systems despite the freedom with which criticism is expressed. The identification with such regimes may not be found in their political formulas, but in the identification with the basic values of the society, its stratification system, and many nonpolitical institutions, which are their infrastructure.

II

Defining authoritarian regimes as a particular type of political system is only useful if we can show that such regimes handle the invariant problems of any political system in a distinctive way. We have already made passing reference to problems like the control of the armed forces, the problem of loyalty, etc., but it may be useful to focus in more detail on a few examples. One is the recruitment and characteristics of the political elite. Another set of questions can be asked about the conditions under which such regimes are likely to emerge and to be stable. Finally, a third set of problems appears when we consider the dynamics of such regimes: whether they will turn totalitarian or democratic, and under what conditions.[55]

The Authoritarian Elite

Let us start with a very specific problem: who constitutes the top elite in authoritarian regimes?

Limited pluralism makes the authoritarian elite less homogeneous than that of the totalitarian system in ideology and political style, and probably in career patterns and background as well. This does not mean that the personalities will be more forceful or colorful. The lieutenants of the totalitarian leader, who rose with him in the struggle for power, often share the demagogic qualities, the marginality and uniqueness, that frequently characterize him; brilliant intellectuals and journalists appear as ideologists in the totalitarian elite's first generation. In contrast, many in the authoritarian elite are less colorful, brilliant or popular; their military, professional, and bureaucratic backgrounds do not breed such qualities.

In a sense both the democratic and totalitarian top elites are composed fundamentally of professional politicians, who live through if not for politics. In the totalitarian first generation, the decisive step was to join the party before it came to power; in most democratic countries there is a slow *cursus honorum* through elected or appointed offices, particularly when the parties are bureaucratized and well organized. The second generation of the totalitarian elite may combine a career in the party apparatus with some technical specialization, as reflected in the expression: "He did party work in agriculture." Research on totalitarian leadership has underscored its marginality [56] in terms of regional origin, religious affiliation, social mobility, stable work life and so on. In contrast, a significant part of the authoritarian regime's leadership had already participated actively in the country's political life as parliamentarians, and through seniority in the army, civil service, or academic world would have been assured a respectable position in the society under any regime. Given the nonideological character of much authoritarian politics, the emphasis on respectability and expertise, and the desire to co-opt elements of established society, a number of those assuming power will have little previous involvement in politics. Occasionally, particularly at the second level, we find people who define themselves publicly as apolitical, just experts. The old fighters of the extremist groups which contributed to the crisis of the previous regime, who participated in the take-over, who hoped to take power, may find their claims rejected, and will have to content themselves with secondary positions. In some cases their political style, their ideological commitments, their exclusivism, may lead them to break away and retire to private life. This has been the destiny of many Falangist and extreme Carlist leaders under Franco.

Participation in the single party may not be a requisite for entering the elite, but it can be quite helpful combined with other qualifications: a brilliant academic or civil service career, identification with other groups in the pluralistic system such as religio-political interest groups. Such multiple affiliations give the elite member wider contacts and legitimize him in the eyes of the groups that will find themselves represented through him. Some biographies of members of Franco's cabinet, described later, will illustrate this point.

Since both totalitarian and democratic governments want to mobilize opinion, intellectuals play an important role as journalists and ideologists. Lasswell and Lerner have stressed that skill in the use of symbols is decisive. In Spain the only effective journalist in the cabinet was there as a minister without portfolio immediately after the war; a minister of labor with demagogic abilities held the ministry until 1957. Both came from the fascist wing of the system. The more rightist an authoritarian regime, the less place is there for the non-professional, nonacademic intelligentsia. Without careful research it is difficult to know if some authoritarian regimes which are described as progressive owe their image to such men; their policies may actually not differ greatly from others not enjoying the same reputation.

Despite their tendency to elect national heroes, in democracies normally only a minority of nonmilitary posts are occupied by officers, and even the defense ministries are often held by civilians. In totalitarian systems a politically neutralized or indoctrinated army may control its own affairs, but few key positions outside that realm are held by military men. Authoritarian regimes that emerge as "commissary dictatorships" (to use Carl Schmitt's expression for those whose intent is to re-establish "order" and then transfer power to the constitutional government) tend to be, initially, exclusively or almost exclusively military: the classical junta. There, a balanced representation of the services, rank, seniority, are more important than personality or political beliefs. If such a regime retains power, shifts are likely to take place, either through reinforcement of a faction like the Free Officers of Egypt or through the co-optation of civilians, as in the regime of Primo de Rivera, Franco, and Perón. These civilians may be professional politicians (as in Eastern Europe during the interwar years), civil servants or experts (Calvo Sotelo in Spain and Salazar in Portugal entered this way), leaders of interest groups or religious organizations (like Artajo, the lay head of Spanish Catholic Action in 1945), or Fascists willing to forgo a state dominated by a single party. Soon the balance of power may shift considerably toward the civilian element, which may even assume leadership as Salazar did, but it is unlikely that the equilibrium between civil and military power will be established at the same level as before. The absence of a relatively large, disciplined, dynamic revolutionary party, or the weakness or death of its leadership, is decisive for the establishment in this period of an authoritarian rather than a totalitarian regime. This was the case in Spain with the death of José Antonio (who probably never would have been a real totalitarian leader in any case) and the weakness and dissension in Falangist leadership described so well by Payne. In Rumania, one of the most authentic and revolutionary Fascist parties had to play second fiddle in the regime of Marshal Antonescu after losing its leader Codreanu, finally to be ousted after four months of collaboration. The strength of the party also decides if the men co-opted from other groups will be able to maintain some degree of pluralism.

The persistence of the pre-crisis social order that goes with limited pluralism and co-optation means that the legal professions, so important in democratic politics and even under traditional rulers, will play a much greater role in authoritarian regimes than in totalitarian systems. The same is true of civil ser-

vants. Their presence may contribute to the strange combination of Rechtsstaat and arbitrary power, of slow legalistic procedure and military command
style, that characterizes some of these regimes. This preoccupation with
procedure ultimately becomes an important factor in the constant expansion
of a state of law, with an increase in predictability and opportunities for legal
redress of grievances. At the same time it may prevent political problems from
being perceived as such, irreducible to administrative problems and not sol-
uble by legislation. Legal procedures are often seen, particularly in the continental legal tradition, as an adequate equivalent of more collective, political
expressions of interest conflicts. [57]

Stability and Change: Patterns of Entry

The top elite of an authoritarian regime, despite its limited pluralism, is likely to
be more limited both numerically and in shades of opinion than the spectrum
of government and opposition in democracies. The existence of a loyal opposition, and the greater dispersion of power, facilitates the training and emergence of new leaders. Limited pluralism allows new personalities to emerge in
the shadows, but their political experience is often inhibited. This slows down
renewal of leadership, and each successive generation is likely to have an
even smaller activated constituency than those of the original group. The emphasis on stability and continuity in such regimes, one of their main claims to
legitimacy against the previous "unstable" democratic system, also contributes to slow renewal. On the other hand a change in the elite's composition
can go on more silently and smoothly than under totalitarianism, where
changes in leadership are associated with crisis. Turnover in authoritarian
elites can take place without purges, by retiring people to secondary or honorary positions, if not to private life. The following incident illustrates how, even
in the case of serious disagreement, a minimum of good manners is maintained within the elite: when two ministers were dropped from the Spanish
regime's elite, the official announcement of the dismissal omitted the customary formula "thanking you for services rendered"; but a few days later a
"corrected" version, including the phrase, was published. [58]

Venomous hatred of defeated elite members is not always absent, but the
lack of ideological clarity, of self-righteousness, contribute to making this
infrequent. On the other hand the more pluralistic, open structure of society
may help make the loss of power less painful.

While the elite is relatively open, predictable ways of entry are lacking,
which frustrates the ambitions of many. Because competition for power is not
institutionalized effectively, paths to it are obscure: neither devoted partisan

service and ideological conformity nor a steady career through elected office is available. Success in nonpolitical spheres, identification with groups like religious associations, particularistic criteria of who knows whom, even accident, may be more important. These processes, which incidentally do not necessarily lead to the selection of incompetent people, exist in all systems, but normally they coexist with more universalistic recruitment criteria. With the increasing complexity of industrial society and increasing emphasis on achievement criteria, universalistic standards are used more and more, but there is no purposive planned cadre training or recruitment through youth organizations, party schools, and so on such as the totalitarians employ. When the educational system is class biased, this depolitization of the elite results in less equalitarian recruitment than that afforded by totalitarianism; formally no one is excluded, but in fact educational requirements exclude many. On the other hand, authoritarian regimes with their universalistic bureaucratic recruitment may be more open than conservative or bourgeois parties in a society at the same level of economic development. But as Kornhauser has rightly noted: ease of entry into elites, and ability to exert influence on them, are not the same thing and may not even vary together.[59]

The first generation totalitarian elite, having come to power together in a revolutionary group, are likely to represent the same generation and to be younger than their democratic counterparts. Authoritarian leadership is likely to be more heterogeneous, combining younger elements (who may have sought a more revolutionary regime) with older men co-opted into the system because of their experience or symbolic value. Obviously the age composition of an elite is likely to differ, depending on whether we are dealing with the period immediately after the conquest of power or years later when the revolutionary group has consolidated its position. From a sociological point of view it is the age at which the group first obtained office that matters. A very interesting problem is how each type of regime handles the problem of recruitment and succession. One interesting feature of the Franco regime, not unrelated to its pluralism, has been its ability to bring a significant number of younger men into the elite. This is the more surprising when we recall that the political channels for selection and socialization into politics, youth organizations, and the party are so undeveloped. Though this very fact enhances recruitment of the young, since it makes political careers less of a *cursus honorum*. So in the present cabinet there are two men, one of them playing an important role, who were under 17 when the Civil War ended. The average of the "victory cabinet" (1939) was 46.1 years, but most have tended to be slightly older; the average for all ministers from 1938 to 1957 at the time of assuming office was 50.5.

Significantly, the average for the Republican ministerial elite was 50.8; in terms of age the Franco regime did not mean a great change, compared to that represented by the younger Peronist cabinets. The average age of the Nazi top hierarchy in 1933 was appreciably younger: 41.9 years, as we would expect in a revolutionary elite. It is only natural that in Spain the Minister Secretary General of the Movement should have, generally, the youngest member (average age 41), while the military ministries where seniority counts have been close to or above the middle fifties.

Political Pluralism in the Elite of the Franco Regime

I   *The Cabinet.* Using some data on the top Spanish elite, I hope to illustrate and to some extent support some of the points made above. The most important decision-making body is the cabinet, both as a collective body and as individual members each in his area of competence. While cabinet members are not equally powerful, they all have control of significant sectors of administrative policy making, and have taken strong initiative in legislative processes. It therefore seems legitimate to concentrate on cabinet members, from the first appointed in 1938 to the last sworn in the summer of 1962, to explore elite pluralism. The number of persons involved is 67, though the number of incumbencies is higher since many have been holdovers from one government to the next and several have held different ministries at one time or another.

Let us start with the political orientations of these men, their former party affiliations, and the groups they may be said to represent (Table 7-1). Since these identifications, a good index of pluralism, are not announced, and political allegiances are not always stable, this involves certain risks. Nevertheless, such classifications are made by participants themselves, as the memoirs of Serrano Suñer reveal. [60] Similarly, Arrese describes how, in a cabinet crisis, Falangists asked for and received various portfolios. [61]

Of the total, 39 per cent have been army officers; a number of them can be classified as pro-Falangist, pro-Traditionalist, or pro-monarchico-conservative, but their primary identification probably continues to be the army; in the case of 24 per cent no political tendency could be assigned easily. In order not to overestimate the role of the army, it is important to note that of the 26 military in the cabinet, 15 have held defense ministries. Professionals and civil servants without any particular group affiliations number at least 10, or 15 per cent. The Falange, in the strict sense, has contributed 17 members, or 25 per cent, of whom only 8 had no other identification prior to the Civil War. Another 4 had been members of the CEDA (Gil Robles' center-right Catholic party) or close to demo-Christian organizations; four could be considered technical with

TABLE 7-1

Political Background or Identification of Members of the Spanish Cabinet (1938 to 1962)

	Total	% of
Falange:		
Falange with no previous political background	8	12%
Falange with CEDA background	5	7
Technical with Falangist orientation	4	6
Total Falange	17	25
Traditionalist	3	4.5
Accion Española and non-traditionalist Monarchist	2	3
Civil figure of the Primo de Rivera dictatorship	3	4.5
Political Catholicism	3	4.5
Opus Dei	3	4.5
Technical or civil service apolitical	10	15
Military:		
With Falangist leanings	3	4.5
With Traditionalist leanings	1	1.5
With Accion Española or Opus Dei ties	2	3
With CEDA background	2	3
Former office holders under Primo de Rivera	2	3
With no particular identification	16	24
Total Military	26	39
Total	67	100%

Falangist leanings. The other official part of the fused party, the Traditionalists (heirs of the nineteenth-century dynastic and ideological conflict between the liberals and the legitimist-Catholic-conservatives) held three posts, particularly the Ministry of Justice where they could enact the pro-clerical legislation in many mixed matters. Three civil figures who were already present in the Primo de Rivera dictatorship (1923-1930) together with two military of that period represent an important element of continuity. The small group of Acción Española, inspired largely by the Action Française of the 1930's, contributes several members, some of whom I have included in other groups with which they were later more closely identified. The CEDA, a party that in the February 1936 election was the second largest in Parliament with 88 of 473 seats, contributes 3 of its deputies, 2 of them military, and 1 (Serrano Suñer) turned Falangist. Three other important figures are closely identified with the ACNDP (Acción Catolica Nacional de Propagandistas), a small elite group of political Catholics. From this group came a younger professor who as minister of education followed an interesting policy of liberalization.

Let us take the biography of Martín Artajo as an interesting illustration of the representation process. He was born in 1905; his father was a member of Parliament under the monarchy; he studied law, graduating summa cum laude, and was president of the Catholic student federation. At 24 he became a *letrado del Consejo de Estado (maître des requêtes)*. In 1934 he participated in a congress of corporative studies in Vienna. He was a member of the ACNDP and before 1936 was Secretary General of Catholic Action. During the war he was on the staff of the military junta's labor commission and of the Ministry of Labor. He was minister of foreign affairs from 1945 to 1957, and up to 1945 had been president of the board of the Catholic publishing trust. His brother was a CEDA deputy; another brother is a Jesuit.

The following excerpts of a letter from the present Cardinal Primate at the time of his dismissal in 1957 illustrate the sense in which he can be said to represent various Catholic groups:

> [Though] I expressed . . . yesterday how praiseworthy [and] effective your action has been in your 12 years as Minister of Foreign Affairs . . . I don't want to leave your letter unanswered. . . . in it you recall that in 1945 you asked my advice about accepting the ministry, and without any doubt I thought I should advise your acceptance, which I expected would result in the common good of the Fatherland and of the Church. Thanks be to God, events have confirmed these hopes. [He goes on listing the minister's achievements in international politics, particularly those in the area of relations between Church and state, mentioning for example the Concordat.] Spanish Catholic Action, of whose Technical Committee your Excellency was respected president, has been honored by your period of office in the ministry of Foreign Affairs, proving by your outstanding example that out of it [Catholic Action] there can come respectable and efficient public officials. [62]

Martin Artajo represents the kind of politician we would find in the right wing of the Italian Christian Democrats, and his affiliations for a lifetime have been of this kind. He was in effect the nonelected representative of certain religious groups. In a cabinet with men of quite different background, he was one element of pluralism. His success in public life would have been almost as certain in a democracy with a Christian Democratic party, and I am certain he does not exclude even that possibility.

There are other men whose background is in itself "pluralistic" and whose success is not unrelated to that pluralism. Take the present minister of finance. Born in a forlorn provincial village in 1914, he studied law, volunteered in the army and became a captain in shock troops. After the war he became an army lawyer through competitive examinations (his rank is now lieutenant colonel) and again through competition became technical secretary of the Sindicatos (corporative structure). He too is a *letrado del Consejo de Estado,* with a top mark in the examination. For some time he was on the board of a bank, and close to the Opus Dei, a very special type of religious group. Then from the undersecretariat of public works he went to finance. In his career he has established ties with the army, the corporative structure controlled by the party, a highly prestigeful group in the civil service, and an ideologically conservative but technocratically oriented Catholic elite group.

In recent cabinets other members or sympathizers of the Opus Dei, a religious secular institute, have played a part; at present at least three ministers and several army men may be so identified. [63]

Occupational Background. A large proportion (42 per cent) have a law degree, but in the Republic this proportion was even larger; 56 per cent (Table 7-2). Many of them were in two of the grand corps of the administration, the Letrados del Consejo de Estado (5) and the Abogados del Estado (6), among them some of the most powerful figures of the regime. The Abogados of the Estado contributed one out of 86 cabinet members during the Republic, while some of the slightly less prestigeful sectors of the civil service contributed more. An interesting datum in support of the multiple affiliations thesis is the number (4) of men coming from the legal service of the armed forces, a dual affiliation that must have furthered their career.

The academic world is represented by 8 (12 per cent) university professors, fewer than in the Republic which had 17, or 20 per cent. But the real change reflecting the lesser importance of the intelligentsia in the regime is the absence, with but two exceptions, of the secondary and primary educational system representatives. In summary the teaching professions contribute 13 per cent, while they made up 30 per cent of the cabinet between 1931 and 1936. The health professions that contributed 8 men to the Republican cabinets, reflecting the leftist-laicist orientation of the medical profession in much of Europe, are absent. In contrast, naturally reflecting the more technical tasks of

TABLE 7—2

Occupational Background of Cabinet Members of the Spanish
Republic (April 1931 to July 17, 1936) and the Franco Regime
(Multiple occupations are coded if important)

	Republic		Franco Regime	
Legal professions:				
Letrado del Consejo de Estado	1		5	
Abogado del Estado	5		6	
Notario or Registrador de la propiedad	7		1	
Diplomats	3		—	
Ministerio Fiscal	2		—	
Juridico militar (legal staff of the				
armed forces)	—		4	
Judge and judicial secretary	5		—	
Legal but not public official	25		12	
Total with legal background	48	56%	28	42%
Academic and teaching:				
University professor	17		8	
Public secondary education	1		1	
Commerce	1		1	
Other higher education	4		—	
Primary school teacher	3		—	
Total	26	30%	10	13%
Engineering	4		8	
Architecture	2		1	
Total	6	7%	9	13%
Medicine and other health professions:				
Physician	6		—	
Pharmacist	1		—	
Veterinarian	1		—	
Total	8	9%	—	
Journalism	21	25%	3	4%
Economics and political science	1	1%	3	4%
Military:				
Navy in the navy ministry	2		4	
Army and Air Force in a defense ministry	2		11	
Subtotal	4	5%	15	22%

TABLE 7—2 (continued)

	Republic		Franco Regime	
Navy and military in other ministries	—		11	
Total	4	5%	26	39%
Business	1	1%	3	4%
Manual Worker	1	1%	—	
Total	(86)	100%	(67)	100%

the government, the proportion of engineers and architects has increased from 7 per cent to 13 per cent. One of the greatest changes is the proportion of journalists: almost one fourth of the ministers of the Republic, but only a small minority (3) of those in the present regime would mention this as a major activity.

Military men holding civilian ministries constitute an important group, numbering 11, or 16 per cent; among them were a general secretary of the party, the undersecretary of the presidency, and a naval engineer who had a decisive role in the creation of the INI (Instituto Nacional de Industria), the state-owned industrial complex.

It would be interesting to continue with the analysis of the changes in the top elite, the early pluralism of the Consejo Nacional, the absence from the top elite, years later, of the Student Movement's youthful politicians, the rise of the technicians, etc., but the examples given so far must suffice.

II   The Elite in General. The political pluralism indicated by the data on the cabinet extends throughout the entire elite. Arrese, when he was secretary general of the party, presented in 1956 to the party's National Council some proposals for new constitutional laws that were received very critically. He felt compelled to defend himself against those who saw these proposals as an attempt by the party to gain greater strength. He wrote that "since some councilors have alluded to the excessive role of the original group of the Falange and of the JONS in the positions of the State and of the Movement," he would give the backgrounds of all levels of the elite at the time by their political origin before July 18, 1936. He stresses the following figures as the share of the Falange:

2 of 16 cabinet members	12.5%
1 of 17 undersecretaries	6.0
8 of 102 director generals	7.8
18 of 50 provincial governors (who are also heads of the provincial party organizations)	36.0

8	of	50 mayors of provincial capitals	16.0
6	of	50 presidents of provincial chambers	12.0
65	of	151 national councillors of the party	43.0
137	of	575 members of the legislature	24.0
133	of	738 provincial deputies	18.0
776	of	9155 mayors	8.4
2226	of	55,960 municipal councillors	9.0

Arrese continues:

> I don't say this to make anyone despair, nor to justify anything, but for the benefit of so many speculators of politics who give as an explanation for not joining the Movement the worn-out excuse that the Falange did not leave a place for their honest desire to collaborate. [64]

In official circles one may hear persons described as "of the regime but not of the Movement," "Falangist but not of the Movement," "Falangist against the Regime," "of the regime but apolitical," and so on through a vast variety of possible combinations which no one would say are meaningless descriptions of political views.

The Dynamics of Authoritarian Regimes. As a final point, let us turn to the dynamics of authoritarian regimes. It could be argued that they are unstable hybrids, subject to pressures and pulls in the direction of democracy or totalitarianism. Undoubtedly their limited ideological creativity makes them unattractive to those who look for logical consistency, meaning, and purpose in political life, for real ideals even at great sacrifice. The intellectuals, the young, those intolerant of ambiguity, soon became disillusioned and turned to the two great political myths of our time, which are represented by the major powers of the world. The unfulfilled promises of authoritarianism may make them more susceptible to totalitarianism, which they believe to be more efficient and idealistic; the immobility of limited pluralism has already disillusioned some of them about the chances of speedy, far-reaching reform under pluralism. Ideological elements from revolutionary movements like fascism and Marxism are a source of tension when incorporated in such regimes and used as standards against which to measure their performance and their pragmatic, often dull, politics. In other cases instability comes from long-standing ideological commitments to constitutional democracy, to which the regime has had to pay lip service, as in most of Latin America. The same is true in new countries where authoritarianism was introduced with the promise of preparing the ground for democracy, as in Turkey after World War I and now in the new states styling themselves "guided," "basic," or "presidentialist" democracies. Another source of tension is felt in countries relying on Catholic organic social theories;

shifts in church policy may subject them to pressure. However, one should not overestimate the impact of ideological pulls, and instead pay some attention to the economic and social factors contributing to the stability of such regimes. After all, some of them have lasted several decades, even in the face of considerable hostility.

If we were to accept the interpretation that such regimes lie on a continuum between democracy and totalitarianism, we should find many examples of transitions from authoritarianism to one or the other without serious crises or revolutionary changes. This however does not seem to be the case; even when the transition to some kind of democracy has been done with little bloodshed, the democracy has often been unstable. Evolutionary cases are rare—Atatürk's Turkey and Vargas' Estado Novo come to mind and the process would deserve serious study. An initial commitment to democratic ideals, and self-definition as a preparatory stage for democracy, seem relevant, as the border-line case of Mexico also shows. Transitions to totalitarianism have not been frequent either unless we agree with the German conservatives (as I would not) that Hitler in 1933 was really pursuing an "autoritärer Staat," rather than a Nazi revolution. Another possible case would be Cuba, if we assume that Castro was initially willing to stop at a left-pluralist authoritarian system and not pursue totalitarianism. Perhaps Peronism is the most interesting case of a shift toward a more totalitarian conception from what was originally a military dictatorship. Political sociology should devote increasing attention to such problems of transition from one system to another, in the way that Bracher and his collaborators have offered a model for the breakdown of Weimar democracy and the process of *Machtergreifung*.

Another question is whether totalitarian regimes, whose transformation into the Western type of democracy no one expects, will look more like some of the present authoritarian regimes if their ideological impetus is weakened, apathy and privatization replace mobilization, and bureaucracies and managers gain increasing independence from the party. Some such tendencies are in sight and undoubtedly the difference between some authoritarian regimes and the Soviet Union today is less than in the Stalinist period. I would even venture to say that a country like Poland seems more authoritarian than totalitarian, but my knowledge of that system is too superficial to document this idea.

A dynamic description of authoritarian regimes should locate factors influencing the development of political and social pluralism and mobilization. It is essential to understand the historical constellations from which such regimes emerge: the breakdown of existing democracy, of a traditional society, or of colonial rule. This limits the alternatives open to the authoritarian ruler, the appeals he may use, the type of legitimacy he can claim, and so on, often independently of his own pragmatic or ideological preferences. But the present cannot be understood only in terms of origins. When these regimes began, their futures were generally very ill-defined (one has only to read the different manifestos and speeches made in the first days of the Spanish Civil War to get a sense of this indeterminacy) and their relative openness makes for considerable shifts if the regime lasts. In the case of Spain it would be extremely misleading to interpret the present only in terms of the past; particularly the forces at play in the late thirties and early forties, for the simple reason that a considerable part of the second level elite of today was not yet adult at the time, and close to half of the population was not even in their teens. In some of these regimes the bulk of existing information deals with their takeover phase and interest dwindles afterwards, which makes comparative study difficult.

Some of you may have missed a judgment about these regimes. I think that as a social scientist I should not express one. As an individual I could, but as a social scientist I would suggest that the problem be broken down into many subproblems, examining the positive and negative implications of such regimes from many points of view. A number of cases would be required to give a general idea of their functions and dysfunctions for social change, but even so the observer's final evaluation of them would depend much on his own hierarchy of values.

Authoritarian regimes can be evaluated on a variety of dimensions: their ability to create stable political institutions articulating the conflicting interests of society, especially in countries where the regime came to power because of the heat of ideological and interest conflicts; their capacity to handle the succession problem; their ability to foster rapid economic development, both rural and industrial, compared with democratic and totalitarian societies under comparable conditions and considering the costs, both social and economic. We might examine the social and political consequences of some typical authoritarian labor policies: stability of employment vs. aggressive wage policy; imposed or voluntary company welfare benefits vs. a more general state or municipal policy; great emphasis on social security legislation combined with limited autonomy of labor organizations. Problems like these require cooperation between sociologists and economists, and I feel that today we have no good studies along these lines.

Among the most difficult questions of all is that posed by the leaders of authoritarian regimes, when they say that national unity can only be maintained or achieved by excluding open expression of political cleavages through political parties. [65] It has been expressed as follows:

> In face of the fundamental problems, the union, the unity of the country is indispensable. Now, without any doubt, the multiplicity of parties ends creating national disagreement about the great questions. No; democracy has nothing to do with the regime of parliamentary assemblies and the agitation of rival political parties. Democracy consists in searching the will of the people and in serving that will. [66]
>
> We don't want democracy to be a source of cleavages, of childish struggles in the course of which the better part of our energies would be wasted. We want . . . to pursue in peace and in union the work of national construction.
>
> Guinea's political unity has been proved by the referendum, and has been growing stronger ever since. It is not our intention to squander this chance of unity by adopting a system which would only reduce our political strength. What Africa needs is a fundamental revolution. It is not too much to ask that all our strength be mobilized and directed toward a common goal. A political system based on two parties would be a certain check on our revolution. The revolutionary dynamism doesn't need any other stimulant than our needs, our aspirations, and our hopes. [67]

Certainly the activation of cleavages in a society where the basic consensus is shattered—as it was in Spain after the October revolution of 1934—or where it has not developed, as in some of the new nations, creates serious problems. Social scientists would have to know much more about the conditions under which the balance of cleavage and consensus required for democratic politics can emerge. Studies of the integration of new sectors into the society under different political and social institutions, particularly by Bendix and Guenther Roth, [68] suggest how difficult it is to weigh the consequences of following one or another path. A comparative analysis of the aftermath of different authoritarian regimes, for example those of Vargas and Péron, would be most important in exploring how authoritarianism can be combined with the expansion of citizenship which characterizes our time.

Evaluation of each authoritarian regime depends finally on the answer to these questions: Could alternative systems work in the societies now under authoritarian rule? What conditions are necessary for these alternative systems, and how could they be created? At what cost? I for one have no definite answers for Spain.

Bibliographic Note. There is no sociological or even political science analysis of the institutions and operations of the Franco regime. Most of the literature on contemporary Spain deals with the historical background of the Civil War, the well-known books by: Gerald Brenan, *Spanish Labyrinth* (Cambridge: Cambridge University Press, 1943); Salvador de Madariaga, *Spain. A Modern*

History (New York: Praeger Paperbacks, 1958); Hugh Thomas, *The Spanish Civil War* (New York: Harper & Brothers, 1961); Franz Borkenau, *The Spanish Cockpit;* D. C. Cattell, *Communism and the Spanish Civil War* (Berkeley: University of California Press, 1955). None of these works is written with a pro-Franco point of view. For that the reader has to turn to Joaquín Arrarás, *Historia de la Cruzada Española* (Madrid, 1940 – 43, 35 vols.) and his *Historia de la Segunda República Española* (Madrid: Editora Nicional, 1956).

For a good general history of modern Spain until the Republic see: Vicens Vives, J. Nadal, R. Ortega, M. Hernandez Sanchez Barba, Vol. IV of *Historia Social de España y America* (Barcelona: Editorial Teide, 1959).

A very important book whose analysis of the early stages of the Franco regime is better documented than most sources in English—that focus on the Republican side—is Carlos M. Rama, *La Crisis Española del Siglo XX* (Mexico: Fondo de Cultura Economica, 1960).

The literature on Spain after the Civil War, both journalistic and scholarly, is largely focused on Spanish foreign policy, but does not add much to the understanding of domestic politics. While, as the title indicates, this is also the focus of: Arthur P. Whitaker, *Spain and the Defense of the West. Ally and Liability* (New York: Praeger Paperbacks, 1962), it contains a lot of material on the basis of the regime, the opposition groups, from the semi-tolerated ones to the Communists, economic policies, etc. We mentioned already the important work of Stanley Payne, *Falange,* but by focusing on only one element in the system, it can only give an incomplete picture. Ebenstein's study of the Church is also useful. Richard Pattee's, *This Is Spain* (Bruce: Milwaukee, 1951) is a presentation from the point of view friendly to Catholic political forces within the regime, but has no scholarly pretensions. For the basic constitutional texts of the regime until 1945 see Clyde L. Clark, *The Evolution of the Franco Regime* (Washington, D.C., n.d.), 3 vols., translations in English.

NOTES

1. Alex Inkeles, "Totalitarianism and Ideology," pp. 87 – 108 in Carl J. Fredrich, ed., *Totalitarianism* (Cambridge: Harvard University Press, 1954), p. 89.

2. Herbert L. Matthews, *The Yoke and the Arrows: A Report on Spain* (New York: George Brazillier, Inc., 1957), p. 100.

3. Raymond Aron, *Sociologie des Sociétés Industrielles. Esquisse d'une théorie des régimes politiques* (Paris: Le Centre de Documentation Universitaire, "Les Cours de la Sorbonne," Sociologie, 1958), pp. 50 – 51.

4. Gabriel A. Almond, "Comparative Political Systems," *The Journal of Politics,* Vol. 18 (1956), reprinted in H. Eulau, et al., ed., *Political Behavior* (Glencoe, Ill.: Free Press, 1956), pp. 35 – 42.

Another formulation of the distinction between totalitarianism and authoritarianism developed independently of ours, but coinciding with it, can be found in an umpublished paper by L. A. Coser, "Totalitarianism, Authoritarianism and the Theory of Conflict: Development Models for the New Nations."

5. To avoid any misunderstanding let it be said that this "mimicry" or "imitation," while not all the reality, is quite real in its consequences. Particularly so since it provides for some participants a concept of legitimacy which does not respond to reality and thereby creates sources of alienation among those initially attracted by the new system.

6. Joseph Schumpeter, *Capitalism, Socialism and Democracy* (New York: Harper & Brothers, 1947), pp. 232 – 302, esp. 269; Raymond Aron, *op. cit.,* p. 38; Seymour M. Lipset, *Political Man* (Garden City, N.Y.: Doubleday & Co., 1960), Chap. II, Economic Development and Democracy, p. 46.

7. William Kornhauser, *The Politics of Mass Society* (Glencoe, Ill.: Free Press, 1959), p. 123.

8. There is no point in referring in detail to the extensive literature on totalitarianism since the works of C. J. Friedrich and Z. K. Brzezinski, Sigmund Newmann, Franz Neumann, Emil Ledere, H. Arendt, Barrington Moore, Jr., Adams B. Ulam, Raymond I. Bauer, and Alex Inkeles are well known. A recent review of the problem with references to the non-American literature can be found in the articles by Otto Stammer, G. Schulz, and Peter Christian Ludz, in *Soziale Welt,* Vol. 12, No. 2 (1961), pp. 97 – 145; Karl D. Bracher, *Die Auflösung der Weimarer Republik* (Stuttgart: Ring-Verlag, 1957); and K. D. Bracher, Wolfgang Sauer, Gerhard Schulz, *Die Nationalsozialistische Machtergreifung* (Köln: Westdeutscher Verlag, 1960); both, sponsored by the Berlin Institut für Politische Wissenschaft, incorporate much of recent German scholarship on the breakdown of democracy and the establishment of Nazi totalitarianism. These monumental works should be used to supplement—and in my opinion modify—much of the dated but classic *Behemoth* of Franz Neumann.

9. Friedrich's definition was formulated in "The Nature of Totalitarianism," (*op. cit.,* pp. 52 – 53, and then expanded and slightly modified in C. J. Friedrich and Z. K. Brzezinski, *Totalitarian Dictatorship and Autocracy* (Cambridge, Mass.: Harvard University Press, 1956), pp. 9 – 10.

10. There is no satisfactory study in Spanish or any other language of the Primo de Rivera dictatorship. Dillwyn F. Ratcliff's *Prelude to Franco* (New York: Las Americas Publishing Co., 1957) is totally insufficient, even when it gives some useful information and translates some documents. The most important partisan source in favor is José Pemartin, *Los valores históricos en la dictadura española* (Madrid: Publicaciones de la Junta de Propaganda Patriótica y Ciudadana, 1929) and the collected writings of Miguel Primo de Rivera himself, *El Pensamiento de Primo de Rivera*, J. M. Peman, ed. (Madrid, 1929).

11. A work on the economic policy of that time by José Velarde Fuertes is in preparation. For a list of the interest groups created during this period see Roman Perpiña, *De Estructura Económica y Economía Hispana* (Madrid: Rialp, 1952), pp. 317 – 320.

The interventions of the dictator in the corporative chamber he created, often in answer to questions from the floor, vividly illustrate the pluralism and autonomy of social forces during that dictatorship. See *Intervenciones en la Asamblea Nacional del General Primo de Rivera* (Madrid, 1930). The comparison with the Cortes of the present regime shows the range of pluralism vs. concentration of power in such systems.

12. L. Vincent Padgett, "Mexico's One-Party System: A Re-Evaluation," APSR, Vol. 51, No. 4 (December 1957); reprinted in Roy C. Macridis and Bernard E. Brown, *Comparative Politics* (Homewood, Ill.: The Dorsey Press, 1961), pp. 193 – 197, see p. 197.

13. Point 27 of the Program of Falange Española, quoted in David Jato, *La Rebelión de los Estudiantes* (Madrid: CIDS, 1953), p. 262. For the English translation see the extremely valuable collection of activities of the regime in various spheres, by Clyde L. Clark, *The Evolution of the Franco Regime*, in 3 vols. (Washington, D.C., n.d.), pp. 611 – 612.

14. The Nazi idea of *Gleichschaltung* is described by Franz Neumann in *Behemoth* (New York: Octagon Books, 1963, reprint of the 1944 edition), pp. 51 – 55. Much of the work of Bracher, *et al., Die Nationalsozialistische Machtergreifung, op. cit.,* is a carefully documented analysis of how this idea was carried out in the most diverse fields.

15. Ramon Serrano Suñer, *Entre Hendaya y Gibraltar (Noticia y reflexión, frente a una leyenda sobre nuestra política en dos guerras)* (Madrid: Ediciones y Publicaciones Españolas S.A., 1947), pp. 38 – 39. This is one of the most interesting books on the politics under the Franco regime by a key participant.

16. Theodor Geiger, *Die Soziale Schichtung des Deutschen Volkes* (Stuttgart: Ferdinand Enke Verlag, 1932), pp. 77 – 79.

As he says with a very graphic German expression: "mentality is *subjektiver Geist* (even when collective), ideology is *objektiver Geist.* Mentality is intellectual attitude, ideology is intellectual content. Mentality is psychic predisposition, ideology is reflection, self-interpretation, mentality is previous, ideology later, mentality is formless, fluctuating—ideology however is firmly formed. Ideology is a concept of the sociology of culture, mentality is a concept of the study of social character." And so on.

17. The recent work by Morris Janowitz, *The Military in the Political Development of New Nations* (Chicago: University of Chicago Press, 1964), shows the difficulty of defining the ideology of the military (often the creators of such regimes) except in some very general terms: nationalism, a certain xenophobia, often anti-communal sentiments, some puritanic tendencies, a proclivity for governmental intervention as an organizational form without much ideological justification and an "antipolitics" outlook (particularly divisive party politics and the mixture of making interest cleavages manifest and afterwards bargaining over them so typical of democratic politics). This "ideology" is so closely related to their professional training, experience, and role, and so little related to any intellectual elaboration, that we would prefer to call it a "mentality." As Janowitz himself writes: "The 'mentality' of the military officer seems to be a mixture of half-developed but strongly held ideology and a deep sense of pragmatic professionalism." (p. 67)

18. General Naguib quoted by Daniel Lerner, *The Passing of Traditional Society* (Glencoe, Ill.: Free Press, n.d.), pp. 242–243.

19. Nadav Safran, *Egypt in Search of Political Community* (1961), p. 253, quoted by Georg Kirk, "The Role of the Military in Society and Government: Egypt," in Sidney Nettleton Fisher, ed., *The Military in the Middle East* (Columbus, Ohio: Ohio State University Press, 1963), p. 84.

20. As quoted in Fernando de Valdesoto, *Francisco Franco* (Madrid: Afrodisio Aguado, S.A., 1943), pp. 115–117. A very similar reference to the liberal values that were not realized can be found in Francisco Franco, *Palabras del Caudillo* (19 abril 1937–31 diciembre 1938) (Ediciones FE, 1939), p. 287 (dated 1938).

21. Getulio Vargas, *Nova Politica de Brasil, Da Aliança Liberal as realizacões do primeiro ano de governo 1930–1931* (Rio de Janeiro: Livraria Jose Olympio, 1938),.p. 63, from a speech on October 4, 1930.

22. Alex Inkeles, "The Totalitarian Mystique: Some Impressions of the Dynamics of Totalitarian Society," *op. cit.*, p. 91.

23. On the relations between Church and State and the different tendencies within Spanish Catholicism see William Ebenstein, *Church and State in Franco Spain* (Princeton University: Center of International Studies, 1960).

24. Immanuel Wallerstein, *Africa: The Politics of Independence* (New York: Vintage Books, 1961), pp. 96–97. Refers to the differences in mobilization in the different single-party systems in Africa, which "at least in theory" are mass parties.

In theory the Spanish single-party is also a mass party and in recent years José Luis de Arrese has spoken of the need to revitalize the party and even initiated—when he was Secretary General—attempts in that direction. See his collection of writings: *Hacia una Meta Institucional* (Madrid: Ediciones del Movimiento, n.d.), pp. 113–126.

25. Raymond Aron, *op. cit.*, p. 50.

26. The notion of "populist" regimes has been used by Monroe Berger, *The Arab World Today* (Garden City, N.Y.: Doubleday & Co. 1962), pp. 418–423, and in some interpretations of Latin American dictatorships to distinguish regimes like Vargas' Estado Novo and Perón's Justicialismo from more old-fashioned military dictatorships.

27. This pattern of passive support rather than mobilization has also been noted by Dionisio Ridruejo, *Escrito en España* (Buenos Aires: Losada, S.A., 1962), when he writes:

. . . the creation of a political desert has gone much further than it went initially: the destruction of specific political forces of the people and the loss of authenticity or increasing neutralization of those that the (civil) war brought about with its enthusiastic and ambivalent pressures toward an emergency politization. . . . Spaniards have been shrunk to their private life without other interests or horizons. This fits the wishes of the groups socially threatened by the popularization of the state and the tastes of the traditional class, attached to its old habits (of passivity).

This makes our case in its superficial style closer to the longing conformity of certain free societies than to the asceticism of imposed obedience in other societies of absolute regimes. [He means totalitarian systems.] In these, in fact, there is no depolitization in the sense of the reduction of the citizens to the sphere of private life as a consequence of the monopoly of public functions in the hands of an all powerful minority. The monopoly exists, but the intense effort of the minority has been precisely to deprive private life of autonomy and scope and to promote a maximum identification of man and citizen, or to say it in another way, infuse to all activities—on occasion even to the most intimate ones—a public dimension. That alternative is something far from pleasant, but it is something different and even the opposite to conformism and, obviously, to the pseudoconformity of which we were speaking.

This work also gives the reader some feeling for the "participatory phase" of the regime under the influence of Fascist ideas and for how the transistion to a more apathetic but more pluralistic political climate took place.

This text of an acute and exiled critic of the regime who, himself, participated in his youthful days in the effort of mobilization under a fascist sign as propaganda chief confirms, independently, our analysis. His book, written as the title suggests as a critic of the regime who had lived the regime "from the inside," is one of the most useful sources if a reader wants to get a feel for the social forces, institutions, political mentalities supporting the regime, and for its evolution since the days of the Civil War. It is a work in the best tradition of the political essay by an active politician. To understand today's Spain, this book is more useful than many by friends of the regime and most of those written by its enemies.

28. See the data on the role of the Mexican PRI at the local level in a forthcoming paper by Linda Mirin and Arthur Stinchcombe on "The Political Mobilization of Mexican Peasants."

29. My research on voluntary associations in Spain shows that the number of all kinds of associations varies directly with per capita income or industrialization, and less so with education. So in the five provinces with highest per capita income, the number of associations was 53.8 per 100,000 in the capital and 46.1 in the rest of the province, in the five of lowest income, respectively 35.9 and 11.4. Even the number of amateur soccer—the national sport—players is highest in industrial regions like Catalonia (3.0 per thousand) and Vizcaya (2.8) and lowest in the economically underdeveloped areas: Extremadura (0.4) and Andalucia (0.9). This relation—with some interesting variations—holds in general even for Catholic Action, and when political traditions are held constant, for the women's branch of the Falange.

30. C. A. Macartney, *October Fifteenth: A History of Modern Hungary, 1929 – 1945* (Edinburgh at the University Press, 1957), pp. 37 – 38. See also pp. 49 – 60 for the excellent characterization of Horthy, who is certainly a good example of one type of authoritarian leadership. The whole book is useful for understanding the ambivalences and contradictory tendencies in such regimes.

31. I use these terms in the sense they have been introduced by G. Almond and S. Verba in *The Civic Culture: Political Attitudes and Democracy in Five Nations* (Princeton: Princeton University Press, 1963).

32. From the study by the Italian sociologist Luciano Cavalli, *Quartiere operaio*, pp. 25 – 64, as quoted by Joseph A. Raffaele, *Labor Leadership in Italy and Denmark* (Madison: The University of Wisconsin Press, 1962), p. 44.

33. Data from a study on voluntary associations in Spain, based on a breakdown by province and date of founding of 8,329 associations registered until 1960. In provinces with a number of associations above the national average, 50 per cent had been founded since 1950, while in a sample of those below the national average it was 73 per cent, 50 per cent of them between 1955 – 56.

34. Georges Lavau, "Les aspects socio-culturels de la dépolitisation" in *La Dépolitisation, Mythe ou Réalité?*, ed. by G. Vedel, *Cahiers de la Fondation Nationale des Sciences Politiques*, No. 120 (Paris: Armand Colin, 1962), pp. 167 – 206.

35. On the creation of the unified party, the Falange Española Tradicionalista y de las Juntas de Ofensiva Nacional Sindicalista, see Serrano Suñer, *op. cit.*, pp. 19 – 39 and Stanley G. Payne, *Falange: A History of Spanish Fascism* (Stanford: Stanford University Press, 1961), Chaps. 13 and 14, pp. 148 – 198. Payne's book is an indispensable source on the history of the Falange and its place in the regime.

36. *Vide infra* the data on the presence of the party in the elite. A report by de Arrese, in *Hacia una . . ., op. cit.*, on the attitude of the Falange toward municipal elections, October 1948, presents the problem of the Falange Movement in these revealing terms:

"In presenting our candidates should we remember that we are a National Movement and include in our lists all those who, at least in theory [an ironic remark], always in theory, are on our side or remember how precarious the collaboration of people who have called themselves our sympathizers has been, and present only men who are unconditionally ours." (p. 61).

Later he notes how others could show dissidence with the regime, while the Falangists were not allowed to do so, during years when the Falange was worn out, as he puts it, with the exercise of powers it was granted fully only when the time came to allocate the blame.

37. For a description of the slowness and false starts in the creation of the Vaterland Front of Dollfuss, see Gordon Brook Shepherd, *Dollfuss* (London: Macmillan & Co. Ltd., 1961), pp. 103 – 109, who writes:

"Though Dollfuss had given the Front a flying start as a propaganda movement, its origins as a political organization were pitiful. For weeks after the Chancellor had issued his first nation-wide appeals for membership no adequate apparatus existed to deal with the response. It was like a publisher advertising a book which he has neither printed nor bound."

Shepherd goes on to describe the bickering and negotiations with the various elements that were to be integrated into the party, to "remain," in terms of membership "basically the old Christian-Socialist camp dressed up in new ornately patriotic garb."

Janowitz, *op. cit.*, also comments on the difficulties found by the military in the creation of mass political organizations, see pp. 84 – 93. The difficulties of creating the National Union in Egypt have been commented on by most observers. George Kirk, "The Role of the Military in Society and Government: Egypt" in *The Military in the Middle East*, ed. by Sydney Nettleton Fisher (Columbus: Ohio State University Press, 1973), quotes a not unsympathetic researcher:

"When I was in the U.A.R. in 1960 I had the impression that no one took the National Union very seriously; certainly hardly anyone could give a clear description of its complex structure of committees and councils, although they were set out with detailed diagrams in many official leaflets and endlessly written up in the press, with the aim of popularizing the new system."

P. J. Vatiokis, *The Egyptian Army in Politics: Pattern for New States* (Bloomington: Indiana University Press, 1961) in the Chapter 5 dealing with the National Union scheme is not much more explicit and does not present data that would allow a comparison of rates of mobilization. Macartney, *op. cit.*, contains numerous descriptions of such dominant, official parties created or reorganized from the top. For an extreme case see Chapter VIII, "Apolitical Politics," on the Union Patriótica of Primo de Rivera, in Ratcliff, *Prelude to Franco, op. cit.*, pp. 57 – 73. See also Pemartin, *Los Valores, op. cit.*, pp. 623 – 647.

38. On the Imperial Rule Assistance Association, see Robert A. Scalapino, *Democracy and the Party Movement in Prewar Japan* (Berkeley: University of California Press, 1953), pp. 388 – 389.

39. On the army and Falange, see Payne, *Falange (op. cit.) passim.*, and particularly pp. 207 – 208 on the maintenance of the monopoly of armed force by the army and the non-emergence of any militia type of units (like the SS or even the Milizia in Italy).

40. Serrano Suñer, *op. cit.*, p. 128.

41. H. Arendt in *Origins of Totalitarianism,* (New York, 1951), pp. 387 ff. Her analysis may be contrasted with this summary by Herbert Matthews:

"The picture of Franco Spain that is firmly believed by the exiles is distorted and in many respects false. They picture a totalitarian police state that simply does not exist. They have no idea of the degree of tolerance that Franco permits so long as his position and the security of his regime is not threatened," *The Yoke and the Arrows, op. cit.*, p. 184, see also pp. 178, 183.

42. Nasser, as quoted by Vaitiokis, *op. cit.*, p. 239.

43. Franco, chapter of a book, reproduced in the "Corriere della Sera" (December 4, 1938), p. 286 of *Palabras del Caudillo: 19 abril 1937 – 31 diciembre 1938* (Ediciones FE, 1938).

44. Nasser, quoted by Daniel Lerner, *The Passing of Traditional Society, op. cit.*, pp. 246 – 247.

45. The alternative outcomes of this ambivalence, to turn over quickly power to the old politicians or to hold on to power without giving it any real political content, are well analyzed in José Antonio Primo de Rivera (the founder of the Falangist party and son of the dictator) in his "Carta a un militar español," pp. 649 – 651, *Obras Completas* (Madrid: Ediciones de la Vicesecretaria de Educacion Popular, 1945), ed. and collected by Agustin del Rio Cisneros and Enrique Conde Gargollo.

46. A good indicator are the weekly lists of officers received by Franco that are as long as those of civilian officials and personalities.

47. In an interview with a leading industrialist and banker, after probing about the influence that men of his prestige and influence in the business community could exercise if they acted united and presented their points of view, I received the following comment: "As a Spaniard you should know better, you know very well that in the army collective remonstrances are never tolerated, only individual protests. So we go each separately through different ways, after agreeing, but never collectively."

48. On charisma and totalitarianism, see Franz Neumann, *Behemoth (op. cit.,)*, pp. 83 – 97.

On Weber's use of the types of legitimacy see Winckelmann, *Legitimität und Legalität in Max Webers Herrschaftssoziologie* (Tübingen: J. C. B. Mohr [Paul Siebeck], 1952). The compatibility of the types of legitimacy with different types of political systems, particularly the coexistance of different types of legitimacy in democracy, is discussed by Wolfgang J. Mommsen in *Max Weber und die Deutsche Politik 1890 – 1920* (Tübingen: J. C. B. Mohr [Paul Siebeck] 1959), Chaps. IX, X.

49. See Francisco Javier Conde, *Contribución a la doctrina del Caudillaje* and *Repre-*

sentación Política y Regimen Español. Ensayo Politico (Madrid: Ediciones de la Subsecretaria de Educación Popular, 1945), mainly pp. 105 – 149.

50. We conceive traditional authority in the sense defined by Weber in his *Wirtschaft und Gesellschaft.* For a summary of this part of his work, only partly translated, see Reinhard Bendix, *Max Weber an Intellectual Portrait* (Garden City, N. Y.: Doubleday & Co., 1962), pp. 329 – 384. While we want to stress the conceptual difference between authoritarian regimes and traditional rule, we also want to suggest that they sometimes have elements in common and that the students of such regimes could gain many insights from Weber's analysis of patrimonial rule and brueaucracy as those of totalitarianism have gained from his thinking about charisma.

51. See Leonard Binder, *Iran: Political Development in a Changing Society* (Berkeley: University of California Press, 1962), pp. 58 – 89 and *passim.*

52. Binder, *op. cit.,* has emphasized the coexistence of different legitimizing formulae and the consequences of this phenomenon, particularly in terms of increased alienation. See pp. 15, 20, and 59 – 63.

53. Many readers of Weber's analysis of legitimacy forget that in the initial paragraphs introducing the topic he notes that: "In everyday routine life these relationships, like others, are governed by custom and, in addition, material calculation of advantages." His point however is that these elements and purely affectual or ideal motives of solidarity are not sufficient bases of domination, particularly in crisis situations, the ones that interest him and political scientists most. He also stresses that obedience by an administrative staff based only on such motives would represent an unstable situation. He does not intend to dismiss their importance, particularly in normal everyday life, nor their importance for the behavior of the mass of the population compared to the staff of the ruler. We feel that it would be as erroneous to ignore the elements of habit and self-interest particularly of the mass of the population as to ignore the role of legitimacy beliefs for rulers and staff in a political system. In this sense a concern with apathetic support and inactive alienation in dealing with political cultures is perfectly compatible with an interest in the problem of legitimacy beliefs. The relevant texts are in *Wirtschaft und Gesellschaft,* Kap. III, p. 122, (Tübingen: J. C. B. Mohr [Paul Siebeck] 1956), the new J. Winckelmann edition; and in *The Theory of Social and Economic Organization,* translated by A. M. Henderson and T. Parsons (Glencoe, III.: Free Press, 1947), pp. 324 – 325.

54. *Op. cit.*

55. Political sociology has centered its attention on the relationship between social structure and political institutions, but with important exceptions has tended to neglect the analysis of how different political systems handle the "invariant problems" and, even more so, the dynamics of political change. While the three aspects are closely interrelated they cannot be reduced to the relationship of society and political institutions. In this paper we have consciously attempted to focus on the organizational aspects and the political process without seeing them fundamentally as reflections of social bases. In a study of specific authoritarian systems and even more their emergence, evolution, and breakdown, we would have to give more attention to the interaction between social bases and the political structure; or, to put it graphically, to add to a Weberian approach a more Marxist one.

56. On this marginality see mainly Daniel Lerner, *The Nazi Elite,* Hoover Institute Studies (Stanford: Stanford University Press, 1951), pp. 84 – 90.

57. For the typical political mentality—ideology—of the bureaucrats see Karl Mann-heim, *Ideology and Utopia* (New York: Harvest Books, 1936), pp. 118 – 119.

58. See Clark, *op. cit.,* Vol. I, p. 289, in the case of José Larraz and Pedro Gamero del Castillo, ministers of finance and without portfolio at the time of the change of government on May 19, 1941, while the dismissal of other officials contained the phrase.

59. W. Kornhauser, *The Politics of Mass Society, op. cit.,* p. 52.

60. Serrano Suñer, *op. cit.,* pp. 60 – 64, 123 – 125.

61. Personal interview, materials of which were incorporated into chapter 16 of Payne's *Falange, op. cit.*

62. From an exchange published in the *Boletin del ACNDP,* 1-15 April, pp. 607 – 608.

63. On the Opus Dei in Spanish politics see Ebenstein, *op. cit., passim.* However there is no good study of this new religious organization, its structure, membership, ideology and much of what is written is undocumented. For the Opus position see Julio Her-ranz, "Opus Dei," in *The Homiletic and Pastoral Review,* January 1962, with a bibliography of articles and official statements.

64. Arrese, *Hacia una meta, op. cit.,* pp. 212 – 213.

65. Social scientists raise similar questions, so Immanuel Wallerstein in *Africa, The Politics of Independence, op. cit.,* writes: "The choice has not been between one-party and multiparty states; it has been between one-party states and either anarchy or military regimes or various combinations of the two" (p. 96), and:

"At present many Africans cannot determine the limits of opposition, do not understand the distinction between opposition and secession. This is what the African leaders mean when they argue that 'our oppositions are not constructive.' It is not that they tend to be destructive of the government in power; this is the purpose of an opposition. It is that they tend to destroy the state in the process of trying to depose the government.

"This is particularly true because, in almost every African country the opposition takes the form of a claim to regionalism—a demand for at least decentralization in a unitary state, federalism in a decentralized state, confederation in a federation, total dissolution in a confederation. Regionalism is understandable because ethnic loyalties can usually find expression in geographic terms. Inevitably, some regions will be richer (less poor) than others, and if the ethnic claim to power combines with relative wealth, the case for secession is strong. . . . But every African nation, large or small, federal or unitary, has its Katanga. Once the logic of secession is admitted, there is no end except in anarchy. And so every African government knows that its first problem is to hold the country together when it is threatened by wide disintegration" (p. 98) and we could continue quoting.

I would surmise that Franco, or the supporters of the Yugoslav-Serbian authoritarian regimes, would fully agree with these arguments. And in the case of Spain one cannot deny a certain legitimacy to the argument if one considers the behavior of a large part of the Socialist party in the opposition during the October days of 1934, or that of Companys, the head of the Generalitat of Catalonia during those days, or the activities of the Basque nationalists, or those of the extreme Right opposition to the Republic. The distinction between opposition to the government, the regime and even the state, was certainly not clear to many Spaniards. (I am sure that Wallerstein would not agree with my application of his conclusions, but then I would suggest that those writing on authoritarian, single-party regimes, the role of the army as modernizer, etc., in underdeveloped areas, would specify further, how in the long-run, such regimes will evolve differently from those in the semi-developed regions of the West.)

66. From the declarations of Franco to the correspondent of *Le Figaro* on June 12, 1958, *ABC* (Madrid), June 13, 1958. The text quoted was important enough to deserve the headlines of the newspaper. Similar statements could be found throughout the political statements of the Caudillo.

67. These quotations are respectively from Camille Alliali, Secretary General of POIC (Ivory Coast) and Sekou Touré (Guinea), quoted by Szymon Chodak, in a paper on the "The Societal Functions of Party Systems in Sub-Saharan Africa," in *Cleavages, Ideologies and Party Systems,* eds. E. Allardt and Y. Littunen (Helsinki, 1964), pp. 256 – 280.

68. Reinhard Bendix, "Social Stratification and the Political Community," *European Journal of Sociology,* Vol. 1, No. 2 (1960), pp. 3 – 32; "The Lower Classes and the Democratic Revolution," *Industrial Relations,* Vol. 1, No. 1 (October 1961), pp. 91 – 116; and R. Bendix and Stein Rokkan, "The Extension of National Citizenship to the Lower Classes: A Comparative Perspective," a paper submitted to the Fifth World Congress of Sociology, Washington, 1962. His study *Work and Authority in Industry* (New York: John Wiley & Sons, Inc., 1956) is also relevant. See also the study by Guenther Roth, *The Social Democrats in Imperial Germany: A Study of Working-Class Isolation and National Integration* (Totowa, N.J.: Bedminster Press, 1963). These studies as well as the comparative research on labor movements, like those of Galenson, should be taken into account before such ideas of unity, rather than painful integration by conflict, are accepted.

8

Spanish Political Attitudes, 1970

Amando de Miguel

(Translated by Ann Kaenig Fleming and Shannon E. Fleming)

Spanish society has been largely apolitical since the Civil War of 1936 – 1939. This is due in good measure to the policies and restrictions of the Franco regime, but it has been greatly reinforced by the wave of consumerism and economic striving that has dominated Spanish society for the past generation. Only in the last few years have timid political opinions begun to reemerge for restrained expression among limited sectors of the population. Preparation for the post-Franco succession crystallized in 1969 when General Franco designated Prince Juan Carlos de Borbón, grandson of Alfonso XIII, as his successor and next king of Spain upon Franco's own death or permanent incapacity. Since that time political concern and speculation have slowly been growing.

The following selection constitutes the first systematic attempt to analyze Spanish political attitudes during the twilight of the Franco regime. Its author, Amando de Miguel, is professor of sociology at the Autonomous University of Barcelona. He is the most active of the new generation of talented sociologists who have emerged in Spain during the past fifteen years and has published numerous books, most recently (with Juan Salcedo) Dinámica del desarrollo industrial de las regiones españolas (1972) and the bestselling Sociología del franquismo (1975). Some of his work has made him the target of official repression and discrimination. The following selection was originally prepared for inclusion in a massive sociological study of Spanish society in 1970, but at that point was suppressed by the censorship. The ban has since been partially lifted, and it is published here for the first time in any language with the permission of the author and of the Fundación FOESSA. (Limitations of space have made it possible to produce only part of the original. Moreover, some of the extensive tables of quantitative data have had to be omitted.)

Prior to the national public opinion poll which we took in 1969,* political polls in Franco's Spain were a problematical matter. Only two were undertaken before 1960, and these were very limited in scope. A 1960 youth poll was a great step forward, permitting very intense political exploration, even though the questions were still very indirect and the results were not widely circulated. Since 1963 the polls of the Institute of Public Opinion have included a growing number of political questions, but their analysis is very descriptive, their diffusion restricted, and some results have not even been published. The 1966 Report of the FOESSA Foundation scarcely dared to include political questions since (in contrast to the previous polls) it was conducted by a private institution.

*Author's note on the methodology of the survey:

The data presented here stem from a series of interviews carried out in 1969. Those that cover the entire country are based on a fairly representative sample of the members of households according to a system of representation proportionate to the size of the district. Within each district households were selected by random sample. Interviews with students, workers, and professional men in Madrid were less representative in so far as they were concentrated on strategic groups, such as a Colegio Mayor, a factory, or a professional group. Data from these latter sources are merely illustrative.

With regard to the trustworthiness of the data, it is necessary to take into account a greater degree of fear or suspicion the farther one descends in the scale of education. That is, students responded with greater liberty than unskilled workers or uneducated housewives. This was practically the first time that such questioning had ever been conducted in Spain. The results, therefore, cannot be interpreted at face value in the same way as polls in other countries where such techniques are common.

In the 1969 poll we not only obtained answers to some of the political questions of an "indirect" type asked up to that time, but we have also measured more direct attitudes. The risk (apart from the actual poll taking, which was not small) is that the results tend to express more moderation, adjustment, conformity, and so on, than may exist in reality. This must be made explicit in order to adequately interpret the following data.

In the polls taken in Madrid we asked for the individual's perception of "the two things which, in your opinion, are of greatest importance to people today." We provided as fixed alternatives two spiritual ideals ("to please God and to obtain eternal life" and "to live in accordance with your individual beliefs") and two material ideas ("to earn money, to have more" and "to have more and more influence, to rule more"). Among all the groups interviewed *the majority opinion was that money is the fundamental motive;* this is especially the opinion of university students. The idea which predominates *in second place is power,* also with more favor among university students. At least in the perception of the people we interviewed, it cannot be said that Spanish society is spiritual, but rather strongly materialistic. Morever, this materialistic outlook is not to be understood as a type of resentment, since it is most notable among the most privileged classes, university students, and professionals. Even among the latter, the higher the level of income the more frequently they mention money in the first rank of importance and power in second place.

In order to gauge even better this materialistic image of those who had designated money or power in first place, we asked them "if the majority of the people (1) are resigned to living with what they earn, have, and are, (2) try to improve their position slowly, or (3) try to have more, rule more, better themselves rapidly whatever the method." Here are the answers:

	High school graduate	University student	Professional people	White collar worker	Blue-collar worker
1. Conforms	1	8	4	5	3
2. Step by step	22	16	14	23	31
3. Rapidly	78	76	82	72	66
Total	100%				
	(221)	(130)	(181)	(139)	(150)

It is evident that this vision of a materialistic society is reinforced by the convulsive rhythm of a society that has decided to become wealthy and to ascend in a great hurry without too many scruples. If diverse social groups see it this way, it is very probable that the society truly lives in a materialistic climate, in a climate of getting ahead whatever the cost. This explains such notorious phenomena in Spanish social life as social mobility, industrial growth, educational growth, and the climate of authoritarianism. Among the professional class the young people represent this norm of rapid ascent in much greater proportion, whatever their means:

	Professional people who have indicated materialistic norms:		
	Under 35 years of age	From 36 to 50	Over 50
1. Conforms	—	4	10
2. Step by step	14	10	22
3. Rapidly	86	86	68
Total	100%		
	(70)	(70)	(41)

An even clearer indication that the group of young professionals is inclined to break with the previous environment and has adopted a critical attitude is found in the comparison of their political ideas with those of their fathers. In the entire group of professional people, 30 percent say that their political ideas are the same as their fathers, 26 percent say they are similar, 37 percent say they are different, and 7 percent confess that they have no political ideas. The oldest group is where we find the greatest identification with the ideas of their father. The group from 36 to 50 years of age is characterized by a high percentage (21 percent) of individuals who have no political ideas; it is a question of a generation which prospered during years of strong authoritarian control. On the other hand, *the generation under 35 years of age is more political and is the one which expresses a greater dissonance with the attitudes of their fathers;* it was formed during a period of greater liberalization and openness and has no memory of the Civil War.

Housewives demonstrated a great similarity of political ideas with those of their husbands, far greater, we suspect, than exists in reality. It is possible that the prevailing norm of the role of the housewife inclines her to affirm that she thinks the same way as her husband in political matters, although in reality this is not so. However, 65 percent of the housewives say that they think the same as their husbands in political matters, while 22 percent indicate that they have no political ideas. Social class makes little difference in this aspect, except that *in the lowest class the proportion of women who say they have no political ideas increases.*

One method of verifying the excessive optimism of the housewives when they compare their own political ideas with those of their husbands is the comparison of responses to the same question asked of upper-middle- and upper-class women and of professional people in Madrid.

Political ideas in relation to those of husband and/or wife are:	According to upper-middle- and upper-class housewives	According to professional people in Madrid
Same	69	52
Similar	10	26
Different	2	13
Have none	19	10
Total	100%	
	(42)	(192)

Naturally with only this data we do not know if the housewives are optimistic or the professional people pessimistic about the similarity of ideas of the spouse. What is clear is that their impressions do not coincide. The objective data does show us that the ideas of both spouses certainly are not the same.

In order to study more in depth the changes in political attitudes which are occurring, a first approximation can be obtained from what we have called an *index of political inertia*. This index is composed of the affirmation or negation of the following concepts:

1. In politics, as in other matters, the known bad is better than a possible unknown good (affirmation).

2. Politics belongs to everyone, and it is necessary to attract people's support and press for one's aims (negation).

3. We are better off if the ones in power decide for us, because we Spaniards don't understand politics (affirmation).

4. Everyone wants to have more than he has, in politics as well as in other areas, and if those in power are not controlled, they tend to go beyond normal limits (negation).

5. I don't want to become involved in politics, because something always happens and the least guilty party is the one who loses (affirmation).

The index of political inertia shows the following values:

High-school students	0.34
University students	0.19
Lawyers	0.16
Doctors	0.25
Skilled white-collar workers	0.26
Unskilled white-collar workers	0.36
Skilled laborers	0.41
Unskilled laborers	0.49

Once more we encounter data which will appear over and over in these pages: High-school students live in a middle-class atmosphere which still maintains a very conservative mentality and is complacent about the status quo. In this case they have absorbed rather well (above all in the upper class) the idea that "one does not get involved in politics." This norm breaks down in the university, and university students and professional people (especially lawyers and the youngest members of the group) are very politicized. In the case of white-collar workers and laborers, the amount of apathy increases as we go down the scale. Finally, in spite of the depoliticization which is sometimes attributed to education, it is certain that the educational system plays a vital role in maintaining interest in politics. An increase in the educational structure will result in an ever-increasing number of politicized persons.

Among the white-collar workers and laborers, and especially among the professional class, it is easy to observe that age signifies a rather notable break in political ideas: *The young people feel a greater urgency to participate in politics.* The data are as follows:

	Index of political inertia	
Years of age	Laborers and white-collar workers	Professional people
Under 25	0.34	
From 26 to 35	0.32	0.16
From 36 to 50	0.34	0.23
Over 50	0.41	0.26

Supposing that the young people do not become more conservative as they grow older (in general one must assume this to a degree), we may predict that when the most qualified youths now under 35 years of age reach positions of responsibility, within a period of five to ten years, apoliticism and authoritarianism will decrease. Such an important development doubtless needs to be determined precisely with greater rigor and a larger informational base. We must take into account not only certain attitudes which measure the degree of politicization, but also delve further into more concrete attitudes.

We need an instrument sufficiently refined to be able to trace the profile of the basic political attitudes found among the groups interviewed. We may begin with a *profile of conservatism-liberalism* composed of the following items:

Conservative items (from greater to lesser acceptance	Mean of the average acceptance	Index of discrepancy among the different groups
In Spain the most important thing is to maintain *peace and order*	58	0.60
What we Spaniards need is *discipline.* The problems of today's youth, for example, as well as many other problems, must be resolved according to a base of authority	34	0.85
Ever since the world has been a world *there have always existed the rich and the poor;* I don't know why it should have to be different now	33	0.53
Only by fixing our gaze on our *glorious history* we can obtain a great Spain	25	0.81
There is only one truth, and to tolerate differences of opinion is dangerous	24	0.88
Things are not going well because *people no longer believe in God*	16	0.54

Liberal items (from lesser to greater importance)	Mean of the average acceptance	Index of discrepancy among the different groups
In Spain things are not going well because the majority of us Spaniards *cannot make ourselves heard*	69	0.18
History is made on the basis of *misery and exploitation of the underdogs,* and it is now time for things to change	70	0.23

Liberal items (from greater to lesser acceptance	Mean of the average accep- tance	Index of discrepancy among the different groups
In Spain what is really needed is *to change many things* so there is more justice	80	0.11
The difficulties which occur from time to time are due to the fact that *many things are going badly* and it is necessary to change them	88	0.11
It is necessary to do whatever is required *to reduce the differences* between the rich and the poor	89	0.02
Every individual should have the *right to think* as he wishes	90	0.08

"Conservatism" in this context means authoritarianism, adhesion to tradition, justification of social differences, and non-secularization. "Liberalism" refers to desire of participation, awareness of the class struggle, desire of change and fundamental liberties. We have based the scale on high-school seniors, university students, lawyers, doctors, white-collar workers, and laborers from Madrid. We see that the *"liberal" beliefs are more acceptable than the "conservative"* and, in second place, that *among the "liberal" beliefs the degree of discrepancy, the difference which separates the various groups, is less than among the "conservative" beliefs.* Although the second conclusion does not fail to result in part as a logical consequence of the first, we feel that it is necessary to expressly point out both because of the practical importance which they may have for the political changes which may be produced. The data shows us the following relationships between political attitude and social class:

1. In general, *laborers tend to say "yes" more often to everything,* a bias that is very common in all types of indices. It is very possible that this bias tarnishes somewhat the trustworthiness of the data referring to the laborers, and also tarnishes its validity from the moment in which this acquiescent tendency reveals a certain fear.

2. *The most decidedly progressive groups (less conservative and more liberal) are, in order, university students, lawyers, and doctors.* It is evident that a university background is the main vehicle of political change in a modern direction. The progressive extreme is found in the 100 percent of the lawyers who affirm freedom of thought and the 97 percent of university stu-

dents who believe that it is necessary to change things which are going badly or who deny that there is only one truth.

3. *The laborers are more liberal with regard to the affirmation of the class struggle and less with regard to defense of freedom of thought.* White-collar workers are somewhat less liberal than the laborers but they are also much less conservative. It is possible that the "acquiescent bias" is not as predominant among them and in this case the lesser degree of progressiveness which they show in comparison with the professional class is more trustworthy.

4. *The influence of the step from high school to university* is very noteworthy in the sense of *somewhat increasing liberal attitudes but above all in the reduction of conservative attitudes.* The socialization of the university could not be clearer.

5. It seems surprising how *the preeminence of "order and peace" as political objectives* has permeated every group. Although in the political theory of many countries they are hardly mentioned, precisely because they are taken for granted, in the Spanish context they become explicit and are placed ahead of all other positive and specific attainments.

6. *The greatest discrepancy is revealed by the authoritarian item that "there is only one truth":* it is affirmed by only 3 percent of university students as opposed to 48 percent of the laborers. As is logical, it is a matter of a declaration incompatible with a university education, because 33 percent of high school seniors are still in agreement with this affirmation.

Within the professional group, the relationship of these attitudes to age is especially clear: *The older people tend to be more conservative and less liberal on almost all counts.* There really is a "generation gap," as the current phrase goes. The proportion, for example, who agree with the statement that: "In Spain the most important thing is to maintain order and peace," is 42 percent among professionals under 35 years of age, 60 percent among those from 36 to 50, and 74 percent among those over 50 years of age.

This slogan of peace and order has profoundly permeated the lower classes, or at least they profess to affirm it in large numbers as these figures reveal:

	% who give preeminence to order and peace
Skilled white-collar workers	49
Unskilled white-collar workers	74
Skilled laborers	81
Unskilled laborers	84

If these levels of authoritarianism are found in samples of males in Madrid, we may imagine what would be the attitudinal profile of the general population, and especially among women. An indication can be found in the responses to the question whether "the State is all of us or only those who govern," which has such important consequences for civil behavior (respect for the law, payment of taxes, cooperation for general well-being, etc.). No less than 66 percent of the housewives polled answered that "the State is those who govern." Curiously, this attitude is more pronounced on both extremes of the social pyramid: among the "poor" class (78 percent) and among the "upper-middle and upper" classes (71 percent).

When speaking of apoliticism in Spain, it is necessary to place things in the proper perspective. One author has spoken of a situation of extreme political "incompetence" (using the expression of Almond and Verba) which produces the question: "What would you do if you were chief of state?" In the most traditional situation, it is difficult to even *imagine* that possibility, much less say something coherent about what one would *do*.[1] Given a similar question: What would you tell Franco if you could speak freely with him? we obtain a relatively moderate percentage of no response (13 percent among high-school students, 21 percent among university students, 9 percent among the professional class, and 7 percent among white-collar workers and laborers). Among the responses, we received an immense variety of answers, from the most positive to the most critical, with a very notable degree of spontaneity among them all.

In general, most responses suggested positive things to do (opening up of democratic institutions, more education, more growth, more freedom, etc.) as well as a vague acceptance of the chief of state. There was also a degree of rejection of Franco which sometimes bordered on insult: It oscillated between 2 percent in the case of housewives to 23 percent among high-school students. Interestingly, once again, the most critical responses were given by the youngest groups, when we distinguish by age within the professional, white-collar, and laborer groups.

We have constantly referred to the difference in attitudes established by age. Historical fate has made the "generational conflict" especially sharp in Spain, separating the generations which "made the war" (Spanish Civil War of 1936-1939) from those who did not make it, and, recently, those who lived during the difficult postwar years from those born later. In this connection, it is worthwhile to consider the answers by housewives and professional people to the question *"if it seems beneficial or prejudicial to you that the country's youth have not lived through the war"*. Eighty-two percent of the housewives *and 79 percent of the professionals,* that is to say, practically the same majority *answered that it is beneficial.* This is not precisely a "heroic" attitude, revealing an attitude of disillusion and generational disenchantment and even, perhaps, a degree of bad conscience for what the war meant for everyone.

But the generational conflict does not arise from this mean percentage alone, but rather from the more important fact that *among the youngest groups it is more probable that the answer will be that it is beneficial not to have lived through the war.* The data are as follows:

Age groups	% who say it is beneficial *not to have lived through the war*	
	Housewives	*Professional people*
Under 25 years of age	89	
26 to 35	84	86
26 to 50	82	75
Over 50 years of age	78	70

The fact that the Civil War was, in part, a class struggle, is revealed in that the lower classes refuse to answer the question more often. When they answer, they are inclined more to the opinion that it is a positive thing not to have lived through the war:

Objective social class	% of housewives who did not answer	*Of the housewives who answered, the % who say that it is beneficial not to have lived through the war*
Poor	12	84
Working	6	85
Lower-middle	5	83
Middle-middle	3	79
Upper and upper-middle	2	78
Total	5	82

After a century and a half of civil wars, the attitudes of Spaniards seem to indicate they want to end definitively this collective trauma which history forced upon them.

Political Awareness

The first condition for the beginning of political participation, for movement toward a "true" democracy, is that politics as a decision-making power be a known fact.

In this sense it is necessary to remember that recent political history—perhaps with the exception of the period of the Second Republic—has signified for the majority of Spaniards a withdrawal from daily political affairs, and more concretely from the vicissitudes of decision-making power.

One feature of this gap between people and government has been a profound lack of information. In a national poll taken in 1960 among a sampling of youth, this low level of information was conspicuous: Only 39 percent of the males were able to name the civil governor of the province and 23 percent that of the minister of commerce (at that time the "popular" Ullastres). The degree of information among women was even poorer. In every case the rural youth were much less informed than industrial or white-collar workers and especially students. The youth of the most industrialized provinces were much better informed. [2]

In the poll among housewives in 1966, even though the means of communication (especially television) had increased notably, the degree of information did not yet correspond to that of a politically developed country. Only 50 percent knew the name of the minister of information, 23 percent that of labor, and 21 percent that of the commissioner of development. Scarcely one in every ten women interviewed was able to name the ministers of commerce and agriculture or the secretary-general of the state-controlled labor unions. Again it is necessary to note that the degree of information was oppressively low in the rural sector. [3]

In the polls taken for this report, we have gathered much more data concerning this first step in the modernization process: political awareness.

To the question of whether they saw the television news on the previous day, heard some radio news broadcast, or read some article in a newspaper, we suspect that the housewives exaggerated somewhat in the direction of the affirmative. Even then, it is surprising to note that only 39 percent of the housewives see the news, 28 percent listen to radio broadcasts, and 25 percent read some newspaper. That is to say, nearly three-quarters of the housewives do not inform themselves regularly of the news through the usual means of information.

As is logical, politicization is much greater among males. In a poll taken in 1960 these results were obtained from young people. [4] It is clear that in general in 1960 one could speak of a high degree of apoliticism among the youth which only decreased among male students.

| Degree of interest in politics | Males | | | Women |
	Farmers	Workers	Students	
Much	3	6	11	7
Enough	8	12	28	15
Little	21	28	32	22
None	64	52	27	53
TOTAL	100% (366)	(626)	(326)	(421)

In 1969 we attempted to determine the degree of interest in politics of various groups in Madrid: high-school seniors, university students, doctors, lawyers, white-collar workers, and laborers. To the question of with what frequency they discussed politics with their friends, they responded thus:

| Frequency with which you discuss politics | Students | | Lawyers | Doctors | White-collar workers | Laborers |
	High-school seniors	University students				
Often	18	26	26	19	14	8
Sometimes	30	50	32	25	20	10
Now and again	34	17	25	25	25	14
Not at all	19	8	16	32	41	68
TOTAL	100% (185)	(243)	(87)	(126)	(172)	(181)

As might be expected, *the degree of politicization is highest among university students and lawyers, followed by high-school students, doctors, and white-collar workers, and lastly by laborers.*

Within the group of high-school students, politicization is somewhat higher among those of a lower social origin: that is to say, among those using education as a means of mobility.

In the case of university students, those who are studying in a general college are more politicized than those who study in specialized schools. With regard to the professional class, it appears quite clear that the younger people are more interested in politics than the older.

In the case of white-collar workers and laborers, we have already seen that the former appear to be more politicized than the latter. The relationship is even clearer because *skilled white-collar workers or those who identify with the middle and upper classes show the greatest interest in politics, while, on the other hand, the least interest corresponds to unskilled laborers and to those who identify with the lowest class.* The depolitization of the working class and the extreme politization of the middle class and professional environment could not be more evident; this is manifestly true at least in Madrid. For example, the percentages of those in the various social strata (subjectively defined) of laborers and white-collar workers who never discuss politics are as follows: poor, 85 percent; working, 67 percent; lower-middle, 48 percent, middle-middle, 46 percent; upper-middle and upper, 39 percent.

A more complete indicator of political information is found in a list of six ministers whose names the people interviewed in several polls were to give: ministers of information, commerce, education, *movimiento,* agriculture, and development. Here is the general distribution:

Number of ministers whose names are known	Students high school	univer- sity	Lawyers	Doctors	White- collar workers	Laborers	Housewives
None	4	2	3	6	3	16	51
One	18	4	—	3	10	19	24
Two	24	5	—	6	21	31	12
Three	20	9	7	17	14	15	6
Four	14	13	13	21	17	9	3
Five	15	22	27	20	14	7	2
Six	5	44	50	28	22	4	2
	100%						
TOTAL	(188)	(249)	(96)	(145)	(200)	(213)	(3826)

Again lawyers and university students appear to be the most politicized: around three-quarters know at least five of the six ministers. White-collar workers are much less informed and laborers even less. Among the latter, 16 percent could not name even one minister. It is worthwhile to consider the fact that a university education presupposes a very notable rise in the degree of political information: High-school students show a notable difference in the degree of information with respect to university students.

The major difference is that between males and housewives, for it separates most clearly the groups interested and not interested in politics. No less than *51 percent of housewives did not know the names of the six ministers and only 2 percent knew all six.*

Among housewives, professionals, white-collar workers, and laborers, the weight of social class is impressive. Among all, *as they ascend in social class or position, the percentage of people who know the names of the ministers rises proportionately:*

	% who did not know any minister:	
Subjective social class	Housewives	Laborers and white-collar workers
Poor	83	42
Working	59	11
Lower-middle	54	11
Middle-middle	30	4
Upper-middle and upper	18	8

The result cannot be more evident that contact with politics is always highest in the highest positions, which reaffirms the idea of a sharp separation between the "actors" in the political arena and the "spectators."

Political Preferences

The evolution of a political life not only obeys the determined actions of politicians or some general values demonstrated by the citizens; it is also essential that the latter express basic opinions concerning the concrete political programs offered by government. In the classic Western democracies, this process has been institutionalized through regular elections, parties, publicity, and opposing candidates: this facilitates analysis by sociologists and political scientists. Since this type of election does not exist in Spain, it is much more difficult to measure the concrete preferences of the citizens.

A curious attempt was made by Linz to judge the eventual political behavior of the Spanish electorate on a basis of accepting the premise (a purely hypothetical "as if," of course) that it would function like the Italian. This would produce 41 percent of the votes for parties of the extreme left, an equal amount for the Christian Democrats, 14 percent for the extreme right, and 5 percent for the Social Democrats.

In the absence of institutional innovations which might elicit political preferences from citizens (for example, multiple "political associations"), we must resort to a casual and relative description derived from questions in a poll. We have no confidence that the results are definitive data and regard them only as clues.

A theme under much discussion currently in Spain is whether a democratic regime without political parties could function in the country. Having asked the question in strategically located samples in Madrid, the following results were obtained:

	A democracy without political parties is not possible
High-school students	55
University students	80
Lawyers	76
Doctors	63
White-collar workers	61
Laborers	57

This is to say, *the majority of those consulted, and an absolute majority in the case of university students and lawyers, consider that a democracy cannot exist without political parties.* The result is interesting given the fact that currently the feeling is practically unanimous that Spain should move toward a democracy; the only difficulty is agreement over which path to take.

Although constitutionally the political form of the Spanish regime has been defined and all is arranged for the succession, we nonetheless inquired about opinions of the groups we interviewed. To the question, "what basic political system would you prefer for the country, when the position of chief of state is vacant," the answers were distributed in the following manner:

	Students		Lawyers	Doctors	White-collar workers	Laborers
	High school	University				
As it has been until now	39	1	8	20	37	55
Regency	3	4	5	9	6	4
Bourbon monarchy	11	11	23	8	5	5
Carlist monarchy	3	3	—	1	1	—
Monarchy	5	5	10	19	7	6
Republic	38	76	53	43	45	30
	100%					
TOTAL	(177)	(227)	(77)	(122)	(179)	(185)

In interpreting these percentages, one must bear in mind that they reflect only the views of those people who answered the question. The proportion who did not answer is quite high: It varies between 6 percent for high-school students and 19 percent for the professional class.

What is really striking in these figures is that *the two most popular solutions in almost every group are the two extremes: the immobility of "continuing as up until now" or the radicalism of a republic.* Two things are truly surprising: *that the laborers should be the group most complaisant with the current situation* (through fear, indoctrination, or conviction, we cannot determine from our data), and that *a university education should be the instrument of maximum radicalization,* as revealed by the differing political spectra of high-school students and from university students.

Again it is necessary to point out that among professionals there is a notable difference of perspective with regard to age: The young are much more in favor of a republic, while older people prefer other solutions. In the case of laborers and white-collar workers in Madrid, it is clearly shown that as one ascends in social position one becomes more favorable toward a republic, while the number of those who wish to continue "as up to the present time" decreases.

Even more interesting than the attitudes about the form of government are preferences about the make-up of the preferred political regime, such as the acceptance or not of political parties. To the question, "if you would like the existence of political parties," the following responses were obtained:

	Students		Lawyers	Doctors	White-collar workers	Laborers
	High school	University				
No party	21	4	13	16	17	31
The Movimiento as the only party	12	1	2	7	8	6
A single party	18	1	—	3	10	17
One party with well-defined political associations	17	10	1	7	9	6
Two parties	14	23	34	30	25	11
Multiple parties	18	61	49	37	31	30
	100%					
TOTAL	(191)	(251)	(83)	(121)	(192)	(193)

In almost every group, except high-school students and laborers, the majority predilection for pluralistic solutions (two or more parties) is overwhelming. As usual, the most radical are, in this order, university students, lawyers, and doctors. Again it is necessary to review the profound change which the few years between high-school seniors and advanced university students signify: Only 32 percent of the former are pluralists as opposed to 84 percent of the latter. Young professionals are more favorable to multiple parties and the older ones to no parties, although in this case the differences are not as striking as on other occasions. The highest level of white-collar workers is characterized by the solutions of moderate pluralism. Laborers stand out by a high degree of preference for the absence of parties or for one single party of the Movimiento.

In order to refer to a more concrete situation, we also asked this question: "Supposing that the new Law of Associations permitted the existence of these groups or political tendencies, for which would you vote if you could?" The possible alternatives along with the proportion of adherents are as follows:

| | Students | | | | | |
	High school	University	Lawyers	Doctors	White-collar workers	Laborers
Traditionalists or Carlists	5	4	1	—	2	—
Falange	7	2	9	5	8	11
Movimiento	17	1	7	11	21	27
Christian Democrats	38	28	26	32	22	20
Social Democrats	20	42	29	24	22	11
Socialists	10	19	19	12	16	22
Regionalists	1	3	1	2	2	3
Others	3	2	9	14	7	8
	100%					
TOTAL	(175)	(234)	(70)	(125)	(176)	(158)

One notes a very clear deflection of the forces which have historically composed the Movimiento. A goodly number of followers remain for the Christian Democrats, but among almost all the groups the Social Democrats or Socialists are predominant. Social Democracy is the majority grouping among university students, lawyers, and white-collar workers; Christian Democrats predominate among high-school students, doctors, and white-collar workers. The percentage who did not respond to the question varied considerably: from 6 percent among university students to 34 percent among laborers. Once again in the case of professional people, a great differentiation is produced by age: *the young are predominantly Socialists and the older people would vote for the forces which make up the Movimiento.*

Perhaps more important than the preference for specific parties is the expression of values as revealed by attitudes about the political programs to be developed by these distinct political groups. As more or less representative of the prevailing values, we have selected these eight: tradition, order, stability, peace, development, justice, liberty, and democracy. The question had been asked previously in a national poll conducted by the Institute of Public Opinion in which 1,119 men and 1,345 women were asked which of these was most important. [5] The percentages were as follows (first figure for men, second for women): tradition, 5, 4; order, 9, 9; stability, 3, 1; peace, 48, 67; development, 5, 2; justice, 20, 9; liberty, 4, 2; democracy, 4, 2; no response, 2, 4. The high consensus revealed by the value placed upon "peace" is impressive. It has been stressed by all media in recent years, especially on the occasion of the recent referendum. Although our data are not strictly comparable, they nevertheless reveal some changes worthy of note. Here are the most general data:

	Students		Lawyers	Doctors	White-collar workers	Laborers	Housewives
	High school	University					
Tradition	1	—	1	—	2	3	3
Order	1	2	7	3	5	6	8
Stability	4	2	7	1	3	1	2
Peace	19	4	11	7	17	32	62
Development	24	13	17	13	16	11	6
Justice	30	54	63	46	39	33	15
Liberty	12	14	4	5	11	10	3
Democracy	9	10	7	7	9	4	1
	100%						
TOTAL	(187)	(247)	(94)	(138)	(200)	(213)	(3,765)

One sees at once that *the value of "peace" has been internalized by housewives and, to a certain extent, by laborers, but it is certainly in the minority among other groups and even has an extremely low value among university students.* Thus there is no total consensus. *Among all groups, except housewives, the value of "justice" predominates,* and this is especially true among lawyers, university students, and doctors.

Among the group of laborers and white-collar workers, it is clear that *the highest white-collar workers have assimilated the values of justice and democracy, while to a high degree, the value of peace is more prevalent among laborers.* Among professional people, justice, stability, and order become more important with age, while democracy, liberty, and development decrease in significance.

Among housewives, social class strongly conditions the desired values: *as one ascends in social class, the importance of justice, stability, democracy, and development are more and more prominent, while the weight given to peace decreases.* Otherwise, the value given to peace is always in the majority.

Another form of detecting the climate of dominant political values, institutionalized in the prevailing political regime, is by means of what we have called an *index of political consensus* and which summarizes the degree of acceptance (or rejection) of the following statements:

1. The entire Spanish people are represented in the Cortes.

2. Unless the present political system changes, Spain cannot be governed with justice.

3. I would like to have this political regime for another thirty years.

4. The present political system functions so that those in power are always the same.

5. The current political regime is made to order for Spaniards and their needs, and it functions better than any other to govern us.

6. There are those who say that Spaniards need a strong hand. The truth is that the Spanish people have always been democratic and we would be better off with a democracy.

Here we shall only give the general results:

	Index of political consensus
High school students	0.44
University students	0.19
Professional people	0.42
White-collar workers and laborers	0.46

Once again it is necessary to note the maximum identification with prevailing values among high-school students, laborers, and white-collar workers and the minimum identification among university students.

One of the most characteristic and prevalent values is doubtlessly *author-*

itarianism: it is not only a matter of an authoritarian political system but also of a basically authoritarian society (which favors this regime and has adjusted to it). In a national poll taken among the youth in 1960, the question was asked: "Is it better for each and every one of us to be interested in our country's politics and to consider ourselves responsible for them, or is it better that one outstanding man have the authority and decide for us." The percentage in favor of authoritarianism were: [6]

	% who prefer that "one man decide for us"
Men	
Farmers	57
Workers	44
Students	42
Women	55

As is seen, women favor authoritarianism more than men, and among the latter, farmers are the most authoritarian and students the least.

We recently repeated the question to a small sampling of housewives and found that 52 percent chose the authoritarianism option. Age, level of education, and social class together condition this attitude: *The oldest women, those who have little education, and those of the lower class are most in favor of authoritarianism.* Here are the data:

Age	% of housewives who favor authoritarianism
Under 25 years	40
From 26 to 35	48
From 36 to 50	52
From 51 to 65	59
Level of education	
None	50
Some elementary	63
Finished elementary	48
Secondary	44
Higher education	40

Subjective social class	% of housewives who favor authoritarianism
Poor	62

Working	53
Lower-middle	53
Middle-middle	49
Upper-middle and upper	37

We find a more concrete attitude with respect to political programs in the subject of economic socialization. The question in this case was "how things would go if the state were the owner of all industries." The responses were distributed in this manner:

	Students					
Conditions would be:	High school	University	Lawyers	Doctors	White-collar workers	Laborers
Better	23	26	29	26	34	54
The same	20	25	4	7	17	14
Worse	57	49	68	67	49	32
	100%					
TOTAL	(187)	(239)	(84)	(133)	(194)	(197)

To the contrary of what we have seen in other political indicators, here *the differences are not very great among the several groups: There are as many partisans as opponents of the idea of the nationalization of industry.* Above all, the laborers are the most in favor of this idea. Those most opposed are the professional people. Here it seems that class interests are more important than the degree of education. The proof of this is that, whereas among white-collar workers and laborers the work category usually determined that the most advanced attitudes were found among the white-collar workers, in this case the laborers are the most in favor of the more progressive attitude. One could also argue that in reality this attitude, without the change of other institutional hypotheses, is the one which is broadcast by many official media or at least those which operate within the Movimiento and, therefore, it is no more than an expression of the authoritarianism of the system and not a radical criticism of it. But in order to demonstrate this contention we would have to undertake an analysis which the length of this chapter does not permit.

It seems quite evident that among professional people the youngest are more in favor of the nationalization of industry than the older. Among them, this attitude parallels the syndrome of liberalism or progressiveness which we have seen before. In order better to interpret these attitudes in favor of or against nationalization, one must look at another more basic attitude: the evaluation of the present degree of state control in economic matters. Is it too strict, normal, or insufficient? The data reveal the following:

State control over the economy is	Students		Lawyers	Doctors	White-collar workers	Laborers
	High school	University				
Too much	26	13	28	13	17	17
Normal	39	21	27	26	34	38
Insufficient	35	66	45	61	49	44
	100%					
TOTAL	(187)	(238)	(85)	(135)	(191)	(189)

Again we find a high consensus among all groups. University students and doctors are those who would like greater state control, which in a certain manner contradicts the previous result in which they did not want the state to control industry. It is possible that for certain intellectual strata there are too many implications to economic nationalization, with the consequence that they do not favor it without a prior change of economic arrangements. Let us repeat that with only this data analysis we cannot verify this hypothesis.

To investigate an additional attitude which reveals the degree of syncretism, tolerance, and secularization represented by ideologies advanced in our time, we put the question of "whether it is possible to be both a Catholic and a Communist." The percentage accepting this proposition fluctuates in this manner: high-school students, 26 percent; university students, 40 percent; lawyers, 36 percent; doctors, 35 percent; white-collar workers, 39 percent; laborers, 34 percent. These percentages cannot be easily analyzed without a prior scale of values or without other comparative data. Since the ideologies which are officially recognized reject this proposition, the fact that at least one-third of the respondents accept the proposition represents a very clear break with the usual values.

Finally, we examined not an attitude, but a behavior pattern, or at least the memory and clear manifestation of political behavior. It concerns the percentage which voted in the last referendum: exactly 89 percent of the professional people in Madrid. Of those who voted, only 17 percent experienced a feeling of satisfaction on voting; 59 percent simply "fulfilled their duty"; voting displeased 7 percent; and 16 percent felt nothing in particular. These percentages do not exactly reveal (among a very small group, we must not forget) a very favorable attitude toward the political system. On the other hand, of those who did not vote, 35 percent could not vote because of illness, travel, and so on, and 61 percent did not vote in order to give a negative significance to their reaction. It will not be surprising if we note that among those who voted, the least satisfied were the young.

NOTES

1. See Daniel Lerner, *The Passing of Traditional Society* (New York: Free Press of Glencoe, 1958).

2. Amando de Miguel, "Estructura social y juventud española. El modelo de la cultura política," *Revista del Instituto de la Juventud,* no. 3 (1966), pp. 94-100.

3. F. FOESSA (I) *Informe sociológico sobre la situación social de España* (Madrid: Euramérica, 1966), pp. 299-300.

4. Amando de Miguel, "Estructura social y juventud española: impacto político e interés pro la política," *op. cit.,* pp. 63-81.

5. The results may be seen in the *Revista de la Opinión Pública,* 9 (July-September 1967), p. 211. The poll was taken in December 1966.

6. See a more ample interpretation of this data in Amando de Miguel, "Estructura social y juventud española: participación política . . .," *op. cit.,* pp. 15-37.

Bibliographical Guide

The best historical introduction to twentieth-century Spain is Raymond Carr's extensive study, *Spain, 1808-1939* (Oxford, 1966). Salvador de Madariaga's *Spain: A Modern History* (New York, 1958) is objective and balanced though rather general. *The Spanish Labyrinth*, by Gerald Brenan (London, 1944), remains a standard work on the sociopolitical background of early twentieth-century Spain.

The most detailed accounts of party politics during the reign of Alfonso XIII are Melchor Fernández Almagro, *Historia del reinado de D. Alfonso XIII* (Madrid, 1934), and *Por qué cayó Alfonso XIII* (Madrid, 1948), the latter hostile to the crown and co-authored by Fernández Almagro and Gabriel Maura y Gamazo. The fullest study of party competition and electoral results is Miguel M. Cuadrado, *Elecciones y partidos políticos de España (1868-1931)* (Madrid, 1969), 2 vols. Another key work on parties is Juan J. Linz's monograph, "The Party System of Spain: Past and Future," in *Party Systems and Voter Alignments,* ed., S. Lipset and S. Rokkan (New York, 1967), pp. 187-282, the best brief treatment from the perspective of political sociology. The role of the army has been studied in S. G. Payne, *Politics and the Military in Modern Spain* (Stanford, 1967). The best works on the two crisis years of 1909 and 1917 are Joan C. Ullman, *The Tragic Week* (Cambridge, Mass., 1968), and J. A. Lacomba, *La crisis española de 1917* (Madrid, 1970).

The principal biographies of major political figures for the first decades of the century are Jesús Pabón, *Cambó,* 3 vols. (Barcelona, 1952 – 69); Diego Sevilla Andrés, *Antonio Maura* (Barcelona, 1954) and *Canalejas* (Barcelona, 1956); Maximiano García Venero, *Melquiades Alvarez* (Madrid, 1954) and *Santiago Alba* (Madrid, 1963); and Vicente Pilapil, *Alfonso XIII* (New York, 1969). Carlos Seco Serrano, *Alfonso XIII y la crisis de la restauración* (Barcelona, 1969), offers an interesting reevaluation.

The best introduction to the politico-cultural reform of the so-called Generation of Ninety-Eight is Pedro Laín Entralgo, *La generación del 98* (Madrid, 1946). On Joaquín Costa, the main civic figure of that disparate group, see Rafael Pérez de la Dehesa, *El pensamiento de Costa y su influencia en el 98* (Madrid, 1966); C. Martín-Retortillo, *Joaquín Costa* (Barcelona, 1961); and E. Tierno Galván, *Costa y el regeneracionismo* (Barcelona, 1961). Gonzalo Redondo, *Las empresas políticas de José Ortega y Gasset,* 2 vols. (Madrid, 1970), deals with the politics of Spain's most famous intellectual of the century. On the only major rightist personality of the group, see Vicente Marrero, *Maeztu* (Madrid, 1955).

Regional nationalism has been one of the three or four major civic problems of twentieth-century Spain. The best analytic introduction will be found in two brief monographs by Juan Linz, "Early State-Building and Late Peripheral Nationalisms Against the State: The Case of Spain," in *Building States and Nations,* ed., S. N. Eisenstadt and S. Rokkan (Beverly Hills/London, 1974), pp. 32 – 116, and "Politics in a Multilingual Society with a Dominant World Language," in *Les états multilingues,* ed., J. G. Savard and R. Vegneault (Quebec, 1974). The principal narrative account of Catalan nationalism is García Venero's *Historia del nacionalismo catalán,* 2 vols. (Madrid, 1967). *Lliga Catalana,* the leading middle-class Catalanist party of the early decades of this century, is the subject of an excellent two-volume study by Isidre Molas (Barcelona, 1971). The history of the Basque movement is treated in S. G. Payne, *Basque Nationalism* (Reno, 1975). On Valencianism, see Alfons Cucó, *El valencianisme polític* (Valencia, 1971).

Gerald Meaker, *The Revolutionary Left in Spain, 1914 – 1923* (Stanford, 1974), presents an excellent account of the left during the crisis and aftermath of World War I. Juan Díaz del Moral, *Historia de las agitaciones campesinas andaluzas—Córdoba* (Madrid, 1929), is still the best source on the peasant revolts in the southern countryside. The social problem of the Catalan countryside has been well analyzed by Albert Balcells, *El problema agrari a Catalunya, 1890 – 1936* (Barcelona, 1968). Development of Spanish capitalism in the era of World War I is treated by Santiago Roldán and J. L. García Delgado,

La formación de la sociedad capitalista en España, 1914–1920, 2 vols. (Madrid, 1973).

There is no adequate study of the Primo de Rivera dictatorship. Gabriel Maura y Gamazo, *Bosquejo histórico de la Dictadura* (Madrid, 1930), is still the chief narrative. Juan Velarde Fuertes, *Política económica de la Dictadura* (Madrid, 1968), provides a brief but useful study of economic policy.

The literature concerning society and politics in twenthieth-century Spain is disproportionately focused on the eight years of the Second Republic and Civil War. There are a number of general histories of the Republic. Ricardo de la Cierva's *Historia de la Guerra Civil española,* vol. I, *Antecedentes: Monarquía y República 1898–1936* (Madrid, 1969) is the most extensive and documented, written from a liberal Franquist viewpoint. It may be compared with Gabriel Jackson's *Spanish Republic and Civil War* (Princeton, 1965), a concise, well-written account from the viewpoint of the moderate, middle-class left. Joaquín Arrarás, *Historia de la Segunda República española,* 4 vols. (Madrid, 1956–67), is the most detailed political chronicle, hostile to the left. Also worthy of mention is the *Historia de la Segunda República española,* 4 vols. (Barcelona, 1940–41), by José Pla, which is devoted mainly to formal parliamentary politics but was an impressive achievement in the immediate aftermath of the Civil War. New perspectives are offered in a symposium edited by Raymond Carr, *The Republic and Civil War in Spain* (London, 1971).

The best monograph on any aspect of Republican problems is E. E. Malefakis, *Agrarian Reform and Peasant Revolution in Spain* (New Haven, 1970). R. A. H. Robinson, *The Origins of Franco's Spain: The Right, the Republic and Revolution, 1931–1936* (Devon, 1970), provides a clear account of the conservative and rightist groups. The only treatment of the left as a whole is S. G. Payne, *The Spanish Revolution* (New York, 1970). Victor Alba, *El marxismo en España,* 2 vols. (Barcelona, 1974), provides a loving account of the POUM by a former militant. The political structure of Catalonia, the most complicated in Spain, is clarified in Isidre Molas, *El sistema de partits polítics a Catalunya (1931–1936)* (Barcelona, 1971). Manuel Ramírez Jiménez, *Los grupos de presión en la Segunda República española* (Madrid, 1969), analyzes the major interest sectors and problems. X. Tusell Gómez, et al., *Las elecciones del Frente Popular en España,* 2 vols. (Madrid, 1971) provides an exhaustive study of the final elections. The two chief political memoirs from these years are José Ma. Gil-Robles, *No fue posible la paz* (Barcelona, 1969), and Joaquín Chapaprieta, *La paz fue posible* (Barcelona, 1971).

The most celebrated treatment of the Civil War is Hugh Thomas, *The Spanish Civil War* (rev. ed., London, 1965). It provides a detailed account, the revised edition corrects some of the earlier errors, and the author has made a genuine effort at objectivity. Other studies must be catalogued according to their viewpoint or affiliation. Ricardo de la Cierva's *Historia ilustrada de la Guerra Civil española*, 2 vols. (Barcelona, 1971), is an impressive, well-informed work, by far the best pro-Nationalist account, and emphasizes the military and political. The leading version of the non-communist revolutionary left is P. Broué and E. Témime, *La Révolution et la guerre d'Espagne* (Paris, 1961; Eng. tr., Cambridge, Mass., 1972). The official communist account is *Guerra y revolución en España*, 2 vols. (Paris, 1966).

The outstanding military study of the Spanish conflict is Ramón Salas, *Historia del Ejército Popular de la República*, 4 vols. (Madrid, 1973), which not only provides an exhaustive account of the Republic forces but analyzes key issues of the war as a whole. The leading blow-by-blow treatment of the war consists of the "Monografías militares de la Guerra de España" prepared by the Servicio Histórico Militar under the direction of Col. J. M. Martinez Bande. Nine volumes have been published to date. The best study of the Guernica incident is Vicente Talón, *Arde Guernica* (Madrid, 1970).

David T. Cattell, *Communism and the Spanish Civil War* (Berkeley, 1955), remains the chief study of that topic. For the communist-anarchist struggle during the first year of the conflict, Burnett Bolloten, *The Grand Camouflage* (New York, 1961), is indispensable. The best economic study of any aspect of the Civil War is Josep Ma. Bricall's excellent investigation of revolutionary dualism in Catalonia, *Política económica de la Generalitat (1936–1939)* (Barcelona, 1970).

The literature on rightiest politics in the Civil War is much less abundant, mainly because there was much less rightist politics. On Falangism, see S. G. Payne, *Falange* (Stanford, 1961), and two works by Maximiano García Venero, *Falange en la Guerra de España* (Paris, 1967) and *Historia de la unificación* (Madrid, 1970). See also V. Palacio Atard, R. de la Cierva, and R. Salas, *Aproximación histórica a la guerra española (1936 - 1939)* (Madrid, 1970). Rafael Abella, *La vida cotidiana durante la Guerra Civil: la España nacional* (Barcelona, 1973), presents an excellent description of society in the rightist zone.

The best biography of Franco is J. W. D. Trythall, *El Caudillo* (New York, 1970), but see also Brian Crozier, *Franco* (London, 1967). The most detailed of all Franco biographies and by far the best pro-Franco account is Ricardo de la Cierva's *Francisco Franco: Un siglo de España* (Madrid, 1971–72), which has thus far appeared only in periodical and not in book form.

The most extensive collection of printed materials on the Civil War is held by the Unidad de Estudios sobre la Guerra de España, in the Ministry of Information and Tourism at Madrid. The Madrid Hemeroteca Municipal contains an excellent collection of Spanish newspapers for the twentieth century. The only major archival collection on any aspect of twentieth-century Spain is the great mass of materials from the leftist zone in the Civil War maintained by the Jefatura de Servicio Documental in Salamanca, including extensive miscellaneous data on all leftist groups throughout the 1930's. Of the several foreign collections on the Civil War, the best is the Bolloten Collection at the Hoover Institution (Stanford, Calif.). The only major published documentary collection for the century is Fernando Díaz-Plaja's *La España política del siglo XX* (Madrid, 1972), 4 vols.

The most general treatment of Spain in the Franco era will be found in George Hills, *Spain* (New York, 1970), and Carlos Seco Serrano, *Epoca contemporánea* (Barcelona, 1968), vol. 6 of *Historia de España*. Jacques Georgel, *Le Franquisme* (Paris, 1970), presents a hostile but incisive analysis of the regime. Joaquín Bardavío, *La estructura del poder en España* (Madrid, 1969) describes the power structure. The formal legal structure of the state is expounded by R. Fernández-Carvajal, *La constitución española* (Madrid, 1969), and the Equipo Mundo's *Los noventa ministros de Franco* (Barcelona, 1970) offers interesting data on the governmental elite. A wide collection of articles and monographic studies on the Franco era and contemporary problems will be found in the three volumes of *La España de los años 70,* ed., M. Fraga Iribarne, J. Velarde Fuertes, and S. del Campo Urbano (Madrid, 1972–74).

Sociological study has proliferated in Spain during the past decade. The best global approach is through the Fundación FOESSA's *Informe sociológico sobre la situación social de España 1970* (Madrid, 1970).

Index